# THE SHATTERED CRYSTAL BALL

# THE SHATTERED CRYSTAL BALL

## Fear and Learning in the Cuban Missile Crisis

by
James G. Blight

*With a Foreword by*
Joseph S. Nye, Jr.

Littlefield Adams Quality Paperbacks

LITTLEFIELD ADAMS QUALITY PAPERBACKS

a division of Rowman & Littlefield Publishers, Inc.
4720 Boston Way, Lanham, Maryland 20706

British Cataloging in Publication Information Available


**Library of Congress Cataloging-in-Publication Data**

Blight, James G.
The shattered crystal ball : fear and learning in the Cuban missile
crisis / by James G. Blight ; with a foreword by Joseph S. Nye, Jr.
p. cm.
Includes bibliographical references.
1. Cuban Missile Crisis, 1962.   I. Title.
E841.B573   1990
973.922'01'9—dc20   89–28558 CIP


ISBN 0–8226–3015–X (pbk. : alk. paper)

Printed in the United States of America

 <sup>TM</sup> The paper used in this publication meets the minimum requirements of
American National Standard for Information Sciences—Permanence of
Paper for Printed Library Materials, ANSI Z39.48–1984.

For j,

Winner of life's triple crown.
Since feeling is first,
tied with cognition and gumption.

# Contents

# Acknowledgments

This book by a psychologist presents a self-consciously psychological perspective. Yet its subject—nuclear crises between the superpowers—is seldom discussed by psychologists and is usually thought of as falling squarely within the domains of political science and history. In addition, the main argument of this book speaks directly to the nuclear policymakers who must actually bear the day-to-day burden of responsibility for trying to avoid another crisis as dangerous as the Cuban missile crisis of 1962.

Because the book was conceived as an interdisciplinary exercise, incorporating the perspectives and literatures of all these diverse endeavors, it could not be written overnight. It is now almost five years since I first realized that a psychologist might eventually have something useful to say about the United States' and the Soviet Union's number one goal: to avoid a nuclear war. This goal in turn is judged by all who concern themselves professionally with these matters to mean that we must therefore avoid any crises that might lead to war. For almost five years, then, I have consulted with, argued with, and learned a great deal from practitioners of all the disciplines with whom I now seek to communicate my findings: psychologists, political scientists, historians, and policymakers. It is with pleasure and respect that I acknowledge here the many whose contributions to this project have been especially seminal.

*Psychologists* who have assisted me over the years include David Bakan, Margaret Brenman-Gibson, Morton Deutsch, William K. Estes, Jerome Frank, Robert R. Holt, Philip S. Holzman, Polly Howells, Charles Kiesler, Ellen Langer, Marion Langer, John E. Mack, Ian Mitroff, Frederic A. Mosher, Ulric Neisser, John A. Nevin, Sherman Roberts, Robert Romanyshyn, Milton Schwebel, M. Brewster Smith,

Eric Werthman, Ralph K. White, and Yuri Zamoshkin. Thanks to one and all for helping me develop a psychological perspective that increased my insight into the experience of nuclear danger in a deep crisis.

*Political scientists* who took this eccentric psychologist under their wing and taught him a few of their tricks include Graham T. Allison, Robert Axelrod, Robert P. Beschel, Jr., Fen Osler Hampson, Stanley Hoffmann, Richard Ned Lebow, Richard Ullman, Stephen Van Evera, Scott D. Sagan, Jack Snyder, and William Taubman. None should be held responsible for my enduring confusion over what, exactly, is "scientific" about political science.

*Historians* who were particularly helpful in acquainting me with the basic documentary facts of the Cuban missile crisis include Robert Dallek, Ernest R. May, Walter McDougall, and Marc Trachtenberg. The documentation on the missile crisis is huge and still growing, and without the interpretive help of these scholars, I would have been overwhelmed and discouraged.

*Policy analysts,* as a group, kept pulling my inquiry back to earth by posing various versions of the "so what?" question. Especially helpful were Richard K. Betts, Bruce Blair, Albert Carnesale, Ashton B. Carter, Abram Chayes, Daniel Ellsberg, Charles Glaser, Morton H. Halperin, Michael Intriligator, Michael MccGwire, and Michael Nacht. The most common question from the members of the policy fraternity was: Why study the Cuban missile crisis now, after all these years? Thus sensitized, I set out to answer by trying to approach more closely the core of the human experience of nuclear danger, which I believe will not change from crisis to crisis.

Special thanks go, in addition, to Linda Healey, J. Anthony Lukas, Sanford Thatcher, and Steve Wasserman for very thorough readings of one or more versions of the manuscript. Special thanks, too, to David Hamburg and Frederic A. Mosher of the Carnegie Corporation of New York, whose generosity supplied me with a research stipend for much of the period during which the writing of this book took place, via the Project on Avoiding Nuclear War, located at the Center for Science and International Affairs, Kennedy School of Government, Harvard University. I wish also to acknowledge the assistance of the MacArthur Foundation, the Alfred P. Sloan Foundation, and the Ford Foundation, which collectively underwrite the activities of the Nuclear Crisis Project, under whose auspices several conferences on the Cuban missile crisis have been held, and from which much that is new and important about the crisis has emerged.

Finally, I want to acknowledge the assistance of a few people whose advice became so important that I now find it difficult to pinpoint where or when specific contributions occurred. Paul Wachtel, psychologist and political commentator, always told me when my psychology was suspect, when my politics were slipping, and when it was time to go to New York to talk about it. Alexander L. George was a kind of "godfather" to me in this endeavor, as he has been to so many others, and his support remained steadfast even though I suspect that he disagrees with some of my conclusions. Thomas Greening, who must be the world's most conscientious journal editor, repeatedly criticized my prose and thereby improved my presentation. Carl Kaysen never failed me when I asked assistance in getting "closer to the bone" of what it was like in the Kennedy administration. Robert Jervis, indefatigable correspondent, psychological and political polymath, and good friend, more than once turned over to me his Columbia seminar on political psychology. The resulting discussions with him and his unique community of scholars were always helpful. Arthur L. Singer, Jr., has been my "coach" in this enterprise, assisting me in all sorts of ways. He alone among my advisors recalled the *other* key event of October 1962: Bobby Richardson's snag of Willie McCovey's line drive, which gave the Yankees the World Series victory over the San Francisco Giants. Fritz Heinzen gave an earlier version of the manuscript an insightful, critical reading, pointing out important possibilities that had eluded me. James E. Lyons, George Zimmar, and Jonathan Sisk have guided me through the publication process with skill and enthusiasm. Janet S. Johnston improved my prose considerably. Thomas C. Schelling has inspired and provoked me more than he will ever believe possible. And Kimberly Blair, an outstanding assistant, compensated wonderfully for my technological innocence, staying late, working weekends, and producing a polished product where only scribbles had existed.

At last, I want to acknowledge the help of those few who saw drafts no one else was allowed to see, those who literally lived through the germination, evolution, and production of this book. They are McGeorge Bundy, Janet M. Lang, Robert S. McNamara, Richard E. Neustadt, Joseph S. Nye, Jr., and David A. Welch. Without the central contributions of these people, there would have been no book. Collectively, they constitute the "invisible college" I attended during its writing.

# Foreword

*Joseph S. Nye, Jr.*

In his biography of John F. Kennedy, *A Thousand Days,* Arthur Schlesinger, Jr., refers to the week of the Cuban missile crisis, October 22–28, 1962, as "The Great Turning," a week permanently emblazoned in the memories of all who lived through it near the center of power and responsibility.[1] Psychologist James Blight takes us in this book back to the experiences of those who managed the crisis, with special attention to the turning point, its final forty-eight hours when events seemed to be spiraling beyond control and when nuclear war appeared to be a real possibility, just before the abrupt and peaceful resolution announced by a radio message from Soviet Chairman Nikita Khrushchev at 9:00 A.M. EST, October 28.

The beauty of this book is that its author is able to convey what the experience of trying to manage that crisis was like. He does so not primarily as would a biographer, historian, or even a psychologist, although he brings these and other disciplinary skills to bear on his material. Rather, he invites the reader into the confusing novelty and uncertainty of the missile crisis in order to make policy-relevant points. He argues persuasively, in my view, that only by understanding clearly what this nuclear crisis was like will we understand the human and institutional requirements any such future episode is likely to involve. Before I encountered Blight, I thought it unlikely that anything significant remained to be learned about this most studied event of the nuclear age. I was wrong. I am now persuaded by this book that until we understand much more fully the nuclear learning of the Cuban missile crisis, our own second-order nuclear learning will be incomplete in important ways. Nuclear deterrence is far more complex than the models in the minds of most academic policy analysts. According to the prevailing models, the American advantage of seventeen to one, and the vulnerability of the Soviet forces, should have deterred Khrushchev from placing missiles in Cuba and encouraged Kennedy to take larger risks than he did. Only by looking more carefully at the psychology of real leaders in crises can we understand such anomalies.

*   *   *

Almost everyone nowadays applauds interdisciplinary research, especially on issues as important as reducing the risk of a nuclear war. Yet few are actually able to practice it to any significant degree, and almost never do we encounter a work such as this book that is so thoroughly interdisciplinary that it is impossible for its author or potential audience to be assigned to any one discipline. It will become clear to the readers of this book that its author is conversant not only with disciplines traditionally connected with nuclear questions, such as nuclear strategy, arms control, and political science, but also with psychology in its many forms, with history, and with moral philosophy.

James Blight is a professional psychologist whose interest in nuclear issues led him to become a research fellow of Harvard's Project on Avoiding Nuclear War (ANW). In 1982, Harvard President Derek Bok responded to the public concern about what was perceived by many to be the dangerously high and rising risk of all-out nuclear war by encouraging a faculty group to publish *Living with Nuclear Weapons*.[2] In that book, my colleagues and I concluded that in the world as we know it, there is no realistic escape from the risk of nuclear war, but that it is imperative to avoid deep nuclear crises in which the risk of nuclear war might suddenly arise. In just such crises, "the shattered crystal ball" of nuclear war (as we put it), may indeed become a reality.[3] We did not provide many suggestions about how to reduce the risk of nuclear war, but this was the central mission of the ANW Project, which Graham Allison, Albert Carnesale, and I launched in 1983 with the support of the Carnegie Corporation. It was the rationale behind the Project's first book, *Hawks, Doves & Owls: An Agenda for Avoiding Nuclear War*.[4] Partway through our research for that book, Blight joined the Project. He was instrumental in causing the members of the Project to focus carefully on *crisis,* especially the manner and extent to which a crisis might constrain the rationality of decision makers, and on the possibility that the psychological effects of nuclear crises, like the physical effects of nuclear weapons themselves, may in certain respects be qualitatively different from their conventional counterparts.

During the period in which *Hawks, Doves & Owls* was being prepared, Blight wrote a series of controversial articles primarily for professional psychologists, inviting those who had taken an interest in issues of nuclear risk to focus attention on nuclear crises.[5] These pieces reflected the prevailing opinion within the ANW group and, indeed, within the nuclear policy community generally: the immediate prerequisite to a major nuclear war would likely be a deep superpower crisis. But, whereas most analysts tend to invoke "crisis" somewhat mechanically as an independent variable, Blight began to develop the concept as a dependent variable. He asked questions such as: How do leaders actually determine when they are in an international crisis? Does their experience of nuclear crises have unique properties? How do leaders' beliefs about the danger in which a nuclear crisis has placed them relate to their actions? With such questions in mind, Blight began to take a new look at the limiting case of the phenomenon: the Cuban missile crisis.

After immersing himself in the vast literature of the missile crisis, Blight noticed a significant point that seemed to him to have been overlooked, which eventually became the starting point for a new research project on nuclear crises.[6] According to Blight, neither form of the paradigmatic psychology used to frame our understanding of international crises allows us plausibly to explain the peaceful outcome of the events of October 1962. The "rational actor" psychology, favored by an entire generation of nuclear strategists, leads us to believe that the Americans, who possessed a vast numerical superiority over the Soviets in deliverable nuclear weapons, should have launched a preemptive strike against the Soviets *if* the crisis was perceived to be a very deep one, close to the outbreak of war. Since Kennedy is reported to have believed during the crisis that the likelihood of war was perhaps as high as 50 percent, the President, according to this simplified view of rationality, should have ordered a nuclear strike to disarm the Soviets and thus to eliminate the possibility that *they* would preempt.[7] Alternatively, what Blight in this book calls the "irrational actor" psychology also leads us to expect the same outcome, although for different reasons. If the Cuban missile crisis carried a risk of war as high as 50 percent, according to this view, the resulting stress, faulty judgment, and eventual panic should have led to war. Both rational actors and/or irrational actors in the White House or Kremlin should, according to prevailing psychological wisdom, have ordered a preemptive nuclear strike, which in fact never occurred.

Blight concluded that either the peaceful resolution of the crisis was a fluke or that the psychological theories whose tenets lead one to expect the wrong outcome—the Cuban war or even a nuclear war—should be regarded as seriously deficient. Of course, such a judgment may reasonably be disputed. One could argue, for example, that in retrospect Kennedy exaggerated his real-time perception of the likelihood of war. If true, this would make the actual decision to withhold any strike more classically rational, just as it would lead us to expect the presence of less stress-induced panic. But Blight had already begun a series of lengthy discussions with members of Kennedy's inner circle, who confirmed to him that the situation by the end of the crisis had seemed very grim, perhaps as grim as the President suggested in his estimate of a 50 percent chance of a superpower war. Thus, to oversimplify a complex decision on his part, Blight chose to go with the outcome of the crisis rather than with the psychologies that, in his view, could not plausibly explain it. This was a bold choice; probably only a psychologist without a strong previous commitment to the virtually paradigmatic psychologies of rational and irrational actors, and one in addition with a primary interest in policy implications, would have moved so quickly and decisively to a new *kind* of psychological analysis of nuclear crises.

He calls his approach a *phenomenological* psychology of crises and avoiding nuclear war. What he means by this term is refreshingly straightforward: if we want to understand the "psychology" of an event like the missile crisis, we should first take the simple but far from easy step of seeking entry into what it was *like,* at the time, to try to manage the Cuban missile crisis. Thus he began to put some empirical flesh on a "psychological" concept that had by then become central to the work of the ANW Project, the "crystal ball effect." Blight asked: What must have been like to look into the nuclear crystal ball when it seemed closer to shattering than at any time before or since? What he found is that, for key American and Soviet managers of the crisis, it was frightening, but not in the sense that one's life is on the line and that one might therefore die in an attack. Rather, each leader appeared to have been struck by the apparently much more disturbing thought that, some finite number of moves down the road, he could conceivably be responsible in some measure for the worst catastrophe in history—a nuclear holocaust.

But there is a second aspect to this commonsense, phenomenological approach; it concerns what this deep fear was *about*. It is on this point that, I would argue, Blight's work presents the greatest challenge to traditional ways of thinking about the issue of nuclear crisis stability. He shows that by the last forty-eight hours of the acute phase of the crisis (roughly, October 26 to 28), the object of the fear for the principal managers of the crisis had shifted from what he calls nuclear *attack* to nuclear *danger*. At the heart of the look and feel of nuclear danger is the conviction that while neither you nor your adversary has any interest in attacking the other with nuclear weapons, the crisis you are both in may still be in danger of spinning out of control and into an inadvertent, unwanted war. This fear of nuclear inadvertence is the fear that, he argues persuasively, led to the nuclear learning that informed our escape without a war in the Cuban missile crisis.

*   *   *

It seems to me unlikely that knowledgeable readers of this book will agree with all its provocative arguments. For example, I am not sure that the Cuban missile crisis is sui generis, the first and only time decision makers experienced the full extent of what he calls the "evolution of situational perversity," leading them to believe that the abstract possibility of inadvertent nuclear war had become a dangerously high and rising probability. My own judgment on this point will be withheld until Blight's data are in on Berlin, a crisis many people at the time believed to be very dangerous. There are bound to be many other points of contention. Strategists and political scientists influenced by game theory will be challenged by Blight's insistence that the resolution of the crisis refutes their rational actor psychology of nuclear crises. Psychologists and some other political scientists will have to come to grips with Blight's data indicating that, in spite of the great nuclear danger (or perhaps because of it), there is little or no evidence of psychological stress or breakdown in Kennedy's inner circle, as many observers have long assumed. It is also possible that many psychologists will find Blight's phenomenological psychology too simple—not complex enough to reflect accurately what they take to be the advanced state of their psychological science. (As a non-psychologist, I find the simplicity of his approach a virtue.) Some historians will no doubt have difficulty with the author's forthright search into the past for policy-relevant answers to contemporary questions, and by his use of many nontraditional sources of data, including interviews, conference discussions, secret tapes made by Kennedy, and statements by Soviets whose credibility is often difficult to assess conclusively. Finally, I imagine that Blight's policy conclusion—that in a nuclear crisis a little deterrence goes a long way, but that some may still be necessary—will upset the many people who seem to doubt one or both of these conclusions.

To all these potential skeptics, I confess that as I observed the unfolding of James Blight's research on the Cuban missile crisis, I too was often skeptical, but I am now compelled by his argument that in the deepest nuclear crisis, leaders were fearful; that their fear was of losing control of events; that this fear seems to have led to learning that produced a peaceful resolution; and, finally, that this cluster of factors is likely to be salient if we ever again face a crisis as dangerous as that of October 1962. I hope that Blight's contribution will bring a whole cluster of nuclear-related disciplines to this common knowledge, by means of this empirical study of the uncommon danger experienced by real people. We must never pass that way again, and James Blight shows us as never before why that is so, by showing us what it was like.

Center for Science and International Affairs
John F. Kennedy School of Government
Harvard University

At that moment . . . there flashed into my mind a passage from the Bhagavad-Gita, the sacred book of the Hindus: "I am become Death, the Shatterer of Worlds!"

> J. Robert Oppenheimer, recalling July 16, 1945,
> at "Trinity," the explosion of the first atomic
> bomb, Alamogordo, New Mexico.

I can recall leaving the White House after it had been decided which message to reply to and after the reply had been drafted and approved by the President, and it was being sent out. It was a Saturday evening. I can remember the sunset. We left about the time the sun was setting in October, and I, at least, was so uncertain as to whether the Soviets would accept [our offer] that I wondered if I'd ever see another Saturday sunset like that . . . That may sound over-dramatic, but that was the way I was feeling at the time. It was that serious a problem. That was Saturday night [October 27, 1962]. [I was worried about] the possible effect on our country of even one of those warheads—nuclear warheads—being launched against us.

> Robert S. McNamara, 1983, recalling the final
> evening of the Cuban missile crisis.

The wick of war had already begun to smolder . . . at the height of the Cuban events, when the smell of burning hung in the air.

> Nikita Khrushchev, December 12, 1962,
> recalling the final hours of the
> Cuban missile crisis.

He who is educated by dread is educated by possibility . . . when such a person, therefore, goes out from the school of possibility, and knows . . . that terror, perdition and annihilation dwell next door to every man, and has learned the profitable lesson that every dread which alarms may the next instant become a fact, he will then interpret reality differently.

> Soren Kierkegaard, *The Concept of Dread,* 1844

# PART ONE: PRELIMINARIES

# 1

# The Thesis: The Shattered Crystal Ball, October 27, 1962

That dread makes its appearance is the pivot upon which everything turns.

Kierkegaard,
*The Concept of Dread*, 1844

In 1983, as fear of nuclear war became widespread in the Western democracies, members of the Harvard Nuclear Study Group published *Living with Nuclear Weapons,* a self-conscious effort to inject dispassionate analysis into a debate growing increasingly strident and adversarial.[1] The book was widely criticized, most notably by Jonathan Schell, for what many took to be its complacency in the face of a risk of nuclear war believed in those days by some to be dangerously high and rising.[2] The authors of the Harvard Group had rejected the nuclear hysteria common at the time, arguing that nuclear risks were generally very low, due to what they called the "crystal ball effect." They pointed out that "the enormous horror of nuclear weapons' effects means that modern leaders have the equivalent of a crystal ball showing them the devastation at the end of a major war. This crystal ball effect," they contended, "helps to give the nuclear world at least some measure of stability."[3] The horror provoked by the prospect of a major nuclear war seemed to these authors so obvious, so catastrophic, and so unequivocally irrational that it was equally obvious why statesmen leading the nuclear superpowers have usually remained far from the brink.

In a chapter called "The Shattered Crystal Ball: How Might a

3

Nuclear War Begin?,'' the authors proposed several imaginary scenarios within which a nuclear war might conceivably commence. They concluded that "this glimpse at the shattered crystal ball should breed neither complacency nor despair . . . The good news for the present is, then, that nuclear war is not probable. The bad news is that nuclear war is, and will continue to be, possible. To make sure that the possible does not become more probable is the continuing task of nuclear policy."[4] And so it is. Day in and day out, nuclear policymakers and analysts fine-tune nuclear deterrence—the threat to retaliate in kind to a nuclear (or massive conventional) attack—in efforts to maintain the robustness of the crystal ball effect and to ensure that hypothetical scenarios for shattering the crystal ball remain wildly improbable, abstract, and thus far from the consciousness of leaders who would shoulder the ultimate responsibility for the use of nuclear weapons.

In this book, I argue that at least once in the nuclear age, perhaps only once, leaders of the nuclear superpowers could honestly have said that nuclear war was not only possible, but probable; that at least for approximately forty-eight hours in late October 1962, leaders in the White House and Kremlin carried in their minds many "scenarios" for nuclear war that, far from being abstract and merely illustrative, were vividly concrete and terrifyingly real; that at the conclusion of the Cuban missile crisis of 1962, American and Soviet leaders did imagine that the nuclear crystal ball was about to shatter, with the full knowledge that if their premonitions were realized, they would bear the responsibility for the worst catastrophe ever to befall mankind; and finally, that some nontrivial degree of vicarious participation in the experience of the shattered crystal ball of October 1962 can yield important insight into how we can learn valuable lessons from the crisis that can and should be applied in the day-in, day-out task of preventing nuclear crises and deterring nuclear war.

Drawing from all available sources, I have tried to articulate what it may have been *like* to be responsible, yet close to being overcome with the sensation that the crisis was spinning out of control and perhaps into nuclear war. Thus, references are included not only to the literature of nuclear policy and to public statements of leaders, but also to declassified documents, memoirs, television programs, films, interviews, novels, poetry, philosophy, psychology, and religion. Throughout, I have tried to find ways to augment our notional understanding of the unacceptability of nuclear war with a sense of what it must have been like to believe that, within hours or days, one would, despite one's best efforts to the contrary, be responsible for the unthinkable.

In a book as unorthodox as this one, I believe it may be useful to identify my central intention: to write a policy-relevant analysis of the limiting case of nuclear danger. If I seem to stray into fiction, or quasi-fiction, it is always in search of greater psychological accuracy and greater realism. The crisis of October 26 to 28, 1962, that I liken to a shattered crystal ball, must have haunted the imaginations of President John F. Kennedy and Chairman Nikita Khrushchev and their key advisers and must also have produced a shattering experience. What, really, do we know about that experience, about what it was like? The answer is "very little," mainly because the members of the community of nuclear strategy and arms control, who have been primarily responsible for interpreting the crisis, have not even interested themselves in the question. In this book, the question is asked and some tentative answers are suggested, in the hope of moving discussion of the psychology of avoiding nuclear war away from a comfortable abstraction and toward a disturbing psychological reality.

For many ordinary people, who had no detailed knowledge of the facts of the crisis nor direct responsibility for its outcome, the experience of watching the crisis unfold on television was shattering. Some may remember that early in the evening of Sunday, October 28, 1962, "The Ted Mack Amateur Hour" was preempted by a CBS News special report on the Cuban missile crisis. The report was interspersed with several commercials for products that normally sponsored the "Amateur Hour." In a juxtaposition of notable, if inadvertent, irony toward the end of the report, Ted Mack, appearing fatherly and relaxed, asked the members of his audience to consider trying Sominex, a sleeping pill to alleviate what he called "simple nervous tension" before bedtime. This commercial came directly after the following remark from Charles Collingwood, narrator of the special report on the missile crisis:

> Wednesday [October 24, 1962] the quarantine line went into effect at 10:00 A.M. Eastern Daylight Time. There was some speculation whether that hour would be remembered as the day World War III began . . . [But] this is the day [October 28] we have every reason to believe that the world came out from under the most terrible threat of nuclear holocaust since the end of World War II.[5]

If ever a week in American history was tailor-made for Sominex, it was October 22 to 28, 1962! Tens of millions of Americans were glued to their television sets, many feeling deeply fearful and totally vulnerable in a way and to an extent that was unprecedented. Collingwood spoke for all who had stocked up on canned goods, moved into their basements, headed for the mountains, or simply been paralyzed into frightened inactivity. In at least one case, this fear was so profound that it gave rise to the fatalistic fantasy that nuclear war had already commenced. An American couple, serving in the Peace Corps in Thailand, later reported hearing (and believing) that during the pivotal week of the missile crisis, New York City, where their families lived, had been destroyed in a Soviet nuclear attack.[6] This was indeed a week of "simple [ but profoundly nuclear] nervous tension."

All this fear about the crisis over the Soviet missiles in Cuba has been discounted by many serious students of nuclear policy as the understandable but hyperbolic enervations of the powerless and ignorant, fed by a sensationalist media. One might therefore regard these extreme reactions to the missile crisis as merely an epiphenomenal sidelight to the causally significant, coldly calculated, political-military drama being played out in Washington, Moscow, Havana, and on the high seas. In fact, this has been the dominant "professional" view of the missile crisis since its occurrence: it was conducted and resolved according to the complex calculations of power and bluff by men who acted much like cool, experienced high-stakes poker players. Lately, another "professional" view has gained favor among a growing number of students of nuclear crises: that the policymakers who managed the missile crisis acted *exactly* like ordinary citizens who provided a panicky, receptive audience for Ted Mack's pitch for Sominex. According to this view, the American policymakers close to President Kennedy entered needlessly into an escalatory spiral of threats and counterthreats that nearly brought on a nuclear holocaust. According to these students of the crisis, we were lucky to have escaped without a catastrophic war, and lucky that Chairman Khrushchev agreed at the eleventh hour to the American demand that he withdraw his missiles.

I argue throughout this book that both views contain some degree of truth, but that both are also highly misleading. There is no question that the calculation, central planning, and control during the missile crisis, at least on the American side, was unprecedented in any peacetime operation. Yet these calculations did not, as one would have predicted based on extravagant American conventional superiority in the Caribbean and overwhelming nuclear superiority at every level, lead the American government to attack and destroy the missile bases in Cuba. Moreover, there can also be no question that during the missile crisis, leaders on both sides were profoundly fearful. Even leaders not directly involved, far from Cuba but presumably within range of Soviet nuclear weapons, have recalled the crisis with recollected horror. British Prime Minister Harold Macmillan, who spoke daily by telephone with President Kennedy during the pivotal week, was quite forthcoming about the way the week affected him. On Sunday, October 28, the same day as Collingwood's newscast, Macmillan reported having had "a sense of anticlimax, after days during which it was difficult to restrain yet necessary to conceal our emotions; on that Sunday afternoon my colleagues and I were able to share the feeling, if not of triumph, yet of relief and gratitude. We had been on the brink, almost over it."[7] These feelings were echoed by the men who *were* most directly responsible for the outcome. Nikita Khrushchev, for example, recalled that week as a time when "the smell of burning hung in the air."[8] Presidential Special Counsel Theodore Sorensen recalled with horror what it was like for John Kennedy to look directly down "the gun barrel of nuclear war."[9] Yet despite an atmosphere of expectant foreboding, the policymakers did not crack; a way out was found, and war was avoided. Thus the key policymakers may have been neither rational actors nor irrational actors, as the commonest competing interpretations would have it. They were certainly fearful, but in spite of the magnitude of the fear they did not permit a failure of nuclear deterrence nor even a conventional war. This leads to the possibility that far from being an irrelevance or an impediment to a peaceful resolution, fear may instead have been connected, in some way, to that great escape of October 1962.

My thesis is this: that fear in the missile crisis was not only connected to the outcome, but that it actually *produced* the learning required to escape the predicament without a war. I believe, therefore, that an appreciation of the role of fear in the missile crisis is an absolutely essential prerequisite to an accurate understanding of why it was resolved peacefully. The key to the puzzle, I argue, is to comprehend how fear in the leaders of the superpowers during the missile crisis was both *profound* and *adaptive*—that is, how the fear of the shattered crystal ball led not to psychological breakdown under stress, as one might have predicted, but to a peaceful resolution. To understand the connection between fear and learning in this nuclear crisis we must, I argue, gain an accurate understanding of the object of the fear: *nuclear inadvertence.* Leaders of both superpowers, who originally believed that their opposite numbers might be willing to risk nuclear war over Cuba, understood by October 26 to 28 that if war came, and if that led to nuclear war, it would occur despite, not because of, the wishes of both parties to the conflict. Once they realized that the real adversary was the uncontrollable situation they had created, they grappled with the perverse situation and reversed its trajectory.

In the end, the fear of a shattered crystal ball may have been even more profound in the White House and Kremlin than it was in those living rooms within which sat the ordinary citizens who were horrified by the drama unfolding around them. Yet, as I will argue, the two types of fear were far from identical. Many citizens undoubtedly felt a visceral feeling of vulnerability to nuclear attack in a direct and immediate fashion. As was emphasized repeatedly in the media and in Congress, Soviet missiles were a mere 90 miles from the coast of Florida. Yet, as far as I can determine, American officials close to Kennedy felt little or none of this sort of fear. National Security Adviser McGeorge Bundy put the distinction this way:

> It wasn't the fear of the foot soldier, afraid of being killed when his time comes to hit the beach or go over the top. It was rather the fear of the commanding officer who, having ordered his men to "charge," suddenly feels that he has given the wrong order, and that he may be leading those for whom he is responsible into disaster. It was the fear of being responsible, not of being a victim; and I can say that it was profound by that last weekend [of the crisis].[10]

This is precisely what we should seek to understand about this fearful nuclear crisis: what the fear alluded to by Bundy was *like,* and what it was *about.* If we can do so with reasonable accuracy we will, I think, be approaching the passionate commitment to preventing its reoccurrence that is warranted by the probable catastrophic consequences of our failure to do so.

A few aspects of the crisis, while certainly relevant to its resolution, are not discussed in this book. The first is that while President Kennedy, all his closest advisers, and the majority of the members of the Executive Committee (EXCOMM) (formed by Kennedy to advise him on the crisis) apparently harbored the dread of nuclear war, a small minority of EXCOMM did not. These "hawks," dealt with at length in *On the Brink,*[11] seemed to have misapplied to the missile crisis the lessons they learned in the era before the Soviets acquired nuclear capability.

A second caveat has to do with the unavoidable asymmetry in this book between the attention given to American and Soviet sides of the crisis. What is available directly from the Soviet leadership is still derived almost completely from Khrushchev's memoirs.[12] We are now beginning to learn more about the Soviet experience of the crisis. (The present state of our knowledge, or impressions, is contained in part three of *On the Brink*.) Yet everything we have learned suggests that the shattered crystal ball was as terrifyingly real to Khrushchev and his colleagues as it was to Kennedy and his advisers.

A third issue, and one sure to trouble some students of international crises, is my claim that the Cuban missile crisis is, in an important sense, unique. No evidence suggests that any other episode in postwar U.S.–Soviet relations seemed to its key participants to carry the potential of a crisis that might spin out of control and escalate into war, perhaps nuclear war. The crisis most often compared with the Cuban missile crisis is the Berlin crisis of the previous year. While scholars are now engaged in a systematic study of nuclear risks in the Berlin situation between 1958 and 1962, it is already clear that the Soviets do not believe Cuba and Berlin were even remotely comparable as to nuclear danger, whatever the ultimate verdict on the Eisenhower and Kennedy administrations in the Berlin crises. But for now, the missile crisis does indeed seem to have involved, as Richard Neustadt said, a whole "new dimension of risk."[13]

Finally, philosophically sophisticated readers will note immediately that while I make extensive reference to Kierkegaard as the great analyst of shattering crises, I ignore the great Dane's strictures about distinguishing between fear and dread (or anxiety, as the newer translations render *angst*). There is a danger here, because the difference is real and important. To Kierkegaard, fear is a response to objects that may cause harm, while dread or anxiety is fear of "nothingness" or "finitude" or, in a typically Kierkegaardian display of paradox, "anxiety is the desire for what one fears, a sympathetic antipathy."[14] At some deep level of psychological analysis the experience of the Cuban missile crisis may indeed have involved something like "sympathetic antipathy." But I use "fear" throughout and try to specify what the fear was about (inadvertent nuclear war), and I try to allude to what it may have been like to feel such fear. I cite Kierkegaard, mainly in the epigraphs, to mark the thematic but not highly specific chords to be played out in the individual chapters.

Yet his relevance to the content of this book and the contribution of his thinking to the writing of it should not be underestimated. In fact, I move that, just as Thomas Schelling is required reading for students of nuclear strategy, Kierkegaard should be required for students of nuclear crises. And these two enterprises are far from identical. Kierkegaard would have understood this immediately, as evidenced by the following entry in his *Journal*: "Eternity is a very radical thought. Whenever it is posited, the present becomes something entirely different from what it was apart from it . . . a person will think it, and he dares not to think it."[15] This is one way to say why it has been so difficult, but why it is so necessary, to recover the psychological life of our leaders during the resolution of the Cuban missile crisis. One can enter, or reenter, this psychological terrain only as an alien, but how much better it is to do so in imagination rather than in the full fury of another nuclear crisis.

## 2

# The Facts: Some Results of the Critical Oral History of the Cuban Missile Crisis

Hardly is the cry of "fire" heard before a crowd of people rush to the spot, nice, cordial, sympathetic people, one has a pitcher, another a basin, the third a squirt, etc. . . . But what says the Fire Chief? . . . He bawls, "Oh go to hell with all your pitchers and squirts!" . . . For a fire is a serious thing, and whenever things are really serious, good intention by no means suffices.

Kierkegaard,
*Attack Upon "Christendom,"* 1854

Those leaders who experienced the shattered crystal ball in October 1962 did so in acts of imagination but not, I believe, in hallucination. This chapter will show that the danger of war between the superpowers was real and, at certain points, substantial. I must point out here, and will emphasize later in this book, that although this is a psychological study of the resolution of the missile crisis, it is *not* a book about what we today consider to be psychological problems. William James, in the finest and most influential text in English on psychology, chose this as his first sentence: "Psychology is the science of mental life, both of its phenomena and their conditions."[1] Much of this book is indeed concerned with the "phenomena," with the experience of living through a dangerous nuclear crisis with substantial responsibility for its outcome. And a good deal of that experience is concerned with the fear of inadvertent nuclear war. But we should continually be aware of the objective and subjective *conditions* that evoked such fearful responses. And, I would argue, the more we learn about the condition of relevant portions of the world in late October 1962, the more likely we are to conclude that the psychological phenomena, the fears, were largely justified. This book, therefore, is about fearful phenomena and the nuclear conditions that produced them.

The bulk of this chapter is occupied by an annotated chronology of the crisis, in which a few familiar facts are woven together with many that have only recently come to light as a result of the efforts of the Nuclear Crisis Project. It is selective, of course: I have emphasized data that accentuate our grasp of the nuclear danger inherent in the crisis. The account is meant only to suggest some of the points at which this crisis was more dangerous than is commonly supposed, or might have become too confusing, dangerous, or difficult to manage.[2]

*   *   *

It is now more than twenty-five years since the Cuban missile crisis, and we are finally gaining access to a flood of declassified documents that greatly clarify just what was contained in the flow of Cuba-related paper within the American government in those days. This is a far cry from the information available to earlier students of the crisis. Mainly, they relied on the often eloquent, but necessarily undocumented, histories written by those closest to Kennedy: Theodore Sorensen, Arthur Schlesinger, Jr., and especially Robert Kennedy.[3] Some of these newly available documents are very revealing, especially the transcriptions of secretly made tapes of the meetings of October 16 and 27, the first and last days of the intense phase of the crisis.[4] These are "real-time" documents, and they have already refuted several mythical "accounts" of the crisis and serve to refute anyone who believes that remembering is a relatively straightforward process. In addition, scores of other documents are keenly interesting and now publicly available.

The release of written documentation is in the end all but inevitable. Sooner or later we were bound to gain access to these documents. But what makes the present period of just a few years' duration so extraordinarily conducive to research on the Cuban missile crisis is that many of the key figures in the event are still alive and anxious to tell their stories and share their diverse thoughts and feelings about it. The juxtaposition of the availability of documents and the availability of crisis participants to interpret the meaning of the documents, especially what was thought or felt but left unsaid or unwritten, has given rise to a research strategy now called "critical oral history."[5]

The main idea behind critical oral history is psychological and derives from William James, who observed that human knowledge falls decisively into two categories: knowledge of *acquaintance,* learned from direct, concrete experience, that is to say from life; and knowledge *about,* which is derived mainly from books or other written or oral means for conveying conceptual understandings and explanations.[6] To take but one Jamesian example, a different *quality* of knowledge is derived from being chased by a bear in the forest and being nearly eaten alive, versus reading about it in the newspaper. While the notion is not profoundly surprising, it has provided an entry into a new way to study the past that has yielded surprisingly fruitful results. We seek to provide structured opportunities for the planned, but still quite unpredictable, collision of these two sorts of knowledge about the Cuban missile crisis: one from life, from having lived through the crisis in positions of power and responsibility; the other from documents, especially from the many declassified documents that have recently become available. Our goal has been to anchor the stories of former policymakers in a thickly woven net of facts and, at the same time, to enrich, to breathe the life of contingent and often ambiguous experience into material to be committed to scholars' notebooks. Originally conceived as a device for investigating American decision-making, we are now extending the use of critical oral history, aided by a steady tail wind of *glasnost,* to Soviet decision-making in the crisis.[7]

In a fine essay, H. R. Trevor-Roper cautioned that "history is full of surprises and if we lose the capacity to be surprised by it, we have lost the sense of it."[8] Critical oral history proves to be a marvelous antidote for this problem. The method has yielded so many surprises (some quite startling, either to scholars or to policymakers or both) that the difficulty is not the tedium of predictability, but the disorienting effect of continual surprise, even bafflement. Several findings already stand out from the rest. First, many policymakers have been astonished at their former colleagues' memories of certain events, leading all who have participated in this process to gain a healthier respect for the constructive, hindsighted, agenda-driven, and sometimes mistaken process of remembering. Many scholars have enthusiastically pointed out the many occasions when policymakers' memories failed to jibe with documentary evidence. Second, a good deal of information that is probably important concerning the Cuban missile crisis exists in no documents or, often, is misrepresented in documents. Chief among these—and this has impressed all the scholars who have participated in the critical oral history—has been the profound fear of inadvertent nuclear war that many policymakers remember feeling by the final weekend of the crisis. That fear exists in no document, but it is burned indelibly into the memories of those who experienced it. At the foundation of this fear apparently lay a heavy burden of potential responsibility for the shattering of the crystal ball that is even now, after all these years, very difficult for those who felt its weight to put satisfactorily into words.

*    *    *

At 7:00 P.M. EST, on October 22, 1962, President John F. Kennedy made a televised speech to the American people. It contained these central points: that the Soviet Union had begun to deploy medium- and intermediate-range nuclear missiles in Cuba, approximately 90 miles from Florida; that in so doing the Soviets demonstrated that they had for many months been lying about their intentions in Cuba; that the U.S. government was prepared not only to blockade the island but ultimately to do whatever might be necessary to remove the missiles from Cuba; and that a Soviet attack on any target in the United States or Latin America would result in what the President called "a full retaliatory response" on the Soviet Union.

Many people in the television audience understood the President to be threatening the Soviets with nuclear war if they tried to respond to American efforts to remove the missiles by striking at the United States. During the days that followed, many bomb shelters were stocked, and Americans stayed close to their TV sets while newsmen described the movement of Soviet ships toward a line of American naval vessels that had been assigned to blockade, or "quarantine," Cuba. The Navy's intention was to squeeze the Soviets in Cuba until they relinquished their offensive nuclear missiles and shipped them back to the Soviet Union. Almost at the last minute, on the morning of October 24, Soviet ships bound for Cuba reached the quarantine line and turned back. Later in the week, on October 27, the superpowers once again seemed poised on the brink of war as the Soviet missile sites reached completion, an American reconnaissance pilot was shot down and killed over Cuba, and the President ordered more than 100,000 combat-ready troops to southern Florida to prepare to invade Cuba. The next morning, however, just before 9:00 A.M. EST, Soviet Chairman Nikita Khrushchev announced in a broadcast over Radio Moscow that he would accept Kennedy's pledge not to invade Cuba in return for a Soviet pledge to remove their nuclear missiles from the island. Thus, the most intense phase of the crisis was over. What seemed like a roller coaster flirtation with oblivion had ended.

How did this happen? How did two governments, each realizing the catastrophic consequences of nuclear war, become entangled in a crisis that brought them perilously close to the catastrophe that neither wanted? Two key events appear to have motivated the inadvertent Soviet slide toward nuclear confrontation. What the Soviets have always referred to as the "Caribbean Crisis" began in earnest on Khrushchev's birthday—April 17, 1961—the day that the abortive American-sponsored Bay of Pigs invasion began. That the invasion failed miserably was far less significant to the Soviets and to the Cubans than that the new Kennedy administration had demonstrated its intention to use armed force to remove from power the Soviet-backed government in Havana, led by Fidel Castro. Soviets and Cubans concluded that the next time the Americans would attack in force, just as they had always done in the region, by sending in the Marines, conquering the island, and setting up a new government more congenial to American interests.

The other shock came later in 1961 during the Berlin Wall crisis. On October 21, Deputy Secretary of Defense Roswell Gilpatric gave a speech in Virginia that confirmed the worst Soviet fears regarding their nuclear vulnerability. The Americans, Gilpatric revealed in numerical detail, were far superior to the Soviets in deliverable nuclear weapons. The Soviets were revealed before the whole world to be so far behind, in fact, that they began to fear that the Americans were entertaining the possibility of what was then referred to in the Pentagon as a "splendid first strike," that is, a massive nuclear attack on Soviet forces sufficient both to prevent any significant retaliation and to destroy the Soviet Union as a functioning society.

These twin fears—of losing Cuba and of losing the nuclear arms race so badly as to invite a successful American attack—drove Khrushchev to his fateful decision secretly to deploy medium- and intermediate-range nuclear missiles in Cuba. The Americans, he felt, would not dare attack Cuba if they knew that Soviet weapons there were capable of striking much of the American homeland. Moreover, in this one secret deployment of a few dozen missiles, Khrushchev well understood that he would suddenly acquire the capability to destroy a substantial proportion of American nuclear forces (nearly 40 percent of the nuclear bomber force of the Strategic Air Command). This would also mean that many American cities and millions of American citizens could be destroyed quickly, without warning, and with missiles against which no defense existed. This was in fact the argument put to Khrushchev by Defense Minister Marshall Rodion Malinovsky who was, we now know, one of only five other men who conspired with Khrushchev in the early planning of the deployment.

Khrushchev planned to shock Kennedy with deeds, just as he had shocked the young President with verbal threats over Berlin at their only meeting, in Vienna, June 3 and 4, 1961. He would give the Americans some of their own nuclear medicine. With the deployment of the missiles, he believed sincerely, he would take a giant step toward establishing the USSR as the other full-fledged nuclear superpower. Furthermore, Khrushchev not only believed he would get away with this daring gambit; he was also convinced that when, according to plan, he announced the deployment at the UN in November, the effect would actually be to *improve* U.S.–Soviet relations. The nuclear balance, thereafter more equal and stable, would usher in Khrushchev's long-sought détente. He believed that Kennedy was too young, weak, and intellectual to resist the deployment forcefully, and that he would simply find a way to accommodate himself to the new situation. It is also likely that Khrushchev believed the deployment would permit him to undertake a deal that, from his new position of military strength, would finally allow him to remove what he called "the bone in my throat"—Allied presence in Berlin and the very real threat, as he saw it, of German reunification and nuclearization. And so the secret deployment of Soviet nuclear missiles to Cuba began, and with it an inadvertent slide toward shattering the nuclear crystal ball.

Khrushchev certainly achieved his immediate goal, although hardly his desired outcome, on October 16, 1962. On that day reconnaissance photographs revealed to President Kennedy that nuclear missile sites were under construction in Cuba and that they would soon be completed. The shock to the White House was profound. The President and his closest advisers could scarcely believe it. In fact, National Security Adviser McGeorge Bundy had explained on national television two days earlier why he believed it unlikely that the Soviets would ever try to deploy offensive nuclear missiles in Cuba. Attorney General Robert Kennedy spent the morning of October 16 in the photo laboratory where the pictures had been developed, certain that there had been some mistake. But there was no mistake. At 11:00 A.M. on October 16, the President convened the first meeting of the Executive Committee of the National Security Council (EXCOMM) to advise him on how to proceed. They agreed at once that the missiles must be removed. But how, and at what cost? During the week that followed, EXCOMM debated their course of action in secret. They eventually chose neither the immediate air strike, which ran the risk of rapid military escalation, nor the purely diplomatic approach, for it was inconceivable to them that Khrushchev, who had in their view lied repeatedly about placing missiles into Cuba, could be persuaded or trusted to remove his missiles merely by gentlemanly diplomacy. (We now know that Khrushchev and his colleagues in the Kremlin lied not only to the Americans but also to their own representatives in the United States, including their U.S. Ambassador Anatoly Dobrynin, UN Ambassador Valerian Zorin, and the courier of the Kennedy-Khrushchev correspondence, Giorgi Bolshakov. They had been deceived by their own government so that their "lies" would be convincing.)

By October 22, EXCOMM had decided on a middle course, a quarantine of Cuba. At 7:00 P.M. the President gave his speech, revealing to the nation and the world the presence of the missiles in Cuba and his strategy for removing them. We now believe, based on information derived from Soviet sources, that Khrushchev, having just returned from a long, well-publicized vacation designed in part to lull American intelligence agencies, was at least as shocked by Kennedy's speech as Kennedy was by Khrushchev's missiles. Khrushchev and the crisis exploded simultaneously. The unforgettable public phase of the Cuban missile/Caribbean crisis had now begun.

Work at the missile sites in Cuba was immediately speeded up to become twenty-four hour activity. Soviet ships steaming toward Cuba approached the quarantine line very closely, then stopped dead in the water before reversing course and heading back to the Soviet Union. We now have reason to believe that the Soviet standstill at the quarantine line almost didn't happen. Only a furious, and still incompletely understood, round of activity in the Kremlin may have brought this about, for Khrushchev, furious with the blockade and with having had his scheme exposed, apparently had initially ordered the Soviet vessels to crash the line, located several hundred miles from Cuba. American standing orders were to sink any Soviet ship that tried to run the line, and there is no reason to doubt that they would have done so. Thus on the morning of Wednesday, October 24, war between the superpowers may have been less than an hour away when Khrushchev's order was rescinded and the Soviet ships and submarines turned back.

During the climactic final weekend of the crisis, October 26 to 28, Americans and Soviets seemed once again to stand squarely on the brink of war. Fidel Castro, fearing that the Soviets were preparing to deal away the missiles he now deemed necessary for the survival of his government, broke away from Soviet control and ordered his several hundred air defense units to shoot down all American aircraft entering Cuban airspace. This order applied especially to unarmed, low-flying reconnaissance planes responsible for close-up photos of the progress of work at the missile sites. The Soviet leadership in the Kremlin, however, maintained its standing order to its surface-to-air missile (SAM) crews not to fire at high-flying American U-2 reconnaissance aircraft. At approximately 10:30 A.M. EST, however, a U-2 was shot down over Cuba and its pilot killed. Word of the U-2 downing reached EXCOMM late that afternoon. All its members seem to have believed that the order had come from Moscow, and that this might mean the Soviets were prepared to risk escalating the crisis to a shooting war. We now know that the President and his advisers were right to believe that the Soviets, not the Cubans, had given the order to shoot down the U-2. But we also know they were wrong to assume that the order came from Moscow, for it did not. The order came from a Soviet commander in Cuba (whose identity is known) in opposition to his standing orders under very confusing and difficult circumstances.

There was also a good deal of confusion in the White House. On Friday, October 26, the Americans received a private letter from Khrushchev, apparently proposing the removal of the Cuban missiles in exchange for a public American pledge never to invade Cuba. Arriving late in the day on Friday the twenty-sixth, the proposed terms were acceptable in principle to Kennedy and his advisers. They went to bed that night believing the end of the crisis was in sight, some returning to their homes for the first time since they first learned of the missile deployment nearly two weeks earlier. But before they could reply on the morning of October 27, American radio broadcast a statement by Khrushchev, who had added a stipulation that most of Kennedy's advisers thought was impossible to implement: trading Soviet missiles in Cuba for NATO Jupiter missiles on the Soviet southern border in Turkey. In putting forth this stipulation, the Soviets made the same mistake the Americans were to make later that day. The Soviets assumed, wrongly, that American-supplied missiles in Turkey were controlled by the American government. But the Soviets were wrong. The Jupiters were under the jurisdiction of the Turks, although the Americans retained custody of the nuclear warheads, and the Turks absolutely refused to bargain away their missiles for what they took to be a local American problem in the Caribbean. The Americans would later assume, also wrongly, that key events at the missile sites in Cuba were controlled by leaders in the Kremlin. Each superpower had great difficulty in appreciating the considerable extent to which the other was *not* in control of crucial circumstances and events.

The second (public) Soviet offer thus thrust the Americans into their own "Turkish missile crisis." Not until late in the evening on Saturday, October 27, was a skeptical President Kennedy persuaded—mainly by Soviet specialist Llewellyn Thompson—to accept Khrushchev's first offer and simply to ignore the second as if he had never received it. We are, in fact, only now beginning to understand just how perplexing was this "Turkish missile crisis" in the White House. The transcript of the secret tapes of EXCOMM meetings on October 27 reveals evident confusion about which Soviet offer was operative. The transcript also reveals a president who was convinced that trading missiles, however distasteful that might have been to the Turks and NATO generally, was certainly preferable to a war, begun in Cuba, that might spread to Europe. Before EXCOMM adjourned that night, Kennedy was persuaded to send off a letter to Khrushchev that, in effect, said "thank you" to the first offer and did not require any public missile trade. It is ironic that few in EXCOMM, including the President, seem to have believed that this ploy would work. Yet it was the only card they felt they had to play short of war, or of some form of capitulation to Khrushchev's latest proposal for a public missile trade.

No one can say for sure what would have happened if Khrushchev had not responded immediately and affirmatively or if, for some reason, his response had been delayed in reaching the White House. But on Saturday evening, Robert Kennedy had been sent to Ambassador Dobrynin with an urgent message: Khrushchev had twenty-four hours to agree to the terms of the American letter or the Americans would move militarily against Cuba; and that no more shootdowns of unarmed American reconnaissance aircraft over Cuba would be tolerated, for the next one would provoke, Robert Kennedy strongly implied, a large-scale air strike against all the missile sites in Cuba. He also conveyed through Dobrynin a private assurance that the land-based Jupiters in Turkey, already scheduled for removal in the near future, would soon give way to sea-based Polaris submarines. If, after sending this message to Moscow, President Kennedy had not gotten a quick and affirmative response, he could have ordered a tightening of the quarantine. He might actually have ordered the air strike and invasion of Cuba. Or he might have averted war at the eleventh hour simply by agreeing to trade missiles publicly with Khrushchev. At one of our critical oral history conferences in 1987, former Secretary of

State Dean Rusk revealed for the first time that the President had, late in the evening of October 27, ordered Rusk to open up a secret channel to Acting Secretary General U Thant at the UN, preparing the way for such a trade, which would have been made to appear as a UN initiative to which Kennedy and Khrushchev would presumably then accede.

The situation on the evening of October 27 looked very grim. As our critical oral history has unfolded, we have discovered that in those moments the men closest to the President were intensely conscious of the nuclear danger, and that Soviet leaders felt the same way. The Strategic Air Command (SAC) was put on airborne alert and, for the first and only time, SAC went to Defense Condition (Def Con) 2, during which the B-52 bomber forces prepared for their missions and the lids were removed from the silos containing American ICBMs targeted on the Soviet Union. In fact, as we discovered not long ago, Def Con 2 was declared "in the clear" via an unscrambled signal. SAC Commander General Thomas Power did so without approval and apparently with the intent of shoving the Soviets' evident nuclear inferiority in their faces, thereby giving every impression that the Americans were in the final stages of preparing for a preemptive nuclear strike against the Soviet Union. We now know that, in response, near-panic broke out at Khrushchev's dacha, 30 kilometers outside Moscow, as he and several aides rushed an immediate and conciliatory reply by car into the city for immediate transmission over Radio Moscow. Having received what he believed to be Kennedy's final offer, and with the knowledge that he no longer controlled events in Cuba and that Castro was apparently trying to provoke a war, Khrushchev could only hope his message would reach Kennedy in time.

Kennedy and Khrushchev went to bed that night having inadvertently moved the world closer to nuclear war than at any time before or since. Was the crystal ball about to shatter? Kennedy and his advisers wondered whether, as recent events seemed to suggest, Khrushchev and his colleagues would actually go to war over a few dozen missiles in Cuba. The men in the Kremlin, meanwhile, wondered whether the American military had overwhelmed the President and were about to destroy the Soviet Union in a nuclear attack. Nothing could be clearer than that neither Kennedy nor Khrushchev wanted war. Each seems also to have believed that the other was looking for a way out. Equally clear is their pessimism on what has become known to many former associates of both as "Black Saturday," October 27, 1962, when the onrush of events toward war seemed to be surpassing their ability to manage them. Yet the solution was found the night of

"Black Saturday" and the early morning hours of the following Sunday, as minds, rather than armies, met in the night. The Soviets would remove their missiles; the Americans would leave Cuba alone; the Turkish missiles would be removed in due course, although they were not to be part of the public deal.

While the crisis may have *seemed* to be over, especially to the Americans, we have recently learned that a later, "November crisis" occurred in Cuba that was very tough on the Soviets and Cubans, in ways the Americans could scarcely appreciate. Castro sought by every means available to thwart the deal. Remembering the 1961 Bay of Pigs, when he had personally led the counterattack against the American-supplied Cuban exiles, he was enraged that his Soviet ally was trying to force him to give up nuclear missiles (and bombers) for what he regarded as an empty and worthless American pledge to leave him alone. When word of the Kennedy-Khrushchev deal reached Cuba, Castro appears to have ordered regular units of the Cuban army to surround the Soviet missile sites, presumably to prevent removal of the missiles. The troops were not withdrawn until November 2, with the arrival in Cuba of Soviet First Deputy Premier Anastas I. Mikoyan, Khrushchev's special negotiator. In the end, Mikoyan persuaded Castro to agree to relinquish not only the missiles but also IL-28 bombers, deemed by the Americans to be "nuclear capable." The negotiations were complex and very difficult, and involved Mikoyan, Castro, and Soviet Ambassador Aleksander Alekseev in Cuba, and Vasily Kuznetsov, John McCloy, and Adlai Stevenson in New York. In the end, all Castro could do was to prevent on-site inspection and air reconnaissance over Cuba, forcing the Soviets and Americans to adopt a procedure involving American inspection, in international waters, of Soviet ships bound from Cuba to the Soviet Union.

This would be the only public recompense Castro would receive for his willingness, first, to accept the Soviet missiles, at the urging of Marshall Sergei S. Biryuzov, commander of the Soviet Strategic Rocket Forces (Biryuzov had been in Cuba in the spring of 1962 on a secret mission to explore for Khrushchev possibilities for the Cuban deployment); and second, for his willingness to return the Soviet missiles for an American promise. During the November negotiations, Castro took Mikoyan to a crocodile farm near the Bay of Pigs. As he fed fish to the crocodiles, Castro lectured Mikoyan and compared Cuba to a little fish, while two large crocodiles were comparable, he said, to the U.S. and USSR. According to Castro, the relevant question was: Which crocodile would devour the fish? To this day, Castro remains bitter about his treatment by both superpowers and is evidently unrepentant about his efforts to defend what he took to be his right of national sovereignty, even at the possible cost of provoking of a war.

On November 19, President Kennedy announced at a press conference that the crisis was at an end, and he ordered cancellation of the nuclear alert. Thus ended the most dangerous crisis in history, an unforeseen event with an unexpectedly swift and peaceful conclusion. At first angry, then by turns confused and finally deeply worried, the leaders of the superpowers and much of the world were deeply sobered by the experience. We have had nothing like it since, due in part to our personal and institutional memories of those autumn days of 1962. Many people believed then, perhaps for the first time, that major nuclear war, barely thinkable, was suddenly quite possible. It became all too clear that it is possible for the superpowers to slide into situations in which, despite its obvious irrationality, a crisis can accelerate beyond control, as it almost did in October 1962.

PART TWO: PROBLEMS

## 3

# The Empirical Problem: Understanding McNamara's Fear

Man has a natural dread of walking in the dark . . . where all relative considerations (the lanterns which are normally a help to us) are quenched.

Kierkegaard,
*Journals,* 1850–1854

A nugget of sensible, radical empiricist wisdom, attributed to Mies van der Rohe, holds that "God dwells in the details." In this chapter, I invite the reader to consider some unusually detailed information from what is undoubtedly one of the most illuminating documents we shall ever have concerning the resolution of the Cuban missile crisis: the transcription of audio tapes, made secretly by President Kennedy, of EXCOMM meetings of October 27, 1962.[1] They provide the fascination of voyeurism of the highest order and induce the feeling that one is, so to speak, sitting under the table at which important decisions are being made that will affect the outcome of history. The thickly textured detail in the recently made available material also strongly suggests, I believe, that neither the public at large nor the strategic professionals have understood exactly what, at the point of its resolution, the Cuban missile crisis was all about. This is because few seem to have understood the character, ubiquity, and power of the fear of inadvertent nuclear war that overtook the American leadership on the last day of the crisis. The document doesn't prove my point about the fundamentally private character and profundity of experienced fear. But the material contained in it suggests, I will argue, that if we are to comprehend the resolution of the missile crisis, we will need to

25

revolutionize the psychological concepts within which we form our understanding of the event, in line with what I take to be the revolutionary characteristics of the crisis. We must therefore begin our inquiry with a different set of assumptions—a different "psychology"—a subject I take up in a more formal way in Part Three.

In title and context, this chapter is focused on the experience of Secretary of Defense Robert McNamara. I emphasize McNamara not because he is in any sense the "key" player or the central guarantor of the outcome. In the White House, ultimate responsibility fell to President Kennedy, just as Nikita Khrushchev bore the burden in the Kremlin. In fact, however, McNamara was, and remains, unusually explicit about whatever it was that concerned him. And in the document that is the focus of this chapter, McNamara spoke more explicitly than most when he arrived at the psychological cul-de-sac that is the shattered crystal ball.

Let us begin with ordinary people's reactions to the crisis. What were they? Although my data base is far from comprehensive, deriving from psychological studies done by others after the crisis and from the memories of acquaintances, my impression is that the episode evoked in ordinary people three sorts of response patterns. All seem to have been either reactions to the possibility of actually being destroyed by Soviet nuclear missiles, or wide-eyed enthusiasm about destroying the Soviets. First, there was *denial,* the nervous refusal to face what almost everyone took to be the fact of the matter, which was that American citizens were at risk of nuclear annihilation. In his fine novel *The Nuclear Age,* Tim O'Brien has vividly captured this most common reaction to the missile crisis:

> At school we practiced evacuation drills. There was bravado and squealing.
> *Hey, hey!*
> *What do you say?*
> *Nikita plans*
> *to blow us away!*
> A convocation in the school gym. The principal delivered a speech about the need for courage and calm. . . . The pastor of the First Baptist Church offered a punchy prayer, then we filed back to the classrooms to pursue the study of math and physics.
>
> How?
> By rolling dice. By playing solitaire. By adding up assets, smoking cigarettes, getting ready for Halloween, touching bases, treading water.
> A dream, wasn't it!
> Jets scrambled over Miami Beach and warships cruised through the warm turquoise waters off St. Thomas.

"How's tricks?" my dad asked.
"Fine."
"Flashes?"
"What flashes?"
He grinned. "That's the ticket. *What* flashes?"
We held together.
By pretending.
By issuing declarations of faith.
"They aren't madmen," my mother said.
"Exactly," said my father.
So we played Scrabble at the kitchen table, quibbling over proper nouns and
secondary spellings.
"They know better."
"Of course."
"Even the Russians—they don't want it—politics, that's all it is. True? Isn't
that true?"
"Oh, Christ," my father said.[2]

Many ordinary families, inundated by media reports of an impending
nuclear showdown but absolutely helpless in the face of it, must also have
told themselves stories they hoped were true, especially about the Soviets.
But in their minds "the Russians" were epitomized by Nikita Khrushchev,
the bombastic Soviet leader who had said he would "bury you," and then
pounded his shoe on a desk at the UN, as if to reinforce the point. But
people tried to get on with life. What else could they do?
    They could have showed two other kinds of response that, during the
public week of the crisis following the President's speech of October 22,
received some headlines of their own. These were the extreme and
antithetical reactions of those who fell into a panic, in fear of a Soviet
nuclear attack, and those who actually seemed to welcome it as the long-
awaited showdown, the outcome of which would be the total destruction
of the Soviet Union, the East Bloc, and the Communists. For these
nuclear warriors, the fear of the crisis was instead anticipation and genuine
excitement. The former group cowered in fear; the latter rooted their
government on to victory over the Communists. In his comprehensive
history of atomic imagery, *Nuclear Fear,* Spencer Weart illustrated these
two phenomena with data and an anecdote:

> a considerable number of people from London to Tokyo thought they might
> not live to see another dawn. Young people in particular became deeply
> alarmed. The public was calm only in Moscow, where the press called for
> peace and did not mention until after the crisis was over that the squabble

had something to do with nuclear missiles. In Washington shovels and sandbags were sold out at hardware stores, while Pentagon employees snatched up civil defense leaflets. In some cities, food hoarding panics stripped supermarkets bare. . . . Not everyone was so afraid. At Cornell University, where I was then a student, when the campus SANE group put a speaker on the steps of the student union building, members of the crowd shouted him down. Some of these students had been approached by the Minutemen, a national right-wing group that was stockpiling materials for guerilla warfare in case of Communist invasion. When the exasperated speaker asked his hecklers, "Are you ready for nuclear war?" they roared back, "YES!" Similar clashes took place elsewhere.[3]

These were the responses of the relatively few: the vocal and the relatively (though by no means exclusively) young. The perceived stimulus was the same: the live possibility of a nuclear attack. Some feared it enormously and said so. Some looked forward to the nuclear attack the Americans were, they hoped, about to launch against the Soviets.

These accounts of reactions of ordinary citizens put into sharp relief the range of options available to people who had no control over, nor responsibility for, the outcome of the crisis. Assuming that a person was aware of the seriousness of the situation, he could speak and act as if it were not all that serious, pretending and hoping that it would turn out all right. Or, if he believed it was a serious confrontation likely to have a nuclear result, he could panic or become aggressive. He could pray for those who were responsible for the outcome to call it off before the world was destroyed. Or he could root for his government to push the adversary into a corner, even to the extent of launching a nuclear attack.

I want specifically to emphasize that the *quality* of this sort of experience of the Cuban missile crisis is that of the spectator, the passive observer whose views and actions, as far as can be determined, count for nothing as regards the outcome. The epiphenomenal quality of this sort of experience meant that those who shared it could be as passively denying, nervously panicky, or blatantly aggressive as they pleased, having only to conform, as usual, to the norms and expectations of those whose opinions of their behavior mattered to them. The Cuban missile crisis was therefore a stimulus not very different from a roller coaster in an amusement park. You could fear it and avoid it; you could ride it and panic and scream and hope that you lived through it; or you could ride it, throw your fist into the air, and thoroughly enjoy the risky thrill of the experience. In any case, you would be responsible for only your emotions. The roller coaster would go where it was bound to go, regardless of your emotional reaction. And that is the point: you are not, you cannot be, responsible for the outcome of the ride, which, while it may feel confining, actually liberates you to respond directly to your emotions.

These considerations are important because, I believe, many influential interpreters of the Cuban missile crisis, including those whose views have come to dominate the "professionals' " understanding of it—those who would apply its lessons to nuclear crisis prevention and management generally, have mistakenly assumed that those most responsible for the outcome of the crisis had the same *kinds* of experiences, the same range of psychological options open to them, as did ordinary powerless people. This is especially true, and therefore significant, when their analyses arrive at the role of fear in the resolution of the crisis. Heretofore lacking the thickly textured data to which I will shortly refer, these analysts have assumed, usually implicitly but wrongly, that the leaders' experience of resolving the missile crisis must have been analogous to that of ordinary people—that is, if they experienced fear at all, it must have been the fear of a nuclear attack, the fear of death for oneself and loved ones. Moreover, analysts have assumed that because those men had awesome responsibilities for the outcome of the confrontation, any fear they did feel must have been counterproductive because it would necessarily have had to mirror the passive denial, panic, or aggression witnessed in ordinary people throughout the crisis. Because the men in the White House and Kremlin *did* have nuclear responsibilities and problems to solve, fearful responses, according to this view, cannot have helped their efforts and may even have hindered them, if the fear was sufficiently severe.

In the Cuban missile crisis, according to all these otherwise quite diverse approaches, the more rational the actors, the better, the more capable, and the more efficient nuclear problem-solvers they were bound to be. That is why (as discussed in more detail in Chapter 4) these approaches should be called the rational/irrational actor psychologies of avoiding nuclear war. Some emphasize the rationality, and relish it; some emphasize the irrationality, and regret it. But the salient dimension is uniformly one whose poles are "rational" and "irrational." So, among those strategists, arms controllers, crisis managers, and others who think professionally about these matters: in the Cuban missile crisis there should have been fearless, rational, and therefore effective leaders who succeeded; and there were (or were not, or may have been) fearful, irrational, and ineffective leaders who were lucky. Fear was not adaptive. *Fear not* has become the first commandment of the enterprise, and the Cuban missile crisis has become its exemplar. People who hold this view cannot possibly understand what I refer to eponymously as "McNamara's fear," the mortifying but adaptive, crisis-resolving fear of the shattered crystal ball.

And that is the problem referred to in the title of this chapter: those who subscribe to the rational/irrational actor approach cannot understand that fear *produced* the peaceful outcome because they do not appreciate that the fear the leaders experienced had nothing to do with the fearful responses of ordinary people, which provide their working models of fear. Lacking hard data to the contrary, and also heavily influenced by disciplinary and ideological and also, one would guess, by their own experience of the crisis as citizens without responsibility for its outcome, the interpreters of the missile crisis have imagined that the experience of fear in the White House and Kremlin (if there was any) mirrored their own—our own.[4] But in this, I believe, they are mistaken, and their mistake has consequences that reach far beyond the missile crisis, because upon this mistake rests the weight of professional thinking regarding the prevention or management of some such future occurrence.

Here I provide only two examples of this absolutely central, mistaken inference about the psychology of the missile crisis. I mean not to close the case but to open it, and I will thus be illustrative rather than systematic, leaving detailed analysis for Chapters 4 and 6, below.

The first example comes from an influential study by Albert and Roberta Wohlstetter, praising the members of the Kennedy administration for slyly and successfully pretending to Khrushchev that they actually feared that the risk of war was uncomfortably high and that events might be spinning out of control. The Wohlstetters profess disbelief that President Kennedy and his advisers could have been fearful, that they thought war so probable as to justify assertions like the President's to Theodore Sorensen that, on the final weekend of the crisis, the odds of war between the superpowers were "between one out of three and even," with all the catastrophic implications of what Arthur Schlesinger called "Kennedy's grim odds." Here is how the Wohlstetters responded to such assertions:

> Some of President Kennedy's statements in the crisis and after may have overstated the likelihood of a nuclear exchange. He was appropriately anxious to express the gravity of his concern about such a catastrophe . . . though control was evident in every one of his moves, President Kennedy's statements did not stress in words that he was in control. It has therefore been possible to misconstrue just what were the risks in the crisis. The matter is of great importance.[5]

Indeed, it is important. We must keep in mind what the President actually said, many times, about feared inadvertence. In his October 28 response to Khrushchev, for example, the President said:

I am replying at once to your broadcast message of October 28, even though the official text has not reached me, because of the great importance I attach to moving forward promptly to the settlement of the Cuban crisis. I think that you and I, with our heavy responsibilities for the maintenance of peace, were aware that *developments were approaching a point where events could have become unmanageable.*[6]

In fact, the Wohlstetters would lead us to believe that the Kennedy administration was extraordinarily clever in their strategy of pretending to lose control; that in doing so, they were able to strike fear into the Soviets, who seem as a function of American cleverness in the matter to have actually *believed* it, thus causing them to back down. Having drained the fear from the White House in their explanation of the crisis, the Wohlstetters dumped it onto the Kremlin, or rather asserted that this is what Kennedy and his colleagues did by design.

Yet the Wohlstetters issued a caution: "Threats," they concluded, "should be administered by prescription, against special dangers, and in small doses. Its use except in extremis is not compatible with a reputation for being both sane and meaning what one says."[7] In other words, contrary to what the President said and contrary to what was reported by most of his closest aides, there was during the missile crisis no appreciable fear of nuclear inadvertence, only the threat of uncontrollability. The Wohlstetters claimed, in effect, that the President and his men, in complete control of the situation throughout the missile crisis, successfully deceived Khrushchev by "threatening" to lose control of the situation.

Where the Wohlstetters perceived a rational, if deceptive, Kennedy administration, fearless and therefore successful, Richard Ned Lebow has seen irrational psychopathology at almost every turn. He has argued, for example, that Kennedy's irrational, Cold War obsessions caused him to manipulate EXCOMM toward ever more aggressive and dangerous actions. According to Lebow: "The evidence of promotional leadership and group-think in the Cuban case raises important doubts in this author's mind about the extent to which leaders are willing and able to take steps to overcome these kinds of decision-making pathologies."[8] Kennedy, like the right-wing Minutemen described earlier by Spencer Weart, would use the opportunity to push the Soviets to the wall, via his "promotional leadership" for military action. Lebow has also suggested that at least some members of EXCOMM, perhaps as a result of Kennedy's bullying them toward unnecessarily aggressive action, became overwhelmed by the experience, caved in and became dysfunctional. Lebow reported that "two important members of EXCOMM had been unable to cope with the stress of that confrontation; they became entirely passive and were unable to fulfill their responsibilities."[9]

For my present purpose, I want only to suggest that the kind of analysis that typifies these characterizations of Kennedy and his advisers could easily apply to the ordinary people I introduced at the outset of this chapter. Being afraid, or otherwise emotional, is in this view a problem for personal management, a psychological problem with a psychological solution. The difference is that if ordinary people acted out their fearful feelings during the missile crisis, it didn't affect the outcome. But, according to the paradigmatic tradition exemplified by analysts like the Wohlstetters and Lebow, top-level decision makers acting on their fear can only harm their ability to succeed. According to these authors, there is no way that profound fear can be salutary. Their theories won't permit it.

Fortunately, concerning what went on in the White House on October 27, 1962, we are not as dependent upon theory as we used to be. A few years ago, the minutes of some of those meetings became available and were indeed interesting, but they constituted a still quite homogenized accounting of EXCOMM's deliberations.[10] But in December 1987, the transcription was released of the actual taped conversations in EXCOMM on that pivotal day. Here I present a small portion, largely devoid of internal commentary, so that the rawness of this data sinks in. The information—"the facts"—in the previous chapter should provide a sufficient guide through the material. As far as we know, only the President knew the sessions were being recorded. The selection concerns EXCOMM's reaction to the shootdown of the U-2 over Cuba, the notification of which arrived late in the afternoon via General Maxwell Taylor. I have edited the material in order to emphasize the reactions of Robert McNamara, to focus and crystallize the points that need to be made. I ask that the reader keep the following questions in mind: Does McNamara appear to be fearful? If so, what does he seem to be afraid of? What, if anything, does this sort of fear have to do with the various expressions for the fear of attack, such as we have discussed thus far in the chapter?

[Late afternoon, October 27, 1962, the White House. EXCOMM has spent much of the day discussing Khrushchev's latest offer, which involves trading NATO missiles in Turkey for Soviet missiles in Cuba, a deal that, as EXCOMM member Paul Nitze has said, is "absolutely anathema" to the Turks and NATO in general.[11] The meeting is now interrupted by the arrival of General Maxwell Taylor, chairman of the Joint Chiefs of Staff.]

ROBERT MCNAMARA:  I think the rush is what do we do—
VOICE:  The U-2.

McNAMARA: The U-2 is shot down—the fire against our low-altitude surveillance—

RFK: U-2 shot down?

McNAMARA: Yes . . . it was found shot down.

RFK: Pilot killed?

GEN. MAXWELL TAYLOR: It was shot down near Banes which is right near a U-2 [sic] site in eastern Cuba.

VOICE: A SAM-site.

TAYLOR: The pilot's body is in the plane. Apparently this was a SAM-site that had actually had the energy . . . It all ties in in a very plausible way. . . .

JFK: This is much of an escalation by them, isn't it?

McNAMARA: Yes, exactly . . . How do we interpret this? I know—I don't know how to interpret—

TAYLOR: They feel they must respond now. The whole world knows where we're flying. That raises the question of retaliation against the SAM-sites. We think we . . . we have various other reasons to believe that we know the SAM-sites. A few days ago—

JFK: How can we put a U-2 fellow over there tomorrow unless we take out *all* the SAM-sites?

McNAMARA: That's just exactly—in fact, I don't think we can.

TAYLOR: . . . It's on the ground—the wreckage is on the ground. The pilot's dead.

McNAMARA: In the water, isn't it?

TAYLOR: I didn't get the water part.

McGEORGE BUNDY: If we know it, it must be either on friendly land or water.

VOICE: It is on Cuban land. [Words unclear.]

TAYLOR: That's what I got. . . .

JOHN McCONE: I wonder if this shouldn't cause a most violent protest . . . a letter right to Khrushchev. Here's, here's an action they've taken against—against us, a new order in defiance of—of public statements he made. I think that—

VOICE: I think we ought—
VOICE: They've fired the first shot.
JFK: They say—uh—that's why I'd like to find out whether Havana says they did shoot it down.
VOICE: We don't have anything from Havana yet, do we?
VOICE: We assume these SAM-sites are manned by Soviets.
VOICE: That's the significant part if it *is* the SAM-site.

. . . . . . . . . . . . . . . . . . . . . . . . . . . . . . . . . . . . . . . . . . . . . . . . .

McNAMARA: This is a change of pattern, now why it's a change of pattern we don't know.
RFK: Yeah.
ALEXIS JOHNSON: It's a very different thing. You could have an undisciplined anti-aircraft—Cuban anti-aircraft outfit fire, but to have a SAM-site and a Russian crew fire is not any accident.
JFK: I think we ought to—why don't we send an instruction to [U.S. Ambassador to Turkey Raymond] Hare to have a conversation, but also have the NATO meeting? And say to them what's happening over here. Otherwise we're going to be carrying a hell of a bag.
DOUGLAS DILLON: I think we're going to have such pressure internally in the United States, too, to act quickly . . .
JFK: . . . That's why I think we'd better have a NATO meeting tomorrow . . . Explain the thing, where we are—uh—I'm afraid of what's going to happen in NATO, to Europe, when we get into this thing more and more, and I think they ought to feel that they've a part of it. Even if we don't do anything about the Turks, they ought to feel that they know.

[President Kennedy momentarily leaves the room. Robert McNamara now addresses the connection, as he sees it, between the shooting over Cuba and the NATO missiles in Turkey.]

McNAMARA: We must be in a position to attack, quickly. We've been fired on today. We're going to send surveillance aircraft in tomorrow. Those are going to be fired on without question. We're going to respond. You can't do this very long. We're going to lose airplanes, and we'll be shooting up Cuba quite a bit, but we're going to lose airplanes every day. So you just can't maintain this position very long. So we must be prepared to attack Cuba—quickly. That's the first proposition. Now the second proposition. When we attack Cuba we're going to have to attack with an all-out attack, and that means [deleted] sorties at a minimum the first day, and it means sorties every day thereafter, and I personally believe that this is almost certain to lead to an invasion, I won't say certain to, but *almost* certain to lead to an invasion—

DILLON: Unless you get a cease-fire around the world—

McNAMARA: That's the second proposition.

BUNDY: Or a general war.

McNAMARA: The third proposition is that if we do this, and leave those missiles in Turkey the Soviet Union *may,* and I think probably will, attack the Turkish missiles. Now the fourth proposition is, *if* the Soviet Union attacks the Turkish missiles, we *must* respond. We *cannot* allow a Soviet attack on the—on the Jupiter missiles in Turkey without a military response by NATO.

LLEWELLYN THOMPSON: Somewhere.

McNAMARA: Somewhere, that's right.

. . . . . . . . . . . . . . . . . . . . . . . . . . . . . . . . . . . . . . . . . . . . . . . . . . . .

VOICE: Frankly, I don't—

McNAMARA: Well, I've got a—why don't I get through— then let's go back and attack each one of my propositions. Now the minimum military response by NATO to a Soviet attack on the Turkish Jupiter missiles would be a response with conventional weapons by NATO forces in Turkey, that is to say Turkish and U.S. aircraft, against Soviet warships and/or naval bases in the Black Sea area. Now that to me is the absolute minimum, and I would say that is *damned dangerous* to—to have had a Soviet attack on Turkey and a NATO response on the Soviet Union. That is extremely dangerous. Now I'm not sure we can avoid anything like that, if we attack Cuba, but I think we should make every effort to avoid it, and one way to avoid it is to defuse the Turkish missiles *before* we attack Cuba. Now this . . . this is the sequence of thought.

. . . . . . . . . . . . . . . . . . . . . . . . . . . . . . . . . . . . . . . . . . . . . . . . . . .

[The meeting begins to break up amid discussion of possible leaks from NATO ministers and about whether or not the U.S. should send fighter aircraft after the MiGs in Cuba, if they fire on U.S. aircraft. The President and McNamara agree to postpone the decision until the following day.]

VOICE: What time did we decide on tomorrow morning? [Mixed voices and laughter and more mixed voices.]

RFK: How are you doing, Bob?

McNAMARA: Well, hard to tell. You have any doubts?

RFK: Well, I think we're doing the only thing we can do and well, you know.

McNAMARA: I think . . . Bobby . . . we need to have two things ready, a government for Cuba, because we're going to need one . . . and secondly, plans for how to respond to the Soviet Union in Europe, because sure as hell they're going to do something there.

. . . . . . . . . . . . . . . . . . . . . . . . . . . . . . . . . . . . . . . . . . . . . . . . . . .

VOICE: Suppose we make Bobby mayor of Havana.[12]

There are no correct or incorrect answers to the questions stated at the outset of the transcript selection. Certain things, however, seem clear about the thinking going on in that room. A plane has been shot down. Who shot it down? Probably the Soviets, for they control the SAM-sites, which are the only possible points of origin for a missile with sufficient range to hit a high-flying U-2. What does this imply? Hard to tell, but possibly that the Soviets are willing to escalate the crisis significantly. What must be done? Pilots must and will be protected. Probably a massive strike on all SAM- and anti-aircraft sites will be required. What follows? First, according to the President, the Turks must be contacted. Why? Because, although they deeply resent having their missiles used as pawns in the crisis, and have in fact refused even to consider the Khrushchev trade proposal, Kennedy wants them to understand that if war commences in Cuba in the next twenty-four to forty-eight hours, they may lose a good deal more than their precious missiles. They may in fact be Target Number One for Soviet retaliation in response to an American attack on Cuba, especially if they don't defuse those missiles. And then what? McNamara shows logically and forcefully where he thinks all this will lead, which is to a NATO response against the Soviet Union, required by treaty in response to an attack by the Soviets on any member state. Despite, or perhaps because of, the gallows humor with which the transcript breaks off, the strain felt by McNamara and Robert Kennedy is palpable. No one knows what will happen. Only a fool would be optimistic.

While the raw data provided by this transcript may prove nothing about the inner lives of those men in that situation, much is strongly suggested if we integrate the real-time conversations in this document with the material in the previous chapter, which outlines the objective facts of the situation. Nothing on the transcript was available before December 1987, and only a small portion of the factual material as well. But now that we have both, it is possible to conclude with confidence that the members of the President's EXCOMM believed they were fast approaching the end of the line. War seemed about to commence if Khrushchev did not respond affirmatively within twenty-four hours, an outcome the President and most of the others thought very unlikely because Khrushchev would first have to repudiate his own public offer. It would be a conventional war begun for reasons of military responsibilities to American pilots and lead to a nuclear war, deriving from political-military commitments of NATO and the Warsaw Pact.

To answer my own leading questions: yes, McNamara is fearful. He is afraid he and his colleagues will be unable to discover an acceptable, peaceful solution to the predicament. His fear appears to be primarily fear of the probable consequences of actions he feels they will be required to take, possibly within hours. The fear has nothing to do with fear of calculated attack, but rather of being locked in a situation in which degrees of freedom for each side are rapidly approaching absolute zero. And in his phrase *"damned dangerous,"* by which he means the situation resulting from a NATO retaliatory strike against the Soviet Union, he comes as close as one can come in a group discussion of this sort to naming the calamity they are all trying desperately to avoid: a major nuclear war.

I suggest that the parting exchange between McNamara and Robert Kennedy is as candid an exposure as we are ever likely to get to sensing the look and feel of the burden of nuclear responsibility, when it is feared that the burden may momentarily prove to be too heavy. I suggest further, in light of these data and those presented and alluded to in the previous chapter, that this fear has nothing whatever to do with the ordinary person's nuclear fears during the Cuban missile crisis. Neither is it irrational, either in Wohlstetter's sense, indicating an unwarranted fear of consequences, or in Lebow's sense, signaling "defensive avoidance" or denial and subsequent, unwarranted risk-taking. It is thus difficult to escape the impression that we are once again witnessing the phenomenon that William James years ago called "the same old story . . . concepts, first employed to make things intelligible, are clung to often when they make them unintelligible."[13] And this means, to me, that to understand the psychological truth embedded in these new details now available on the Cuban missile crisis, the old theory won't do. It does not predict the data. It cannot explain them. We need an approach that will allow us to identify, predict, understand, and evaluate McNamara 's fear, and with it, the resolution of a crisis that we must now try to look at anew. We need, to return to that radical empiricist William James, to "turn our backs on our winged concepts altogether and busy ourselves in the thickness of those passing moments over which they fly."[14] In the following chapter, I offer some thoughts on how to begin.

# 4

# Psychological Obstruction: Rational and Irrational Actors

The objective tendency, which proposes to make everyone an observer, and in its maximum to transform him into so objective an observer that he becomes almost a ghost . . . refuses to know or listen to anything except what stands in relation to itself.

Kierkegaard,
*Concluding Unscientific
Postscript,* 1846

In this chapter I want to provoke a crisis about our lack of understanding of nuclear crises. For even if the reader has found the argument of the previous chapter convincing—that "understanding McNamara's fear" should, so to speak, be our goal—convincing a good many people of this is unlikely to happen quickly. This is because the present state of the study of psychological principles underlying the avoidance of nuclear war in crises is dominated by a two-headed monster of an entrenched discipline, the devotees of which are either blithely uninterested in crises, although they are intellectually rigorous, or they are obsessed with the ostensible danger of nuclear crises, but their views are theoretically incoherent and empirically empty.

The former, proponents of a rational actor psychology, can explain the outcome of the Cuban missile crisis, although only implausibly, because its proponents can make no sense of the recollections of most of its key participants, who recall with horror their sense of profound nuclear danger. The latter, whom I call irrational actor psychologists—because they fear the risk-inducing effects of irrationality in a nuclear crisis—have no good explanation as to why nuclear war did not commence in October 1962, although they sympathize with its participants who recall their nuclear fear. Each psychology has its rightful place: rational actor psychology in nuclear strategy and arms control; irrational actor psychology in studies of the failure of conventional deterrence. But neither, in my view, has anything of psychological interest to say about the resolution of a nuclear crisis like the Cuban missile crisis. Yet each has powerful constituencies; thus, together, they constitute a formidable obstruction to intellectual progress in our understanding of whatever connections there may be between nuclear crises, fear of inadvertent nuclear war, and nuclear risks. In this chapter I try to take the measure of these psychologies, note their deficiencies, and thus lead the reader to the following section, which contains the outline of a psychological approach sufficient to explain the Cuban missile crisis. We need to shatter a few psychological myths before we can fully appreciate the psychological significance of the shattered crystal ball.

*   *   *

If we are to avoid a nuclear war while the United States and Soviet Union continue to coexist under a condition of mutual nuclear deterrence, our most important task is to prevent a situation in which the leaders of these countries forget, or "unlearn," the central lesson of the Cuban missile crisis of 1962. The lesson is simply stated: nuclear war must be avoided. All presidents since John Kennedy have learned this, although none in quite as dramatic a fashion as he had to learn it, over Berlin in 1961, and particularly over Soviet missiles in Cuba.

More recently, the nuclear learning of former President Reagan was particularly dramatic. As a private citizen and as a newly elected president, he made vague but often bellicose threats to best the Soviets in a nuclear war, if one should arise. But after a short time in office, where he became more acquainted with the risks and consequences of a nuclear war with the Soviets, he became convinced that "a nuclear war cannot be won and must never be fought."[1] This phrase took on bilateral significance when it was included in the joint communiqué issued by the 1985 meeting in Geneva between President Reagan and then General Secretary, now President Gorbachev. This is recent evidence that both superpowers have learned, as Thomas Schelling said many years ago, to transform the nuclear balance of terror into a "balance of prudence."[2] Pro-nuclear war factions do not exist. Neither does the prospect of leaders who are anxious to begin a nuclear war. These facts reflect a remarkable evolution in thinking about nuclear weapons and nuclear war. With not a single nuclear weapon fired in anger since World War II, and thus by means of thought experiments alone, the leaders and citizens of the nuclear superpowers have learned to abhor the prospect of any sort of nuclear war.[3]

But does abhorrence necessarily translate into avoidance? Few would argue that it does, although opinions regarding the likelihood of a nuclear war range from the nearly panicky to the complacent. No serious student of nuclear risk, however, rates the probability of nuclear war at zero. Those who worry about how to avoid a nuclear war are concerned with two factors: first, a nonzero probability of an event with a potentially catastrophic outcome; and second, our belief that in certain situations—we usually call them "crises"—the probability of a nuclear war might rise alarmingly high. Such an abhorred but, paradoxically, initiated nuclear war would occur by means of *inadvertence:* a not-fully-imagined, insidious concatenation of technology, psychology, and politics that results in a situation so relentlessly perverse, so apparently devoid of satisfactory options, that nuclear war is actually initiated. When we speak, therefore, of the task of avoiding nuclear war nowadays, we generally mean avoiding inadvertent nuclear war.

The problem of framing our understanding of inadvertent nuclear war is bound up entirely with what we believe constitutes a nuclear crisis, and answers to both sets of questions—regarding inadvertence and regarding crises—will depend on our success in addressing what is fundamentally a psychological process. In the worst conceivable situation, often described simply as a "crisis deeper than the Cuban missile crisis," leaders' basic beliefs will become inverted regarding the relative worth of initiating a nuclear war. It is an inadvertent process because in normal times, or even at the outset of such a crisis, leaders would not have believed that they eventually would come to believe such a thing. The nature of the difficulty encountered by anyone who tries to say anything sensible about these issues of inadvertent nuclear war, arising out of a crisis, can be illustrated in a set of propositions. The first four are generally believed to apply uniformly in all noncrisis situations, while a fifth may, under the most desperate circumstances, apply in a nuclear crisis. The trick is to answer the question that follows the propositions in a way that has enough empirical content to be convincing.

Under normal conditions:

1. Nuclear deterrence—the mutual capacity for total annihilation—promotes caution and political stability.

2. No sane leader will want to start a nuclear war under any circumstances.

3. Purely accidental nuclear war or nuclear war via insanity is practically inconceivable.

4. Nuclear deterrence is robust, stable, and very unlikely to fail.

Under nuclear crisis conditions:

5. Instances 1–4 may be false.

Question: What will happen between [1–4] and [5]?

Somehow, a nuclear crisis will work its psychological black magic on leaders responsible for nuclear arsenals. Minds will change; deeply held beliefs will be jettisoned. In this way, for reasons just barely imaginable, the most basic lesson of the nuclear age will somehow be forgotten or repudiated: that a nuclear war must never be fought. A psychological revolution will have occurred just before the world is blown up.

Thus a great strain is inevitably placed upon the imaginations of students of paths to inadvertent nuclear war, and upon the credibility of their enterprise. In certain respects, the task of avoiding nuclear war is somewhat akin to avoiding earthquakes or falling meteorites. Everyone wants to do it. But no one really knows how, other than to specify in unreassuring probabilistic ways the conditions under which the likelihood of their occurrence may rise or fall. Schelling has recently proposed an even more interesting metaphor, which brings the discussion of avoiding nuclear disaster to some of the basic principles of deterrence. Our learning (a) to abhor and (b) to avoid a nuclear war, according to Schelling, are nearly functionally equivalent to one another. As Schelling argues: "People regularly stand at the curb watching trucks, buses and cars hurtle past at speeds that guarantee injury and threaten death if they so much as attempt to cross against the traffic. They are absolutely deterred. But there is no fear. They just know better."[4] Because he believes we "know better" than to enter into a nuclear war, it is difficult for Schelling to imagine a situation in which this salient knowledge would be forgotten or superseded. Having once worked with Stanley Kubrick on the planning of the film that eventually became *Dr. Strangelove*, Schelling believes the film turned out to be an absurdist comedy for precisely this reason: no one involved in conceiving it could imagine it as a believable tragedy.[5] That is why the inadvertence in *Dr. Strangelove* became a function of certifiable lunacy among all the major characters in the film. Thus, while one may find *Dr. Strangelove* entertaining, most of us do not believe that the highest levels of nuclear policy-making are anything like analogous to its insane goings-on.

We should notice the psychology that underlies Schelling's difficulty in imagining inadvertent nuclear war as a live possibility. Traditionally, many of the most influential students of nuclear risk have had the same difficulty, and for the same reason. The reason is this: the psychology—the cluster of assumptions, concepts, and data we use to interpret aspects of mental life deemed relevant to nuclear risk—is not derived from commonsense psychology, or from academic, scientific, or clinical psychology, but rather from economics. This made perfectly good sense in the late 1950s when Schelling, the Wohlstetters, and a number of other nuclear strategists made their first seminal contributions.[6] The great fear in that dawning of the missile age was a nuclear surprise attack—a "bolt out of the blue." The task of Schelling and the others was to spell out the conditions under which rational individuals, continually calculating the ratio of costs and benefits to be derived from initiating a nuclear war, might actually arrive at a decision to do it. This was the imagined mental event of interest par excellence, and the contributions of Schelling and his colleagues may indeed have played a significant role in deterring nuclear war, in part by revolutionizing what he called in 1960 "the retarded science of international strategy."[7]

This psychology has proved to be very durable. It remains, in fact, the ostensible (although, as Schelling has recently pointed out, quite inconsistently applied) psychological basis for our arms control policies and for strategies for deterring nuclear war.[8] The concrete result of applying this economics-derived rational actor psychology to nuclear strategy and arms control has been to render demonstrably irrational the initiation of a nuclear war by either superpower against the other. This is what we have learned. And to the extent that we believe in the salience, ubiquity, and power of human rationality, inadvertent nuclear war may to the same extent seem almost like a contradiction in terms or, at most, a very remote possibility, and avoiding it as easy and predictable as not stepping in front of a speeding bus. In fact, continued deterrence of nuclear war is fully deducible from the rational actor psychology, together with the presence of mutually redundant, survivable strategic nuclear forces. Under these conditions, the initiation of a nuclear war is probably tantamount to committing irrational suicide. Thus, according to this view, leaders just won't do it. They will just "know better."

By seeming to many people to have radically raised the risk of nuclear war during his first term in office, President Reagan by his bellicose anti-Sovietism inadvertently ended the virtual hegemony of the rational actor psychology of avoiding nuclear war. Of course, there had been movement in this direction for years within the strategic and nuclear policy communities. Most notably, Graham Allison and John Steinbruner had a decade or so earlier begun to amend the rational actor "model" in important ways, especially by noting how rationality is constrained by the standard operating procedures of large bureaucracies.[9] Steinbruner was especially concerned about inadvertent nuclear war deriving from a process analogous to that which he believed produced World War I: "An unintended and unexpected consequence of a limited strategic maneuver."[10] But with the great nuclear fear that swept the Western democracies in the early 1980s, this trickle of derationalization and attention to nuclear inadvertence became a flood. As professional psychologists and psychiatrists began to enter the nuclear debate in large numbers, and as their views found their way into the arguments of nonpsychologists, the ensuing discussion became increasingly strident and radically divergent from the rational actor psychology and the policies for which it seemed to provide justification.[11] Unlike students of nuclear policy who came to an interest in the subject from economics, game theory, or political science, the new psychological radicals tended greatly to minimize the role of rationality—in planning, in deployment, in strategy, and, most of all, in crises. As a result, inadvertent nuclear war, which had previously been regarded by most of the people who thought about it at all as distinctly improbable, came increasingly to be regarded as, under certain (likely) conditions, almost a sure thing. As the hypothetical irrational actor started to replace the hypothetical rational actor, inadvertent nuclear war suddenly seemed far from mysterious and improbable. The wonder, according to irrational actor psychologists, was that one had not already occurred.

This new psychology of avoiding nuclear war has focused almost exclusively on inadvertence: on some hypothesized process by which the mechanisms of deterrence become inverted and thus the cause of, rather than the antidote to, nuclear war. This event is imagined to occur along three more-or-less canonical paths. The first, and least plausible, is by what we may call (following Murray Sayle) *a conspiracy of circumstance.*[12] Roughly speaking, this is the argument that "Murphy's Law" is the guiding principle of international affairs, that accidents are "bound" to happen, and that sooner or later any system as complex as that which buttresses mutual nuclear deterrence simply must fail.[13] Advocates of this view often use as analogies the Soviet shootdown of Korean Air Lines 007 in September 1983 or, less plausibly, the nuclear accidents at Three-Mile Island and Chernobyl. The argument is simple and, to some, compelling: systems break down; nuclear deterrence is a system; deterrence will break down. Thus, this particular approach may be thought of almost as an a-rational antipsychology, according to which the relative rationality of actors is less important than the law of large numbers. Sooner or later, it is believed, if the wheel of fortune is spun often enough, it will come up with any number, including those as improbable as that "representing" a major nuclear war. When this occurs, it will be a case of fallible matter triumphing over unwitting, unintending minds.

A second variant of the irrational actor psychology of avoiding nuclear war may be called war by a *conspiracy of crazies or craziness.* A substantial number of antinuclear radicals apparently believe that the leaders of the superpowers are, in fact, crazy and desirous of provoking a nuclear war. Helen Caldicott, for one, has put forth an elaborate argument to demonstrate that former President Reagan and former Defense Secretary Weinberger were paranoid psychotics while in office.[14] She is far from alone in holding this view; it is quite popular among psychiatrists and clinical psychologists. Thus, according to advocates of this view, the most likely sort of nuclear war will occur inadvertently, against the wishes of the vast majority of humanity but not contrary to the wishes of certain sick leaders, many of whom are believed to crave the chance to fight such a war. In this way, a Strangelovian scenario will actually unfold as life imitates art in the most catastrophic fashion imaginable.

A more sophisticated version of this general approach holds that *systemic craziness,* not deranged leaders, will bring about an inadvertent nuclear war. Surprising as it may seem to many nonpsychologists, this view has become virtually paradigmatic in the American psychological establishment. Morton Deutsch, a distinguished social psychologist, calls the process leading to nuclear war the "malignant superpower relationship."[15] The central idea is this: the villain is the arms race, which, because it requires one to "demonize" the enemy, leads to a phenomenon labeled (by psychoanalyst Erik Erikson) "pseudospeciation"—the belief that a national adversary is composed of subhuman devils. Erikson sees powerful parallels between the pseudospeciation of the Jews in Nazi Germany and what he takes to be the advanced stages of the same process occurring presently between the

United States and the Soviet Union.[16] When this process runs its course, according to believers in malignant, systemic superpower craziness, war can easily break out between the superpowers, leading ultimately to nuclear war and planetary catastrophe. The slightest spark could provide the impetus, because both sides would have become caught up in a crazy process of threat and counterthreat whose natural terminus is a war to eliminate an enemy who is by then regarded as both subhuman and superdangerous. In this kind of scenario, a nuclear war occurs despite the relevant leaders' full knowledge of its consequences, because of the irresistible evolution of enmity that derives from the crazy social process in which both sides are trapped.

None of these conspiratorial theories of nuclear inadvertence is given much credence by strategists or even by political scientists. Indeed, many of the best-known advocates of these views are almost unknown outside the subset of psychologists who concern themselves with nuclear matters. But a third conspiratorial view, in its various formulations, has begun to find a wide audience among more traditional students of nuclear risk. Advocates of this view believe an inadvertent nuclear war is likely to begin because of what may be called a conspiracy of *circumstantial craziness*. The psychology informing this approach is focused on situation-specific lapses in the rationality of decision makers under the stress of trying to manage deep and dangerous crises. These scholars worry about such decision-making pathologies as defensive avoidance, "groupthink," cognitive closure, selective attention, and the many other ways in which the quality of foreign policy decision-making can be degraded under the stress of crisis.[17] In a recent important book, Richard Ned Lebow has illustrated the ways in which crisis-induced stress may have been causally connected to radical lapses in the powers of perception and reason in the leaders of Great Britain and Argentina in the 1982 Falklands/Malvinas War. In the same book, Janice Stein has put forth an analogous argument in regard to the two most recent Middle Eastern wars.[18] Moreover, the Harvard Project on Avoiding Nuclear War has identified crises and crisis-induced degradation of rationality as important but imperfectly understood factors that may contribute to raised risk of nuclear war. They have begun to suggest measures for combating what they call "Model II Factors"—breakdowns of rationality in crises, or of the *belief* in mutually ubiquitous rationality, that may lead to the initiation of a nuclear war undesired by all parties at the outbreak of the conflict.[19] For all these students of nuclear risk, the enemy is the crisis because under conditions of high risk, high stakes, and apparent shortage of time to decide, leaders may do (and have often done) what look in retrospect like very crazy things.[20] They may even, as Richard Betts has argued, conclude for some reason that nuclear war is inevitable, or that it has already begun, and on this basis launch a nuclear attack that, under ordinary (noncrisis) conditions, would have been inconceivable to them.[21]

Recall the Peace Corps couple (mentioned in Chapter 1) who feared New York had already been destroyed. Advocates of a psychology of avoiding nuclear war that emphasizes circumstantial craziness fear the results of just such a piece of misinformation being believed by an American or Soviet president. What would he (or she) do if he believed New York had been attacked? If he "retaliated" for this chimerical Soviet strike on New York, what would the Soviets do in response? And so on into nuclear catastrophe. Students of the circumstantial craziness of crises have no trouble envisioning an American president, aloft in his airborne command post and surveying the ruins of a postnuclear war United States, updating the famous lament of Shakespeare's Richard III. The president could say quite literally: "Information, information, my country for a piece of accurate information."

How should we evaluate the evolution of the psychology of avoiding nuclear war over the past decade and a half? In particular, what are we to make of these radical departures from the mainstream rational actor psychology that has held nuclear policy in its grip for so long? First, and perhaps most important, the psychological radicals have injected into the nuclear debate an urgency that has been missing for a generation. John Steinbruner spoke the discomfiting truth in 1976 when he argued persuasively that "the entire topic [of nuclear strategy and arms control] has become established, familiar, middle-aged and—let us admit—rather boring."[22] This is no longer true, mainly because of the recent radical challenges by those whose psychological views permit them to imagine plausible paths to an inadvertent nuclear war. Taken together, these purveyors of the newer psychologies of avoiding nuclear war can imagine several classes of scenarios during which we might, in effect, forget the singular lesson of the nuclear age: a nuclear war must never be fought. This influx of assumptions and arguments from sources of psychology other than economics and game-theory may eventually transform the nuclear debate in ways, which are, at present, difficult to predict.

Then again, these new psychologies may prove to be epiphenomenal, for much of the literature of these new psychologies of avoiding nuclear war is either so flawed logically, so empirically dubious, or so reductively and esoterically psychological that it may in some of its more extreme forms be doomed to policy-irrelevance. For example, arguments that rely for their credibility on the putative insanity of leaders are unlikely to have much impact, particularly on leaders themselves. Moreover, arguments that rely, as do those of the pure circumstantialists, on analogies between international affairs and the spinning of roulette wheels or the flipping of coins are just plain false. These analogies fail to take into account the possibility of human learning, whereby the risk of nuclear war might gradually be reduced, because of the superpowers having made conscious decisions that make war between them less likely.[23] Furthermore, analogies between the clinical consulting room and international politics, which are extraordinarily popular among psychiatrists and psychologists, are also highly dubious. In fact, the quasi-anarchic world of sovereign states is, in important respects, the inverse of the artificially supportive environment the psychological clinician tries in most cases to establish.

Finally, we must not fail to notice the implications of an important anomaly confronting the psychologies that emphasize the significance of stress in crises. As many studies have shown, although indirectly, the psychological effects of stress in nuclear and nonnuclear contexts may be quite different. For whereas the top-level decision-making in recent cases like the Falklands/Malvinas War and the two recent Middle Eastern wars seems to exhibit the full range of psychological devolution, the reverse appears to have occurred during the Cuban missile crisis, the capital case of nuclear danger.[24] In the cases of conventional conflict, leaders' judgments seemed, as the crises wore on, to become increasingly detached from the constraints of objective reality and equally unable to distinguish between their fears and the probable intentions of the adversary. But in the missile crisis President Kennedy, to take only the most obvious example, moved rapidly from relatively simplistic judgments about the Soviets to a very intense effort to discover Khrushchev's motivations and constraints. It may well be that, psychologically speaking, nuclear danger really is unique in certain respects. If it is, then we ought to be very skeptical about attempts to generalize the psychological analyses of nonnuclear crises to hypothetical nuclear cases. (I will come back to this point in Chapter 9, where I examine the different roles fear seems to play in nonnuclear and nuclear contexts.)

In sum, the new psychologies of avoiding nuclear war have so far shown themselves to be policy-irrelevant, for various reasons. This has been admitted by several leading exponents of the conspiratorial approaches, especially Lebow. In a passage remarkable for its courage and honesty, he has pointed out the source of the difficulty facing all those seeking to replace the rational actor psychology of avoiding nuclear war with a psychological perspective that permits a serious investigation of the risk of inadvertent nuclear war—that takes this possibility seriously as an event that, under certain (specifiable) conditions, is very likely to happen. According to Lebow: "Deterrence, which, relatively speaking, is easy to implement, may nevertheless not be a very effective strategy of conflict management, because it does not address the most important sources of aggression. On the other hand, efforts to alleviate the kinds of insecurities that actually encourage or even compel leaders to pursue aggressive foreign policies do not seem very likely to succeed."[25]

This is Lebow's paradox: the rational actor psychology underlying classical deterrence theory is *psychologically* bankrupt; it has no place in its lexicon for the psychological implications of the fear engendered by attempts at deterrence. And an irrational actor psychology focused on the degradation of rational decision-making in crises is *pragmatically* bankrupt; policymakers do not like its message, nor do they understand it, hence they have no idea how to implement policies in accord with it. Lebow is quite direct about why the irrational actor psychologies, even those emphasizing stress and crises, are likely to remain pretty much academic exercises. Neither he nor anyone else has so far imagined a plausible means for intervening directly into the lives of leaders so as to reduce the intensity of the psychological needs that seem to motivate many failures of nonnuclear deterrence (and which, by analogy, are believed to be primary psychological culprits in some hypothetical failure of nuclear deterrence). Leaders, even (or perhaps especially) in crises, are unlikely to believe that they are becoming progressively less rational, let alone believe that psychological counseling of *themselves* is the key to resolving crises successfully. Thus Lebow is correct, I believe, to ask: What is the practical point of the new irrational actor psychologies of avoiding nuclear war? How will the new understandings they generate help to reduce the risk of inadvertent nuclear war?

Having briefly surveyed the rational/irrational actor psychologies of avoiding nuclear war, let us observe in conclusion why neither can, even in principle, provide assistance to those who want to understand avoiding *inadvertent* nuclear war arising out of a crisis. We have already seen that Schelling, the fountainhead of the rational actor psychology, seems to believe that rational actors will survive through and beyond a nuclear crisis. He acknowledges the problems that might arise from "nervousness," but he finds the issue much less interesting than do the proponents of irrational actor psychology. This accounts for Schelling's interesting account of the Cuban missile crisis in *Arms and Influence*. Instead of trying to describe the sequence of psychological events—possibly leading to a decision to launch, Schelling explained, strategically, why no such decision was ever reached.[26] The reason he couldn't imagine it was that the observable data bearing most heavily on the outcome (the strategic nuclear balance), combined with the theory of rational actors, fully determined the decisions of leaders not to go to nuclear war. While one can dispute Schelling's interpretation, it is consistent with the outcome of the missile crisis. One gets the distinct impression from Schelling's work, in fact, that a "crisis" is only a linguistic convention with which he has reluctantly agreed to go along. Certainly, people may become nervous during these particularly intense competitions in risk-taking, as he first called them a generation ago and as they have generally been understood ever since. But one never gets the impression that competitions of this sort are somehow or other qualitatively different sorts of enterprises, to which, perhaps, different psychological principles apply. In fact, this was the point of Schelling's collaborative book with Morton Halperin, *Strategy and Arms Control:* the same principles apply, whether bargaining in easy chairs in Geneva or deep in a so-called "crisis."[27]

The irrational actor psychologists say they reject all this, and that crises are special, qualitatively more dangerous episodes in the conduct of international relations. Why? Because risk of nuclear war will rise dramatically in a nuclear crisis. Yet because they agree with a lot more of Schelling's assumptions than they know or admit, they are forced into an awkward situation that Schelling and other rational actor traditionalists have avoided. Schelling had only to observe the outcome of the missile crisis and conclude that, just as one would have expected, people acted rationally: Khrushchev noted his inferiority, backed down, and thus ended the crisis.

But the irrational actor psychologists must try to offer convincing explanations—general, vague, and usually drawn from data unrelated to the missile crisis—as to why in certain circumstances one might do what is inherently unimaginable. And so they endorse vague truisms like "Murphy's Law" will prevail, or that stress can often lead to clouded judgment, which, while perhaps true, tell us little about any particular crisis. Alternatively, one can imagine in great detail what might have happened, say in the missile crisis (but did not), that would have pushed the crisis into war.[28] But again, it is impossible to attach meaningful probabilities to such possibilities, leaving the arguments quite unconvincing.

Notice what happens as purveyors of the irrational actor psychology, deeply worried about the risk-inducing effects of nuclear crises, try unsuccessfully to fit this square psychological peg into the round hole of a psychological approach, assuming ubiquitously rational action, developed to deal with a totally different problem: calculated surprise attack. For Schelling et al., the psychological variables remain constant; the actors remain rational (in theory). The central determining factors influencing a decision to launch a nuclear war, within or without a crisis, reside in the constituents of the strategic balance of nuclear forces. The values of these factors are empirically derivable, within estimable ranges of error. But for irrational actor psychologists worried about the decisive, catastrophic effects of a nuclear crisis, constants and variables are reversed. Since the strategic balance of forces will not change merely because of the onset of a crisis, the balance is taken as given and constant. If the risk of war is to rise dramatically, *psychological* variables must become altered; something will change fundamentally in the minds of leaders charged with nuclear responsibilities. The ultimately significant question is, of course, *what* changes? But the prior question, one that presents a real conundrum, is: Where do we look for data, for evidence, concerning the nature of this supposed psychological revolution that is a logical prerequisite to a decision to launch a nuclear war? What is to be the evidentiary analogue to Schelling's empirically derivable description of *his* relevant variability, the state of the strategic balance? What is to be the psychological analogue of ground intelligence and satellite reconnaissance that would inform Schelling's rationally acting leaders, crisis or no?

The answer is that there is no such analogue. Borrowed from every sort of psychological literature imaginable, arguments are put forward emphasizing the deleterious effects of stress, denial, and so forth. "It might happen; you cannot say it cannot happen" is the only conclusion one can justifiably draw from this literature. The proponents are in fact hung up on the "N = O" problem, the lack of an actual, two-sided nuclear crisis that exploded into war. And the missile crisis, the closest call, only serves to reinforce Schelling's point, if one is predisposed toward it, which is simply that it is just very difficult, "crisis" or no, to have a nuclear war. Those who emphasize the connection between crisis, fear, irrationality, and risk of nuclear war can say little more about the missile crisis other than that we were lucky. We may or may not have *been* lucky, but the irrational actor psychologists cannot provide what they need to provide to people who disbelieve them: an empirically rich description of the perverse psychological revolution required in a nuclear crisis that produces a nuclear war.

Several facts seem obvious. First, the rational actor psychology has done the job required of it. Surprise attack, having been rendered totally irrational, is unlikely. Second, for those whose intuitions or experience tell them that nuclear risk rises in a crisis, the rational actor psychology has little or nothing to say. It is crisis-irrelevant in the sense that it has no place for a state called "crisis" that yields a qualitatively different and more dangerous psychological evolution. Third, the irrational actor psychology is crisis-obsessed but still crisis-irrelevant. Its advocates are correct to believe that something like a new discipline—psychology and arms control—is now required to augment the venerable tradition of strategy and arms control. But the irrational actor psychologists have, for various reasons, chosen to emphasize imported theory over indigenous data. They have failed to appreciate that a crisis-relevant, and therefore potentially policy-relevant, psychology of avoiding nuclear war must begin with Schelling's question: Why have we *not* had a nuclear war explode from a crisis? Rather, they have, in effect, asked: How *would* we explain the nuclear war we have *not* yet had? In regard to the missile crisis, we must ask, if we are to have anything psychologically useful to say: Why was the missile crisis resolved peacefully? If we believe nuclear crises are really different, then we must turn our descriptive focus inward on the evolution of psychological life during that crisis and try to understand what it was like when, psychologically, the crystal ball shattered, and how that is connected to the fact that the world did not.

# PART THREE: PROPOSALS

# 5

# The Empirical Goal: Recovering the Psychological Life of the Cuban Missile Crisis

It is perfectly true, as philosophers say, that life must be understood backwards. But they forget the other proposition, that it must be lived forwards.

Kierkegaard,
*Journals,* 1843

In an engaging and challenging essay published on the twenty-sixth anniversary of the day the Cuban missile crisis peaked and was resolved, H. R. Trevor-Roper has argued for the inclusion in our understanding of the past what he calls "The Lost Moments of History."[1] He means to reintroduce into serious historical inquiry the idea of "turning points," those moments when the flow of historical life might have moved decisively in directions quite different from the paths that ultimately were taken. Trevor-Roper himself is most interested in such "moments" in the past when calamities, such as the Thirty Years' War or the rise of Hitler in Germany, might have been averted. He realizes immediately, of course, that he has embarked upon a hazardous course. For playing the game of "lost moments," while eternally popular among amateurs with a fascination for the past, is regarded as entirely off-limits to serious students of history. So after announcing his intention to discuss a number of such "moments," Trevor-Roper admits that already he "can hear the objection. The lessons of history, it will be said, must be deduced from what has actually happened, not from what has not happened. And of course I must agree that this is true."[2] So must we all. The Thirty Years' War was the worst man-made disaster to befall Europe before the world wars of our century; Adolf Hitler did exert a demonic influence upon our time that continues to shape the world we live in. These are hard facts that cannot be wished away in games of wishful thinking.

This much admitted, what makes Trevor-Roper's argument relevant for investigating the experience of nuclear danger is his liberal and liberating criteria for inclusion in the category "what has actually happened." He wants to include, indeed he wants to emphasize, the *sense* of what it must have been like actually to participate in the unfolding of what we now call history, but which was, in one lost moment after another, the contingent, confusing, largely shapeless and unmanageable present. He wishes, in other words, to include *psychological* facts in our telling and understanding of history, but not just as they have come down to us in ordinary documents.

And this, of course, leads to a methodological conundrum: What has actually happened psychologically—the look and feel of the texture of a lived situation—is not available from the lifeless, dusty documents that make up the stock-in-trade of the working historian. Such psychological facts are not even available from a real-time, verbatim transcript like that of the October 27, 1962, EXCOMM meetings. Such "facts," therefore, must be inferred from the most thickly descriptive data we can acquire. But even if we accept the necessity of including in any inquiry the sense of the forward movement of history, it is not at all obvious how to justify to professional colleagues, or perhaps even to oneself, the guesses and inferences that would constitute any attempt to turn the historian's past into the historian's subjects' future, and then make all this comprehensible to other historians who are far from inclined to join in the exercise. In announcing his intention to pursue this sort of inquiry, Trevor-Roper says he feels like he is standing at the open door of an airplane in flight, about to be sucked into the maelstrom. For what rules govern such an enterprise? Won't methodological chaos and anarchy set in? Despite this danger, he says, the alternative is worse, "which is keeping the corpse [of history] unburied and refrigerated, on a cold mortuary slab, for anatomical demonstration."[3] If we cannot recover the psychological life of the past, with its sense of forward movement, then our analyses, in his view, bear the same relation to the data they ostensibly describe as a corpse does to a healthy, vital, living human being. Instead of trying to become the caretakers of a living history, the professionals seem to Trevor-Roper to have become, by and large, its undertakers.

Trevor-Roper could easily have been describing that intellectual's mortuary science that is the historiography of the Cuban missile crisis. No episode of modern times can have suffered more inadvertent abuse from history's learned undertakers than the missile crisis. It was our closest call to major nuclear war, to the end of life as we know it, and an event that is recorded in the memories of tens of millions of living people. Yet one could not deduce from the mountains of studies devoted to it that the event was managed by people who did not yet know that all would be well after thirteen days. There are exceptions. Robert Kennedy's memoir, for example, crackles with palpable fear and tension.[4] But he was not an analyst, not a professional "undertaker" bent on explaining the event. In fact, the missile crisis provided perhaps the most significant "lost moment" of modern times, but in a sense that is exactly the opposite of Trevor-Roper's favorite lost moments. For during the missile crisis, events might have transpired to produce not peaceful resolution, but a catastrophe beyond imagination and with horrible, impossible-to-calculate consequences for subsequent history. It was *the* calamity of modern times that did *not* happen. As with all such lost historical moments, in Trevor-Roper's phrasing, "it was not a historical necessity, a consequence hanging in the stars, but the result . . . of particular human accidents or decisions or events that in themselves were not necessary: it could have been otherwise."[5] This, of course, is what I referred to previously as "McNamara's fear." How do we breathe some life into the refrigerated, intellectualized corpse that this event has become? How might we reenter some portion of the actual Cuban missile crisis, as it was lived, and in so doing recover some of the sense embedded in the home truth that it could have been otherwise, and thus next time, may be otherwise?

We need a different approach to the event, a different point of departure, and I suggest that we take our cue from Kierkegaard. He well understood that the experience of moving forward through the perplexing maze of what *will* become history often bears little resemblance to the experience of what *has* become history. And as Kierkegaard emphasized so often and so eloquently, fear of an unknown and highly uncertain outcome is what is characteristically omitted from after-the-fact accounts. Looking backward, we know how the missile crisis turned out. From our vantage point, we can never *not* know this. But looking forward, as indeed its managers were required to do, this knowledge was unavailable. If we therefore seek a better understanding of the psychological requirements for peace in a nuclear crisis, we ought to try to recover the psychological lives of the managers of the missile crisis, as they were lived forward. Of course, we can never approach complete success in this endeavor. But what Trevor-Roper says about history in general is true in particular of the Cuban missile crisis: the alternative is riskier, and by remaining content to explain the event, we risk contributing yet another dead body to the great morgue of scholarship on the crisis.[6] So let us begin with the common-sense assumption that life in the White House and Kremlin in October 1962 was lived forward, with its participants ignorant and fearful of its outcome.

In my discussions of the missile crisis and nuclear policy with specialists over the past several years, I have found that the common-sense psychological approach I advocate is far from valid to them. I am often regarded as naive—naive to believe that the missile crisis is psychologically unique and that feared inadvertence is (or should have been) central to its resolution, and naive to think that the recovery of the psychological lives of leaders, as lived and experienced, is what the psychology of avoiding nuclear war should be about. These critics, I admit, are fundamentally correct about my theoretical "naiveté." It is in fact cultivated. I do believe that theoretical and disciplinary naiveté is precisely what is required to move this field closer to a description of evolving, real-time psychological reality. Obviously, for analysts weaned on game theory, microeconomics, comparative political science and, more recently, on the psychologies of stress and decision-making, my mode of analysis is likely to seem foreign and rustic. It is. As I contend in Chapter 6, "psychology" is for our purposes best taken to indicate the actual, living sense of a situation—what are (or were) the objects of attention and what was it like, then and there, to be so attentive. But as we shall see, in beginning our analysis here, where the person (not the psychologist or other analyst) begins, we come upon methodological issues as complex as the approach is conceptually simple.

But a relatively simple approach need not necessarily be regarded as simplistic and therefore irrelevant. An important assumption underlying the argument of this book is that if the missile crisis is apprehended in a way that is closer to what amounts to a commonsense explanation, and less as a deduction from some implicit or explicit psychological theory, we will get much nearer to the psychological core of a nuclear crisis and to the experience of living imaginatively through the shattering of the nuclear crystal ball, To show that my proposal, although radical and simple in relation to present disciplinary norms, has a substantial ring of truth to it, I offer the following anecdote, borrowed and adapted from Robert Romanyshyn. If one story cannot convey the prima facie credibility of a dozen case comparisons or a hundred references to learned psychological literatures, it can still argue persuasively for the common sense of my psychological analysis of the Cuban missile crisis that occupies much of this essay.

The following is a methodological parable emphasizing the critical importance of recovering the psychological life of a fearful experience. It describes a perfectly ordinary experience that could happen to anyone. Yet in its emphasis upon psychological recovery, upon fear, and upon the centrality of the experienced fear in accounting for behavior, the parable comes uncannily close to the heart of the argument of this book, an attempt to recover the psychological life of a lived experience of leaders of the nuclear superpowers: the fear of participating in a perverse process that may lead to inadvertent nuclear war.

### The Experience: Living Forward

It is a dark evening, and my car is the only one on this deserted country road. I am preoccupied with the events of the day, thinking about the things I have not yet done and those which I still must do when I arrive home. Thinking of these things, I have more or less given my eyes over to the task of searching the road. They are there on the road before me, guiding the car through my hands and feet before I do. Suddenly my foot presses the brake and the car jerks to a halt. It takes a moment for the one who was considering the events of the day to rejoin his eyes on the road. But when I do it is easy to see why my foot pressed the brake so suddenly. There in front of me, at a distance which is already too close looms a dark and sinister-looking shape. That is what I saw, that is what my eyes saw while I was thinking of the day.

I wait, and as I wait that shape in the distance begins to change. What was only a moment before a dark and sinister shape now appears to be the twisted and gnarled trunk of a tree which has fallen across the road. I blink my eyes and I move my head slightly forward to get a better look. But the light is dim and I still cannot quite make out what I am seeing. Cautiously and not without some misgiving I leave my car and approach the object in the road. Now at this distance I am sure. Yes, there is no doubt about it. Lying across the road is a fallen, twisted tree trunk. I certainly will not be able to drive my car around it. I will have to turn around and take another way home . . .

### The Explanation: Looking Backward

What is the reality which is there on the road to be seen? The answer to this question seems obvious. It is a fallen, twisted tree trunk which is on the road. That is a fact, and with this knowledge of the facts I am convinced that the dark sinister shape which I saw earlier was a mistake. A moment ago I was in error about what I saw and this later experience proves it. What I see now corrects what I saw before. The fact replaces an illusion.

### The Importance of Recovering Psychological Life

We should not however be so ready to accept this answer which seems so obvious, because it discounts the earlier experience too readily. To be more precise this obvious answer commits a retrospective fallacy. It replaces an earlier experience with a later one, and in this process it establishes an illusion where none previously existed. At the moment when I saw the dark and sinister shape, I was not seeing an illusion. The dark and sinister shape was there before me on the road, and the conduct of my foot proves it. If I do not want to deny that earlier experience, I cannot deny that first appearance as unreal. . . .

### Looking Backward at Living Forward: The Return of the Fear

To appreciate this point [the psychological reality of the first experience] consider what might happen when I return to my car to recommence my journey home. Initially I may feel embarrassed by my earlier fear. How silly of me, I might think, to have reacted so emotionally. Confident now with this later knowledge and engaged in scolding myself for being so foolish, my eyes may again catch one more glimpse of that object on the road as I turn my car around to drive home. And again out of the corner of my eye I may see that dark and sinister figure, and in *that* moment I will not be able to suppress an anxious feeling. Despite what I have just recently seen, despite what I know, I cannot deny that I am only too ready to leave this place.[7]

This parable of fear, action, and reflection poses a fundamental question for anyone engaged in almost any sort of psychological inquiry. Where does the inquiry begin? Do we take the path of experimental science and begin by seeking a detached, objective view of the situation as it "really" exists (or existed)? Do we then follow this up with an attempt to measure the psychological distance between what we take to be objective reality and the mere appearance of it, according to some individual or group? And do we finally seek to explain some event by attributing it to error or illusion? In this way of explaining behavior, the efficacy of human action is at least implicitly, but often quite explicitly, taken to be the difference between what individuals would have done if they had known as much as the psychologists (or other analysts) examining their behavior and what, in their ignorance, they actually did.

The parable demonstrates, I believe, just how hegemonically persuasive this kind of explanation is to modern sensibilities. We begin, in the marvelous phrase of the philosopher Thomas Nagel, seeking "the view from nowhere," a neutral corner of the universe from which objects and situations will appear as they really are, not just as we believe they really are.[8] Nearly every force in the contemporary intellectual *Zeitgeist* pushes us to try to begin our psychological inquiry there—nowhere in particular, within no one's view at all—so that we can claim in the end to have achieved an objective explanation of whatever it is we wish to understand. But if we try to begin with a view from nowhere, then I believe we must stand, like it or not, for the annihilation of psychological life as it is experienced, and the elevation of abstraction, especially more-or-less well developed theories of human behavior. Thus in the parable, the driver may be seen simply to have made an error, an incorrect judgment. Perhaps, having learned of his error, his judgment in the future will improve. In any case, we will want to use this data—the estimated psychological distance between fact and illusion—as part of our effort to construct an ever more inclusive and predictive theory of human perception and behavior. Using our corroborated theory, we would hope thereby to suggest ways of narrowing the gap between illusion and reality.

Alternatively, as the narrator of the parable suggests, we may choose to begin our inquiry with a view from somewhere—somewhere deep inside the viewpoint of the person whose action we seek to understand. If this is where we choose to begin—where experiencing persons begin—then we will seek not an objective assessment of the gap between perceptual illusion and actual reality, but instead a systematic *description* of the experience in which the action is embedded. Instead of getting as far as possible outside an individual's viewpoint, we will instead seek ever deeper entry into it. Our goal will be to provide a description of what the experience seemed to be about and what it was like to have had such an experience. In effect, we will seek to get so far into the viewpoints of others that we begin to appreciate just how their situations looked and felt to them. We will seek to recover their psychological life, not to annihilate it. So if, for example, we begin our inquiry into the behavior of the driver of the car from his viewpoint and ask why he stopped the car so suddenly, we are likely to begin with the conjecture that he stopped because he was afraid to go on. The bulk of any subsequent inquiry would be given over to seeking a deeper and broader understanding of why the situation seemed so fearful when he slammed on his brakes. In other words, instead of focusing our inquiry on establishing the distance between illusion and reality, we will instead try to understand the connection between the experience and the behavior. We will want to know not why the driver was mistaken, but why he was afraid.

A causal account of a given behavior can be generated from within each perspective. Looking backward at the action in the parable, seeking an objective view from nowhere, we might conclude that the driver slammed on his brakes prematurely and unnecessarily hard because he was paying insufficient attention to the road, because his vision was obscured by foggy conditions, and so on. This would explain the observable behavior. But looking vicariously forward, seeking entry into the evolving psychological life of the driver as it was lived, we might conclude that he slammed on his brakes because he experienced a wave of fear in the presence of the frightening apparition that seemed to rise up in the road. It is important to recognize that causal accounts such as these do not necessarily compete with each other, in the sense that one must be correct and the other mistaken. They are instead complementary; both may be correct. There *was* a tree in the road. It did *seem* at the moment of braking that something much more menacing than a tree was blocking the driver's path. He slammed on his brakes in a panic because of a mistaken perception. He slammed on his brakes in a panic because he was afraid of the apparition he saw before him.

Thus it is impossible to choose one account over the other on the basis of factuality or even of the internal coherence of the explanations. For although they purport to explain the same action, the accounts appeal to different universes of facts: as viewed backward from nowhere or vicariously forward from somewhere. Yet one must choose. It is obviously impossible to *begin* a coherent inquiry from within both perspectives. But in acknowledging the necessity of choosing a place to begin from these complementary modes of psychological inquiry, we come to an absolutely basic fork in the methodological road. The choice of paths therefore is of fundamental importance to the sort of endeavor the psychology of avoiding nuclear war in crises is going to be.

On what basis, then, should we choose? The conclusion of the parable provides the clue. Despite knowing, after the fact, that his panic was unwarranted, despite realizing that it had not been a sinister apparition that he had seen, despite having concluded that it was only a dead tree in the road, the narrator confesses that a parting glimpse of the scene in his headlights makes him shudder all over again. With speed and glee unwarranted by the facts, he hurries from the place. As he reenacts the original encounter, even with the facts fresh in his mind, his fearful, panicky reaction is recapitulated. One is inclined to predict, on this basis, that any future encounters of this sort will also evoke the same response pattern: Fear → Sudden Stop → Examination of the Facts → Flight from the Scene → Backward Glance → Fear All Over Again. In other words, the knowledge that one has made an error, and that an objective view of the situation yields the conclusion that one's fear and subsequent action were unwarranted by the facts, is often unlikely to alter one's perception and action the next time a similar situation is encountered. This of course should not be taken to mean that we are incapable of learning from our mistakes. We obviously can. But it does mean that in situations of surprise, uncertainty, potentially high stakes, and thus considerable fear, the fact of our past mistakenness may not be nearly as compelling as the fearful facts that seem to be emerging before us. Looking backward with certainty, we understand that we have often been mistaken in such situations. Looking forward uncertainly, and with a great deal apparently at stake, we cannot help feeling that this time our worst fears will be vindicated.

This has implications that should be immensely troubling to practitioners of the paradigmatic psychology of avoiding nuclear war who are united in their enthusiasm for discovering errors in the decision-making of leaders with nuclear responsibilities. In this already large and rapidly expanding body of work, nuclear decision makers are characterized as irrational, mendacious, paranoid, close-minded, shortsighted, and by many more psychologically based epithets. But as I argue in what follows (and as I have argued at great length elsewhere), these attributions of mistakenness have failed to have any impact whatever on nuclear policy-making.[9] The reason is clear: the accounts emphasizing errors, or gaps between the illusions of policy-makers and the reality as determined by the psychologists, strike the policymakers almost universally as psychologically unreal, as merely disguised attempts to demonstrate that, in fact, nuclear policymakers know considerably less about avoiding nuclear war than do nuclear psychologists. Even former policymakers, looking backward at their efforts to manage nuclear risks in a crisis, see nothing in the psychological accounts that reflects an understanding of what they faced, and what their successors will face in any future nuclear crisis. Thus, on the basis of policy-relevance, we should choose to begin our inquiry with a psychology that seeks entry into the forward-moving psychological life of policymakers. However much or little we may learn from such an endeavor, we stand a far greater chance of actually communicating those lessons to nuclear policymakers. In that case, we psychologists, whether we call ourselves "psychologists" or not, will have learned to speak their language rather than (implausibly) requiring them to learn ours. We will in that case, to reinvoke the morbidly vivid image of Trevor-Roper, have become the caretakers of the psychological life of decision makers, rather than its undertakers.

Finally, there is a more important reason for seeking to recover rather than to annihilate the evolving psychological life of nuclear policymakers. It is this: although fear can often lead to mistaken judgment, profoundly emotional reactions to situations are seldom wholly without foundation. Our mental life is, in a word, usually adaptive. If we are very fearful, for example, there is usually a reason: something to be afraid of. As William James (following Darwin's lead) pointed out more than a century ago, our emotional reactions are at the very core of our capacity to survive, and it is not for nothing that our emotions are often stubbornly resistant to cognitive control.[10] We evolved and survived as a species because we developed the ability to sense and avoid danger. In the chapters that follow, I will cite much psychologically based criticism of the managers of the missile crisis and of nuclear policymakers in general. All of this criticism is predicated on the assumption that emotional reactions to nuclear danger are either unimportant or to be avoided. What we should seek, according to this view, is greater rationality.

I disagree. Greater "rationality" should not be our goal. This is not to say, however, that I believe "irrationality" is required to reduce nuclear risks. But it does mean that such a conclusion—to improve the rationality of nuclear policymakers in specific situations—derives from beginning the whole inquiry in the wrong place, seeking a view from nowhere. Once again, the key to the proper response is in the parable. "The dark and sinister shape was there before me on the road," the narrator recalls, "and the conduct of my foot proves it." Indeed it does. For although he was mistaken, as he later discovered, in his estimate of what was before him, he was absolutely correct to discern danger and thus to stop before colliding with whatever was in the road.

I argue likewise in Part Four, below, with regard to the nuclear danger present in the missile crisis. The key participants may (or may not) have overestimated the degree of nuclear danger they were in. But the fact—the living psychological fact—that they feared they were in mortal danger had everything to do with why they, too, slammed on their own brakes and sought a peaceful retreat from the dreadful apparition of major nuclear war that seemed to be before them. Thus, the more we discover about the way the look and feel of inadvertent nuclear danger evolved, the greater the likelihood that we will eventually articulate a psychological approach that seems real to policymakers, and the greater will be our understanding of the adaptive role of feared nuclear inadvertence in the nuclear crisis of October 1962 and in the one we are ever trying to prevent.

# 6

# Psychological Transparency: The Theory and Practice of Phenomenology

The majority of men are subjective toward themselves and objective toward all others, terribly objective sometimes—but the real task is to be objective toward oneself and subjective toward all others.

Kierkegaard,
*Journals,* 1848

The question to be addressed in this chapter is Rousseau's classic question: is it possible to overcome obstructions to full, open, and honest communication with others? Is it possible to achieve some degree of transparency? Rousseau, in his life, was disappointed. In our more modest research effort, we hope to do better. The rational and irrational actors posited by the present alternative psychologies of avoiding nuclear war in crises are totally inadequate. They respond to theoretical rather than to empirical imperatives and, as such, obstruct the view we seek into the look and feel of nuclear danger. A more fully transparent psychological approach is therefore required, one that enhances rather than retards the clearness of our vision into the experience of events in which we ourselves played no part. In what follows, I present a few basic principles of phenomenology, followed by a short case study of ''McNamara's fear'' that has emerged from our critical oral history of the missile crisis. We seek ultimately something of the feel of the forward movement of a nuclear crisis, and phenomenology, pure and applied, is where I argue we should begin.

67

Let us return to our point of departure. Over the long run, if we are to have a major nuclear war, it will very likely be an inadvertent one, occurring because the perverse circumstances of an evolving crisis lead one or more parties of the conflict to forget the fundamental lesson of the nuclear age, at least since the Cuban missile crisis: a nuclear war cannot be won and must never be fought. As we have seen, advocates of a rational actor psychology have a good deal of difficulty imagining such an occurrence, while many of the purveyors of the newer irrational actor psychologies can do so with ease, even virtuosity. The most extreme formulations of these views, which unfortunately are among the most popular to each of their constituencies, lead to the opposing conclusions that under anything like present conditions, an inadvertent nuclear war is either virtually impossible or virtually inevitable. Both formulations take an awful lot for granted about the actual psychological life of leaders in a nuclear crisis, the one assuming blithely that rationality will prevail, the other seeming to shout in a virtual panic that it will not. Neither offers much insight, if any, into the psychological process according to which nuclear risk would be raised, lowered, or remain about the same. Each is so heavily theory-driven, so dependent for its credibility upon the acceptance of a vast network of theoretical propositions about the human mind, that it has proved impossible so far to imagine a way to adjudicate the debate raging between them. Even the sensible framework of *Hawks, Doves, & Owls* has helped little in this regard. The authors posit "Model I" (rational) factors and "Model II" (nonrational) factors, but the relative applicability of each, and especially the process by which one or the other comes to dominate, are left quite mysterious. The result has been that rational actor psychologists like Schelling have voiced great perplexity over what a "Model II" factor actually is, while proponents of the irrational actor psychology are likely to doubt the salience of "Model I" factors, at least in a nuclear crisis.[1] Neither proponents of rational nor of irrational actors appear to believe, based on this strategy of dividing and thus hoping to account for the psychological variability in nuclear risk, that they need regard the other as, in effect, separate but equal.

Yet the authors of *Hawks, Doves, & Owls* are obviously correct to assert that there is something in both the rational and irrational actor psychologies. It is also obvious that it will not do to hold merely that people are sometimes rational, other times not so rational, or that such a difference in behavior is to be accounted for by postulating "factors" that are responsible. In fact, it is not the axiomatic rationality or irrationality that ought to attract one's interest in these approaches, for these are usually given as assumptions within which one is expected to interpret facts, rather than as having been empirically derived in any meaningful sense.

What, then, is central to each sort of psychology that might in turn lead on to a more empirical, less abstract examination of the actual psychological life of actual leaders in actual nuclear crises? What is it about them that might help lead us methodologically to circumvent the rather arid and fruitless polemics over whether politicians are rational? I would argue, first, that the important kernel of wisdom in the rational actor psychology exemplified by Schelling is its insistence on placing purposeful human action at the center of any inquiry into avoiding inadvertent nuclear war. "Inadvertence," as Schelling has written, "is in the steps that lead up to where somebody believes . . . it is safer to launch than not to."[2] This is fundamental: we begin with *belief*, especially with the psychological shift in belief that will (or might) run counter to the central lesson of the nuclear age and compel a leader to decide to go to nuclear war. This shift in belief, from regarding nuclear war as anathema to nuclear war as the only remaining option, is the basic psychological problem to be solved if we are fully to understand the phenomenon of inadvertent nuclear war. For it is simply inconceivable that we could move from a standing start to the initiation of a major nuclear war without the causal intrusion of an enormous number of conscious decisions leading, finally, to an anguished but conscious decision to launch. How this mental evolution would occur ought to be our first question, and it begins with Schelling's assumption that human thought and action will be at the center of any series of events leading to nuclear war.

What of the psychological revisionists, those who are convinced that irrationality lay at the heart of the puzzle of how we might one day find ourselves in nuclear war? What is their centrally useful insight? I believe it is this: serendipitous circumstances, craziness, and the circumstantial craziness of crises *must* be significant contributors to any process leading to a totally destructive, major nuclear war. If a path to any potential nuclear war were actually as familiar, controlled, or ordinary as waiting on the corner for a bus to pass (rather than inviting disaster by stepping in front of it), then, short of a suicidal mental breakdown, inadvertent nuclear war would seem to everyone, as it seems to Schelling, virtually unimaginable. Yet in a nuclear crisis, the irrational actor psychologists believe, the situation is likely to seem stranger than fiction, events will seem to be racing beyond human control, and the resulting sense of nuclear danger may appear anything but ordinary. They are no doubt correct to believe these things; most American and Soviet leaders in the Cuban missile crisis believed them. Therefore, in any nuclear crisis leading to nuclear war, unintended consequences of the actions of leaders will without doubt play a central role.

How might these diverse requirements—the dual emphasis upon the centrality of human action and of unintended consequences of human action—be combined in a way that leads us deeper into the psychological requirements for initiating (or avoiding) an inadvertent nuclear war? We can combine these insights if we merely make one simple assumption: that leaders in a superpower crisis will be at least as aware of the centrality of their actions, and of the unintended and only partially predictable consequences of their actions, as are psychological analysts who examine their thought and behavior after the fact. Indeed, leaders are likely to be far *more* sensitive to their responsibilities and limitations than are analysts. But if we admit this much, as indeed we should, then we arrive at a somewhat folksy but nonetheless highly significant principle: *the evolving psychological life of leaders in a deep nuclear crisis will be characterized by intense awareness of the rising risk of inadvertent nuclear war.* By granting our leaders, past and present, roughly the same degree of prescience that we psychologists, and other students of nuclear policy, customarily attribute to ourselves, we would expect leaders in such crises to act much as we believe we might. That is, far from confronting a superpower crisis in a ho-hum manner, like the experienced, curb-bound pedestrian confronts a speeding bus, leaders are likely to be preoccupied with exactly the sorts of contingencies that psychologists concerned with inadvertence worry about: unintended consequences, odd circumstances, bad information, shortage of time, and so on. President Kennedy is said to have made a remark during the missile crisis that exemplifies this principle of responsibility and feared inadvertence. "The great danger and risk in all of this," he said to his brother Robert, "is a miscalculation—a mistake in judgment."[3] Embedded in this statement are the two central aspects of the psychology of a nuclear crisis we are seeking: the sense of the significance of human judgment and action, and the deep fear that actions taken to avoid war and to attain the ends of foreign policy that seemed to warrant entry into the crisis might lead, instead, to war and even to catastrophe.

In fact, the fear of nuclear inadvertence seems to have preoccupied American political leaders increasingly as the missile crisis evolved.

The President and his closest associates came greatly to fear the unintended, potentially catastrophic consequences of actions taken to keep American commitments to prevent the establishment of a Soviet nuclear arsenal in the Western Hemisphere. Secretary of Defense Robert McNamara foresaw the possibility of inadvertent nuclear war at the first imagined step of escalation beyond the naval quarantine of Cuba, which was to be the bombing of all four missile sites under construction there, followed by a massive invasion of the island. Here is one scenario of inadvertence McNamara recently recalled:

> Those of us who were concerned about Soviet reaction to air strikes or invasion didn't believe that the Soviet political leaders, even in the face of a massive air strike or invasion, would authorize—or thought it unlikely, I should say—that the Soviet political leaders would authorize the launch of a nuclear weapon from the island of Cuba against the U.S. But we didn't know that they had the power to prevent it. And in the face of a military strike by the U.S. against a missile site or an invasion, we couldn't be sure that the second lieutenant in command wouldn't, perhaps quite properly in his mind, feel that it was his responsibility to launch the nuclear weapon before it was destroyed.[4]

For McNamara, the essence of understanding what it was like to try to manage the missile crisis is a poignant paraphrase of the dilemma at the heart of feared nuclear inadvertence: the fear of an event neither side wants to happen but may happen anyway, as an unintended consequence of actions that appear necessary to protect one's vital interests. A necessity for action is felt, but so is the fear of the ultimate consequences of the action, which would be self-obliteration.

According to Robert McNamara, "nuclear weapons really didn't play a part in the Cuban missile crisis, in the sense that we never intended to use them. . . . But it is not true that they weren't on our minds."[5] In other words, nuclear weapons had no role in the outcome, other than that their use, while not intended, was an ever present possibility and therefore threatening. I believe we must seek a psychology pertinent to this evolving fear in a crisis. We must seek to understand what, exactly, was on McNamara's mind, and would be on anyone's mind who is caught in a situation such as the leaders faced during the last weekend of the missile crisis. What, exactly, is this fear of nuclear inadvertence about, and what must it be like to have such thoughts and feelings in those contexts?

This psychology of inadvertent nuclear war will focus on *the evolu-*

*tion in crises of the fear of nuclear inadvertence itself,* on the fear of circumstances beyond one's control, the fear of the effects of stress, the fear that the adversary is having the same fears, and the fear, finally, that he may therefore conclude that no option is available other than war, perhaps a nuclear war. This is not a psychology designed to distinguish between rational and irrational actors. It is instead a psychology of actors who are keenly aware of their responsibility and their vulnerability, and of the effects the stress of the crisis is having on their ability to manage it. It is not a psychology of leaders who are likely to forget the cardinal lesson of the nuclear age, but rather the psychological narrative of leaders who *fear* that they, or their adversary, may soon forget it. It is therefore centrally concerned with understanding how leaders of the superpowers in a deep crisis might lose their confidence in the mutuality and robustness of the nuclear learning that they have uppermost in their own minds: the futility of a nuclear war.

Some attempt to articulate a set of narratives of feared nuclear inadvertence would fulfill the basic requirements of what, in the lexicon of psychology, would be called a *phenomenological* description. The goal of phenomenological psychology is to obtain as accurate a description as possible of the evolution of "the stream of thought," as William James called it, as it flows creatively onward and as it is experienced by individuals.[6] Phenomenologists tend to distinguish between two complementary characteristics of evolving mental life: its *intentionality,* or what the mental life is about; and its *subjectivity,* or what it must be like to have such thoughts and feelings within just those situations that a person is experiencing.[7] These two sorts of descriptions together constitute an attempt to pry open the meaning a given pattern of thought and feeling has for a person. In the context of a nuclear crisis, therefore, we should seek to address these questions: First, what types of events signify to leaders in a deep crisis that the risk of inadvertent nuclear war is high or low, stable, rising or diminishing? Second, what would it actually be like, operating within the bounds of some estimate of the extent and directionality of nuclear inadvertence, to confront the situation in a position of great power and responsibility? If we focus on these canonical questions, a phenomenological approach to the psychology of avoiding inadvertent nuclear war can meet the requirements we have set for a useful psychological approach to these questions, an approach that avoids the essentially fruitless controversy over the rationality or irrationality of nuclear policymakers, and which begins with the central methodological propositions of both the traditional rational actor psychology and the revisionist irrational actor psychology. We would focus our inquiry on conscious, purposeful human thoughts and actions concerned with the implications of the evolving fear of inadvertent nuclear war. Such an attempt would open up a new way of approaching questions of inadvertent nuclear war, a way of seeing them in a less reductive psychological light, and a way that is tied far more closely to the lived experience of policymakers than to the theories of advocates of both rational and irrational actor psychologies.

Let us recall the two categories of fundamental significance to a leader in a crisis who begins to fear nuclear inadvertence. First is awareness of absolute, irremediable vulnerability. As Robert Jervis has written, "it is not an exaggeration to speak of the nuclear revolution [because] the side that is ahead is no more protected than the side that is behind."[8] Leaders of the superpowers in a nuclear crisis will (and have come to) know in a profoundly visceral way that they cannot defend themselves and their citizens from nuclear catastrophe. Further, they have faith in the ubiquitous rationality that will keep leaders on both sides from initiating a process leading to national suicide. But as fear of inadvertence begins to emerge, and as leaders begin to realize that rationality alone may not prevent nuclear war, the fact of vulnerability to holocaust should become more prominent.

Second, there is the related fear of the momentum of the crisis itself—fear that in some way the crisis will cause one or more of the central actors to ignore, deemphasize, or even forget about their vulnerability. Schelling believes that these worries can lead to great danger. "Nothing is more dangerous to either side in a nuclear confrontation," he writes, "than the anxiety on the other side, the reciprocated anxiety about the breakdown of confidence in the ability to keep the crisis from exploding into war."[9] Schelling has long believed that some such process of mutually escalating anxiety in a nuclear crisis greatly increases the risk of a preemptive attack by whichever side gives in first to the anxiety. Whether or not this is so, and it is not borne out by the resolution of the missile crisis, it seems clear that these are likely to be the brute psychological facts of a nuclear crisis: deep awareness of mutual vulnerability to catastrophe, and mutual fear that unimpeachable knowledge of the potentially dreadful consequences of total vulnerability will become swamped by fear of losing control of the course of events.

It is important, finally, to appreciate the various dimensions of the methodological rationale for beginning any psychological, phenomenological inquiry into inadvertent nuclear war, by seeking a detailed description of the look and feel of inadvertent nuclear danger. First, it will permit a greater degree of confidence in our attempts at prediction than we are likely to attain if we subscribe to one of the theory-driven, abstract, rational or irrational actor psychologies of avoiding nuclear war. For all we know, leaders in any future nuclear crisis will think, feel, and act as did the leaders who managed the first (and perhaps the only) such crisis so far—the Cuban missile crisis.

A second reason for preferring to begin any inquiry into nuclear inadvertence within the perspective of phenomenological psychology is that it provides a means for pursuing relatively straightforward and convincing explanations of the actions of leaders in the missile crisis. It is almost impossible to overemphasize the perplexity common to many serious students of the missile crisis, and a few of its more important participants, in the face of what they regard as the mysterious (and to some totally inexplicable) behavior of the American government in October 1962. An anecdote told by Richard E. Neustadt will illustrate this perplexity. He reports hearing the following syllogism argued at a Rand Corporation briefing by an air force general shortly after the missile crisis.

1. The Soviets are rational.

2. The United States was publicly committed to removing the missiles from Cuba by force, if necessary.

3. The United States had overwhelming tactical *and* strategic superiority.

Therefore:

4. The Soviet Union *had* to capitulate, pull back, and remove the missiles.

5. There was absolutely no need to hurry the crisis to a premature conclusion, no danger of war (certainly no danger of nuclear war), and no need to offer Khrushchev a "deal" by promising not to invade Cuba in exchange for a promise to remove the offensive weapons.

6. The only reason the deal was struck and a needless compromise reached was [what the general referred to as] "the flap in the White House."[10]

General Maxwell Taylor put the same view somewhat more picturesquely. "We had Khrushchev over a barrel," he recalled, "but then we offered him a piece of cake."[11] The important point is that the White House behavior, the "flap," and the giving of unnecessary gifts (as it is argued) is perplexing and unexplained. To attribute it to "irrationality," even when the account is presented within the framework of a psychological theory, is hardly an explanation that can be expected to persuade, or even be scarcely comprehensible to, policymakers. It is more likely to be regarded as a conceptual void where an explanation ought to be, as evidence that those doing the explaining do not have an accurate idea of what needs explaining. And the participants will have a valid point. For these "explanations"—whether throwing up the hands, an accusation of a "flap" of irrationality, or a typical psychological analysis of behavior under stress—all have in common a preconceived notion of what, a priori, ought to have been done. The "explanations" are attempts to explain the functional distance between their own "ought" and the Kennedy administration's "is." They are attempts to understand why one group of people—the actors—failed to do as another group—the explainers—believe the actors should have done.

In just such situations, where explanations and actors pass one another like ships in the night, phenomenological psychology can help. Its goal, in the phrase made famous by Edmund Husserl, is to get "back to the psychological facts themselves."[12] This goal has of course been ridiculed as simplistic. We can never, say the critics, get to any such place; thus we must begin with our theories. True enough. But we ought to keep in mind that what Husserl had in mind, and what phenomenology stands for, is a goal, a direction, a way of approaching perplexities of human mental life and action, not an achievement. Phenomenologists begin with this proposition: if you are perplexed by an action, ask the actor what he or she was trying to do. Actors can often give helpful reasons for acting as they did. The second proposition: if the reasons actors give for their actions still perplex you, try to understand the meaning the situation and action had for the individual actors. Do not turn first to theories derived from "literature" or elsewhere. Turn to the actors; try to get inside their own view of the situation. There will always be time later to criticize them for being wrong, if in fact they have been guilty of misapprehensions or delusions, or cowardice, or irrationality of one sort or another. The phenomenologist begins with what passed for ordinary common sense before research literature became the new common sense of professional psychological analysis.

It is well to recall what an explanation is for. "Explanation," Charles Taylor has reminded us, "involves . . . bringing the strange back to a place in the normal course of events."[13] Phenomenological psychology thus begins with the acting, experiencing person's view of "the strange." It seeks to do so by means of *intentional* explanations. Implicit in the general's remark about "the flap in the White House" is the claim that the "flap" was unjustified. But justified or not, when compared with some preconceived notion of what was factual and correct, the intensity of the look and feel of nuclear danger was psychologically real to President Kennedy and his closest associates, and it eventually seems to have become the principal motive force driving their perception and action. In general, as Theodore Mischel has argued, an intentional explanation of the actors in such a situation seeks entry into "how it is that people . . . acquire conceptions of their engagement in the world, conceptions which may or may not be justified by the facts, and with how their conceptions enter into the generation of their behavior."[14] This is an important point, for it dispels the common but unfounded hearsay that phenomenology is relatively primitive or superficial, a mere preliminary exercise to orient oneself until one gets on with the real business of constructing causal explanations. But intentional explanations are also causal explanations. They seek entry into evolving streams of thought of individuals, so as to clarify how beliefs, fears, and thoughts *themselves* contribute to the causal chain leading to the behavior that needs explaining. In an important sense, much of the material in the following chapters represents an attempt to transform, by means of an intentional explanation, the mysterious "flap in the White House" into a comprehensible phenomenon with a point of origin, an evolutionary history, and an outcome explained by the psychological evolution that produced it.

Explanations of human action as controversial and, in the view of some, as strange as the behavior of the American managers of the missile crisis often follow the same pattern. We have encountered it in the remark about the White House "flap," in Maxwell Taylor's quizzical comment about why we offered an allegedly optionless and defeated Khrushchev a "piece of cake," and also in the first explanation of the driver's panicky stopping on a shrouded road (in Chapter 5). They all take the following form:

1. The outcome was suboptimal.
2. The actors did "X."
3. *The actors should have done "Y."*
Therefore:
4. The bad, unfortunate, or unnecessary outcome is explained by the conceptual distance between "X" and "Y."

I have already tried to show that the validity of any such explanation is contingent on at least two important factors. First is the validity of the general theory upon which rests the claim that the explainer sees the situation relatively accurately, in hindsight, while the actor, moving through the action without benefit of this theory, was the victim of illusion. Second, in order for such an explanation to be valid, one must argue convincingly that the reasons given by actors for their actions are unnecessary epiphenomena—not really the causes of the action. Of course, it is also possible to refuse to enter into any controversy about which explanation is correct. In this case, one would adopt a kind of live-and-let-live philosophy with regard to explanations that do and do not draw on the actual intentions of actors.

But in the field of nuclear policy, as with all questions of public policy, a relentless Darwinian principle is always at work, selecting some explanations, predictions, and policies as plausible, while rejecting others as beside the point of what sensible policy should be. In the world of nuclear policy, for example, the survival-of-the-fittest explanations of policy-making derive from an environment composed of policymakers, former policymakers, and those who aspire to be policymakers. We have already seen that the irrational actor psychologies of avoiding nuclear war have been more or less ignored by the policy community, in large part because the assumptions and language in which they are embedded are foreign to those of policymakers. This brings us to the third salutary feature of intentional explanations: they are far more likely to be perceived by policymakers as policy-relevant. Because intentional explanations are meant to reconstruct, elaborate, and refine the mental evolution of policymakers, rather than to replace it with concepts and content that is foreign to their experience, intentional explanations will tend to "make sense" to them. In other words, the explanation of behavior is split off from the justification of behavior, resulting in a process that leads first to a far greater understanding of the psychological phenomena that are later to be deemed justifiable or lamentable. Thus we encounter another salutary byproduct of focusing on intentional explanations of actors: far from being a mere rubber stamp for the actors' view of the situation, the intentional approach characterizing phenomenology actually holds greater promise of policy-relevant criticism. For as actors come to believe that they are truly understood, that their critics—psychological critics in the present instance—understand why they believed they had to do as they did, their criticism is more likely to be regarded as pertinent. The criticism will be seen as criticism of them, the actors, rather than criticism of some fictional, psychopathological, deluded creatures with whom they are totally unfamiliar.

A phenomenological psychologist will therefore in every case seek first to understand before accusing or praising. This ordering of priorities ought to make sense not only to the policy community, for it constitutes good epistemological sense as well. As William James once sensibly said, we ought to try to begin our investigation of any sort of mental life with a single assumption: "thought goes on."[15] But this is far more difficult to accomplish now than it was in James's era. James himself lamented in 1890 that professional psychology had entered what he called its "less simple phase," with its ritual genuflections to hard science, the pursuit of facts for their own sake and, in general, a greatly diminished respect for the integrity of persons and their own view of why they do what they do.[16] Today it is almost axiomatic that psychologists, or those who have taken the time to become somewhat sophisticated in the vastness of psychological literature, know far more about us than we can possibly know about ourselves. Phenomenological psychology rejects this attitude and is in this respect a throwback to an earlier time, a time when psychological inquiry began by talking to people, by asking them why they behaved as they did. This approach does not require an audience of policymakers and policy analysts to swallow the scientific baggage of a century's accumulation before the digestion of a psychological explanation of policy-making can occur. On the contrary, it represents an attempt to get the policymakers' stories straight. It tries to make sense of them, for policymakers. In effect, whereas the "less simple" psychology with which our entire society is saturated has been appropriated in order to *teach* policymakers how to behave, phenomenologists will try to *learn* from policymakers something of why they acted as they did. In other words, phenomenologists begin with persons, not with theories.

In the present context, this means we should try, initially and vicariously, to reenter the evolving mental life of the President and the men surrounding him during the Cuban missile crisis, and to reconstruct as best we can the look and feel of inadvertent nuclear danger as it appeared to them. We must go *backward* and take a closer look at the psychological reality of the crisis, but in so doing we must try to step figuratively into streams of thought and feeling that moved *forward*.

Can phenomenological psychology be made to work? Can uncovering the meaning of the then and there, out of reconstructions in the here and now, really lead us to a better understanding of an experience very few people have ever had? As usual, William James put it most pithily: "What, in short, is the truth's cash value in experiential terms?"[17] In this concluding section I want to suggest that a phenome-nological approach can, and in fact already has, demonstrated some "cash value" in our experience of investigating the Cuban missile crisis. I will discuss briefly a process of discovery that derives from the ongoing critical oral history of nuclear crises that has been under-taken at the Nuclear Crisis Project.

Critical oral history is applied phenomenological psychology and is such by design. In search of greater insight into the meaning an experience has had for a person at a particular place and time, phenomenologists seek, as I have outlined, information regarding what may be called the "objective" context of the experience: what it was about, what was in the focus and periphery of attention. Since memory is a relatively poor guide in these matters, critical oral history requires those former policymakers who participate to do two things: first, to familiarize themselves with hundreds of pages of documents that, in the event in question, would likely have provided them with the particular information on which their decisions were based. But they must also agree to submit to what amounts to cross-examination by scholars who are experts on the documents, the players, and the issues of that time. In this way we try to reconstruct, however imperfectly, important objective aspects of the situation faced in a nuclear crisis.

But that is only half of the phenomenologist's mission. The other half is concerned with understanding what it was like to be in that situation whose objective elements are represented by documents now interpreted by scholars. Here, memory is a better guide and, in fact, virtually the only guide. So in order to discharge our phenomenological responsibilities regarding the feel of the situation, we try to listen carefully. And we try to provoke the former policymakers, in some cases by bringing to mind former colleagues' opinions of their conduct, or by introducing views that are greatly at variance from their own. The goal, in effect, is to elicit a response, such as "Wait a minute! He wasn't there! He doesn't know what it was like!" after which, perhaps, they are able to be more explicit about what they recall it *being* like. In this way, we try to arrive at a more enriched description of what we call "the *look* and *feel* of nuclear danger." Transposed into the jargon of phenomenological psychology introduced earlier into this chapter, critical oral history helps us arrive at more accurate descriptions, we hope, of our subjects' intentionality and subjectivity.

Let us return then to "McNamara's fear," discussed in Chapter 3 and earlier in this chapter. There appear to have been two main parts of his fear of inadvertent nuclear war on October 27, 1962. The first was emphasized in the selection from the transcript of the secret tapes of EXCOMM meetings of that day: a Soviet retaliatory strike on NATO bases in Turkey, followed by escalation to nuclear war. The other was the "second lieutenant" problem: McNamara's fear that the Soviet missiles in Cuba were fully operational, and that in an attack, a Soviet "second lieutenant" might have the ability and inclination to launch his missile, possibly causing the deaths of hundreds of thousands of Americans. These two fears together constitute the basis for much of that "flap in the White House," so described by missile crisis hawks who believe McNamara, Kennedy, and the others were utterly mistaken, that there was no nuclear danger, and that there should have been a simple, quick, decisive air strike on Cuba to remove the missiles. No crisis, no "flap," no endless EXCOMM deliberations. According to the present "anti-flap" view, we should now remember the successful Cuban air strike of October 16, 1962—the one that never occurred—rather than the thirteen days of surpassing nuclear danger that ended on October 28.

McNamara's reflection on fear of a "second lieutenant" was included in the documents that were distributed for a critical oral history conference in March 1987.[18] At that time, the discussion included some hard questioning of the validity of McNamara's fear by EXCOMM hawk Douglas Dillon. David Welch and I decided to follow up this introductory inquiry into McNamara's fear by arranging private interviews with EXCOMM hawks Paul Nitze and Douglas Dillon, in part to get their detailed views on McNamara and his fear without the constraints imposed by the collegiality of a conference. We also looked much more carefully into the objective situation McNamara faced, what he probably knew at the time. In short, we tried to determine whether the fear of the "second lieutenant" was valid.

Both Nitze and Dillon believed McNamara's fear was yet another example of what they took to be his excessive caution (which they also believed was in evidence in his conduct of the Vietnam War.) According to Nitze, "I thought we were being awfully pantywaist about what it was we wanted to stop [at the quarantine line], [and] from a military standpoint, I thought we were in a position where we could safely bring greater pressure and that we should bring greater pressure earlier."[19] Dillon was even more forceful:

> I didn't understand then, and I don't understand now, why people worried so much about one limited, conventional action leading to nuclear war. The idea is preposterous! The only explanation I can think of is that

[George] Ball's (and McNamara's) relative inexperience in these matters caused them to draw unwarranted conclusions. I think they may have let their fears run away with them, mainly because they had never been through anything like this before.[20]

In this view, the fear in the White House was pure "flap," with no substance to support it.

Next we looked into what McNamara would have known about the various aspects of a possible air strike on Cuba. We looked especially closely at material contained in the briefings of General Walter Sweeney, the head of Tactical Air Command and the man who would direct operations in the event of air attack. Our conclusions, based on all the available information regarding firing procedures at the Soviet missile sites, likely warning times, and dozens of other factors, were that a Soviet second lieutenant would have needed the help of divine intervention to launch an MRBM while under attack from the U.S. Air Force.[21] In fact, such an occurrence seemed to us wildly improbable, so improbable that we could not imagine any plausible way it might occur.

These results led to our initial set of unexpected conclusions. First, we decided that McNamara's fear had probably been baseless, for it seemed to us to have been unwarranted by the facts. Second, the hawks had been right all along, at least on this particular issue, and the fear had been merely the "flap" of the uninitiated. Third, McNamara had therefore exhibited what looked like classically irrational behavior, driven by fear. Fourth, paradoxically, and in complete contrast to the concerns of irrational actor psychologists, fear seemed in McNamara's case to have led to excessive caution, rather than to belligerence.

These surprises concluded the first phase of a phenomenological investigation of a particular fear that seemed even more peculiar than it had at its outset. Robert McNamara, a paragon of rationality, indeed seemed to have lapsed—his critics said "flapped"—into an irrational fear of Soviet second lieutenants at missile sites in Cuba.

Finally, having become familiar with much of what McNamara would have known about the probability of a launch under attack from a Cuban missile site, we went to McNamara to ask him about what we had been told and to tell him what we thought we had discovered. I believe we may have expected him to defend himself against the (implicit) charge of fear-based "irrationality" embedded in the remarks of Nitze and Dillon. I, at least, did not anticipate his response, for nothing we said seemed to surprise him. Nitze's and Dillon's opinions were familiar to him, and so were many of the details relating to the joint probability of events prerequisite to a successful launch under attack from Cuba. He agreed entirely with our conclusion: a launch by a second lieutenant had been very unlikely. He explained his point of view this way:

> I'm not interested only in probable risks. I'm interested in less than probable risks, if they may lead to disastrous consequences. That was what motivated me. I think it is too easy to be analytical about all this after the fact. I mean, was I worried more about a conventional war or nuclear war, or a Soviet second lieutenant or a Soviet response in Berlin or Turkey, or about Khrushchev's irrationality? That's putting too fine a point on it. I just don't know the answer to such questions, because that's not the way it was. The point you had to keep coming back to was that *any* of these routes could lead you into disaster. All were possible. We should not accept even a small risk of any of them, therefore, if we could avoid it.

Why, we asked, suspend the rules in a nuclear crisis of what ordinarily passes for "rational" probabilistic thinking? Why act merely on the basis of what is possible? Because, he said:

> If you go to nuclear war, and the other side retaliates, and only a few—maybe even only *one*—bomb gets through to destroy an American city, you—the one who just initiated the nuclear war—will have had to shoulder the responsibility for the worst catastrophe in the history of this country. So you won't do it.[22]

In this fashion we arrived at a richer understanding of what the missile crisis had been like for Robert McNamara. The burden of responsibility for a possible nuclear catastrophe was what he seemed to recall. McNamara's fear seemed (to us) to have been a fear of being culpable for a catastrophe that, as Richard Neustadt had pointed out earlier, would, in the best nuclear case of one bomb falling on one major American city, have killed approximately the same proportion of American citizens as were killed between 1861 and 1865 in the Civil War, a tragedy from which America has still fully to recover.[23]

Does this research vignette have, in James's terms, "experiential cash value"? I believe it does. It raises large questions about how (or whether) questions of rationality or irrationality enter into our understanding of the look and feel of nuclear danger. It helps focus attention on the burden of responsibility felt by those for whom the crystal ball began to shatter in October 1962. And it begins to help us make a tentative connection—a point of contact—between fear in a nuclear crisis and avoiding nuclear war.

After the interview just quoted, I saw a videotape of McNamara, to be used later for a television special, talking about his fear of the second lieutenant. He said again, as he has on other occasions, that when he went to bed on Saturday, October 27, 1962, he feared he would not see another Saturday. I now understand him a little better, I thought. He was afraid millions of innocent people wouldn't see that Saturday, and that it would be his fault. Then I noticed tears in his eyes as he spoke, and I realized I still didn't fully understand what he was trying to say. It will take much more hard phenomenological work to carry our understanding forward from McNamara's fears to Mc-Namara's tears, and beyond that to those of his colleagues and adversaries, and finally to the outcome of the Cuban missile crisis. Time will tell whether a psychological approach to the experience of intense nuclear danger can be developed that is sufficiently transparent to allow some nontrivial access not only to the look but also to the feeling of responsibility for the shattered crystal ball. In the following two chapters, I outline a framework and an example with which to begin the journey.

# PART FOUR: POSSIBILITIES

*7*

# The Crystal Ball Effect: A Framework for Imagining Nuclear Catastrophe in a Crisis

Now the dread of possibility holds him as its prey . . . He who went through the curriculum of misfortune offered by possibility lost everything, in a way that no one has lost it in reality.

Kierkegaard,
*The Concept of Dread,* 1844

The rational actor psychology articulated by Thomas Schelling and a few other pioneers of the late 1950s and early 1960s represented an attempt to come to grips with the nuclear revolution. Nuclear weapons were capable of unthinkable mass destruction; this was a fact. A fierce Cold War between East and West was being waged; this too was a fact. Thus the problem for which the rational actor psychology provides an elegant theoretical solution: to win the Cold War without having to fight a disastrous nuclear war. This was to be done by engaging in a competition in risk-taking, in tests of will, resolve, and nerve, and in issuing credible threats that left something to chance. Strategy thus became all-important to these pioneers of Cold War psychology because capabilities existed sufficient to destroy both competitors, the United States and the Soviet Union. This meant that thenceforth the competition would have to be more abstract, more psychological—much like the competition in the game called chicken. The winner of the war of nerves would, in this view, be the side whose leaders were most persuasive in their efforts to convince the other side that they would be willing to go all the way to the brink and even over it to achieve their absolutely vital interests.

Brilliant and persuasive though these Cold War analysts were, they made the mistake of assuming that this psychology also applied to nuclear crises, those supposedly supreme tests of nuclear resolve in which the Cold War might be won or lost. These economists, political scientists, and physicists could not know that a second nuclear revolution, also psychological, would occur in a very close brush with major nuclear war. When this finally occurred, as it did during the Cuban missile crisis, the manipulation of risk, of the *probability* of nuclear war, would in the darkest hours of the missile crisis be transformed into tremendous fear of the *possibility* of nuclear war by an inadvertent path not yet imagined. In that moment, the goal would become a compromise that left nothing to chance and an intense cooperation in risk reduction. This is the phenomenology of a nuclear crisis. In this chapter I suggest, based on evidence from the missile crisis, a framework for thinking about the evolution of the crystal ball effect from the rational world described by Schelling (and others) to a situation so perverse as to constitute its very opposite. The framework is the story of what appears to happen psychologically when one's nuclear threats seem to be on the verge of leaving nothing to chance.

In his dialogue *Meno,* Plato has his protagonist put the following question to Socrates, a question heavy with implications for any psychological inquiry, but one that is especially pertinent in the present context in which psychological analysis and its subject matter seem so incommensurably separated from one another.[1] Meno asks: "And how will you enquire, Socrates, into that which you do not know? What will you put forth as the subject of your inquiry? And if you find what you want, how will you ever know that this is the thing which you did not know?" In paraphrasing his interlocuter, Socrates means to show that the question is absurd. "You argue," says Socrates, "that a man cannot enquire either about that which he knows or about that which he does not know." As is evident in his reply to Meno, Socrates believes that this line of reasoning leads to the preposterous conclusion that learning is impossible. He escapes both horns of the dilemma by postulating innate forms—"Platonic" ideals—that are present in all human beings from birth, and that are most efficiently learned by a "Socratic" method designed to draw out this innate knowledge.

The psychology of avoiding nuclear war, in contrast, is hung up on both horns of Meno's paradoxical question. On the one hand are policymakers, past, present, and (perhaps) future, who literally have no conception of any psychological problem to be solved. Their job is the analysis, formulation, and execution of those aspects of foreign policy that seem to relate to nuclear risk. They are ignorant of the complex theories of rational actor or irrational actor psychologies that dominate psychological discussion of nuclear issues. If we ask how policymakers will therefore inquire into that which they do not know, the answer, following Meno, is obvious: they won't. They wouldn't know a psychological problem in the formal sense if they crashed into it.

On the other hand are the many purveyors of various sorts of psychologies of avoiding nuclear war. Heavily armed with their theories, supremely confident that these theories are both empirically corroborated and capable of covering a vast array of domains within foreign policy analysis, these psychologists (in function, if not always called such) see examples and confirmations of their theories everywhere. Yet they know, I believe, almost nothing of the complex psychological life of nuclear policymakers in the situation in which nuclear risk is greatest, a nuclear crisis. Once again following Meno, if we ask how the psychologists of avoiding nuclear war might inquire into the evolving psychological life of nuclear policymakers, a life they believe their theories permit them to understand with perfect ease, the answer is once again obvious: they won't. This is why, in my view, so little learning takes place between the psychologists and policymakers who claim an identical goal: to avoid a nuclear war. Both groups are too ignorant of their own ignorance of one another to see any point in a collaborative inquiry.

Phenomenological psychology seeks to avoid just such a situation by deriving its data on mental life, and by pitching its analyses of those data, so as to remain interesting and comprehensible to the actors whose actions need explaining while also addressing questions of causation, of prediction and, ultimately, of policy. The trick is to articulate a framework in which a mutually informative dialogue can occur between actors and psychologists. And it *is* a trick. No hard and fast rules dictate an ideal ratio between abstraction and concreteness, or between the use of a psychological idiom and those deriving directly from the lexicon of the actors. One rule, and one rule only, must always prevail: the psychological accounts of the thoughts, feelings, and actions must ring true to actors, psychologists, and ordinary people alike. The descriptions of evolving mental life must tease out, to whatever extent possible, the meaning the events had for the actors, and these meanings must be capable of comprehension by those whose participation in the events in question can never be closer than second-hand. All must have a compelling sense of what it was like, and the sense must conform to the psychological facts as best they can be determined.

If one gets the impression that a phenomenological account may be highly dependent on the artistry of the psychologist, or more idiosyncratic than might be ideal, or more derived from unusual sources and methods than scientific psychology would warrant, one would be absolutely correct. Phenomenological psychology is not a science, in the sense that physics is a science. But one must keep constantly in mind, as one proceeds through this central conceptual chapter, that the goal is to get as close as possible to an understanding of forward-moving psychological life; we want to participate in small chunks of lives, as they were lived. And life is not a science. If anything, it is an art. So is politics, which forms the general outline of our inquiry into questions of the psychology of avoiding nuclear war. Politics, conducted by human beings, is not governed by general laws, but is governed by conscious, sentient, complex *governors*. We can study the moon and the stars and the atoms. This is how we have come to understand them. But if we are to understand politics and the people who make policy, we must come to know them. This is what phenomenology, stripped of a certain amount of obfuscatory jargon, is about.

It is important to keep in mind that the phenomenon that really interests us, toward which all psychologically oriented students of nuclear questions must continually turn their attention, is this: the possible crisis between the superpowers that eventually becomes so perverse that nuclear war is chosen as the least-worst (or perhaps only) remaining option. Fortunately for the world at large, but unfortunately for purposes of comparative analysis, this has never occurred in the nuclear age. This truism should be a reminder that trying to understand the psychological life in a crisis that might lead to all-out nuclear war is to work largely in the dark, and that analogies must frame the inquiry. Some of the most popular classes of analogy have been nonnuclear crises that exploded into war, psychological experiments on decision-making under stress, and the results of analyses of the game called "prisoners' dilemma."[2] In each of these classes of examples, students of the psychology of nuclear risk say, in effect: "The initiation of a nuclear war would be like 'X,' so let's study 'X' and then generalize to the nuclear situation." Only analogical exercises are possible.

Only analogies are available to phenomenological psychologists, although analogies will play a role different from that which they customarily play. Normally, analogies to the initiation of nuclear war must bear a good deal of the explanatory weight. A lot depends, for example, on whether the documented failures of nonnuclear deterrence are convincingly "like" some hypothetical failure of nuclear deterrence in some imagined superpower crisis. A phenomenological account is far less formally demanding of its analogies, which are meant merely to orient the reader, to suggest the steps in the analysis of actors that is to follow. The purpose is to encourage the reader to participate vicariously in an experience that is both common and held to be something like the analysis of the less common, perhaps even unique, action to follow. Nothing hangs on the specifics of the analogy. But the plausibility of the analytic framework for inquiry may (or may not) be greatly enhanced if it seems to the reader to exemplify certain aspects of the psychological phenomenon to be explained.

What we seek by means of analogies is this: to participate vicariously in the evolving psychological life of persons in a certain situation, one that seems to actors to be becoming so perverse that they eventually commit the act that many of their previous actions had been designed to avoid. Does everyday life provide us with any examples in which individuals undergo a radical shift in outlook, as a function of the increasing complexity of their situation? I believe it does, although considerable artistry is required to convey its sense in print.

In Iris Murdoch's novel *The Bell,* we meet Dora, a young woman who boards a train to meet her husband. It is an extremely hot day and, as the train begins to fill up, an elderly lady halts in the doorway to Dora's compartment. The elderly lady appears to be a friend of the person sitting next to Dora, so it occurs to Dora that perhaps she should give up her seat.

> She had [Dora thought to herself] taken the trouble to arrive early, and surely ought to be rewarded for this. . . . This was an elementary justice in the first comers having the seats . . . [the] corridor was full of old ladies anyway, and no one else seemed bothered by this, least of all the ladies themselves! Dora hated pointless sacrifices. She was tired after her recent emotions and deserved a rest. Besides, it would never do to arrive at her destination exhausted . . . She decided not to give up her seat.[3]

From the moment Dora begins to entertain the possibility of giving up her seat, her situation becomes increasingly difficult. Perhaps she notices the old lady begin to weaken in the heat. Moreover, the old lady is obviously anxious to ride with her friend. With the passage of time, the probability rises that Dora might either be asked by the old lady to relinquish her seat (which would be embarrassing to Dora) or, far more humiliating, the old lady might faint from weakness, an event for which Dora would then be responsible. Dora must also prepare for a possible rapid escalation of her internal conflict if the old lady's knees begin to wobble furiously and her face become ashen; and in the worst possible circumstance, the old lady might collapse in a heap at Dora's feet, humiliating Dora and, after reviving, getting Dora's seat anyway. So Dora offers the lady her seat and cuts her losses. She won't arrive fresh and rested, but she won't arrive guilt-ridden. To preempt her own escalating sense of guilt and foreboding, she "got up and said to the standing lady, 'Do sit down.' "

While this vignette does not prove anything about the behavior of policymakers in a nuclear crisis, the general outline of Dora's crisis is familiar to us and also fulfills some of the psychological requirements of any imaginable nuclear crisis. Among these are, first, the dilemma presented by a set of conflicting goals. The moment Dora recognizes that the old lady is feeble and wants Dora's seat, the crisis begins. An internal struggle ensues in which personal comfort struggles against moral obligation. Second, if we are to understand the meaning Dora's experience had for her, we need some insight into her own personal "crystal ball effect." My brief interpretive passage following the selection from *The Bell* is an attempt to see and feel some of what I imagine anyone would experience in such a situation. As the situation evolves, as Dora envisions more (and more humiliating) possibilities, she feels the pressure becoming increasingly intense. Finally, she encounters what I call, later, full "situational perversity": a situation in which all the options seem bad and the stakes seem high. In Dora's case, the possibility of arriving tired, sweaty, and more than a little embarrassed to meet her husband must be weighed against a state of possibly profound embarrassment.

If leaders in a nuclear crisis remain sane, and there is little to suggest they will not, we would expect them to undergo a similar sequence of psychological evolution. For if there is to be an initiation of nuclear war, it will come only in a situation where there appears to be no alternative. But before that, leaders will *fear* that their situation will become intractable. For what Dora really fears has not overtly happened nor, as far as she can tell, is presently happening. She instead fears inadvertence, which, if it did happen, would be disastrous from her point of view, and which she is incapable of preventing in her seated position. And it may be useful to keep in mind, as we proceed through the evolution of situational perversity in a nuclear context, that Dora's moral precepts turn out to be the decisive contributors to the way she chooses to end the crisis.

In the following pages there is more discussion of active, working morality than typically occurs in either philosophical works on nuclear questions or in works on psychological aspects of avoiding nuclear war. In situations that are at least as perverse as Dora's—and this would certainly include one facing the leaders of the superpowers on the brink of war—moral considerations may become controlling. In the Cuban missile crisis, the sense of distress may have derived in large measure from moral anguish over not being able to envision a way around committing an act, or being responsible for committing an act, that one takes to be profoundly wrong, that is, immoral. Cuban missile crisis veteran Dean Rusk believes that "at the end of the day, moral and ethical considerations play a very important part, even though people don't wear these things on their shirtsleeves or put these things in official memoranda. . . . People act in reference to their basic moral commitments [which] are likely to come to the fore when situations become critical."[4]

The following framework contains a number of illustrative figures, many in the form of graphs. No numbers are on the axes of any figure. The figures should be taken no more (but also no less) seriously than the analogy between Dora's train crisis and a nuclear crisis. For these too are meant not to prove, but to evoke the sense of the evolution of a certain sort of psychological life. In other words, these "humanist graphs," as they have been dubbed by a friend, should be treated as pictures, as attempts to illustrate several dimensions of the fear of nuclear inadvertence that must, I argue, become controlling aspects of psychological evolution through a nuclear crisis. In fact, however, these humanist graphs do derive from something. Participants in the missile crisis whose styles of thinking are as different as the strategist Robert McNamara and the historian McGeorge Bundy have said that during the crisis, the members of President Kennedy's EXCOMM did indeed carry risk fractions for nuclear war around in their heads, fractions not greatly dissimilar from those suggested by the pictures that follow.[5] With these caveats, (regarding analogies, morality, and illustrative pictures) we may move directly to a consideration of the phenomenological framework for studying the evolution of the crystal ball effect in a nuclear crisis.

## A. The Dilemma: Conflicting Goals

Deep crises, although they may catch leaders by surprise, do not arise out of a void. They require at least two major actors with at least partially overlapping vital interests. When such competing interests exist, and when one side is perceived by the other to have threatened one of its nonnegotiable interests, a crisis may occur that produces what Alexander George has called "the basic paradox and dilemma of crisis management": "The paradox is that there need be no crisis if one side is willing to forego its objectives and accept damage to the interests at stake. The dilemma, in turn, arises from a desire to do what may be necessary to protect one's most important interests but, at the same time, to avoid actions that may result in undesired costs and risks."[6] This leads to an obvious but sometimes neglected conclusion: that avoiding a nuclear war is only one of the goals of the leaders of any superpower who find themselves in a crisis with another. The leaders must also strive to protect whatever interests were deemed sufficiently prized and threatened to warrant a tense confrontation in the first place.

Upon entering a crisis, therefore, a leader faces the situation represented in Figure 7.1. At least two "curves" will be filled in before the crisis is resolved: one represents the estimated risk of inadvertent nuclear war; the other(s) represents the estimated risk of a more traditional foreign policy defeat, such as President Kennedy's fear of *not* getting the Soviet missiles removed from Cuba in October 1962. The goal, so obvious but so difficult, is to achieve one's initial purpose, or something akin to it, without initiating a disastrous war.

The dilemma of crisis management—protecting one's interests while avoiding unacceptable costs—was acutely felt from the first meeting of President Kennedy's EXCOMM, the morning after the offensive Soviet missile sites were discovered in Cuba. President Kennedy asked Secretary of State Dean Rusk to lead off the meeting with a general survey of the situation and what was to be done about it. It was clear to Rusk that the missiles had to be removed and that, by whatever means they were to be removed, the risk of an all-out nuclear war (what Rusk calls "General War") would be raised considerably. Here is how Rusk opened the first meeting of EXCOMM the morning of October 16, 1962:

Mr. President, this is a, of course a . . . serious development. It's one that we, all of us, had not really believed the Soviets could, uh, carry this far. . . . I do think we have to set in motion a chain of events that will

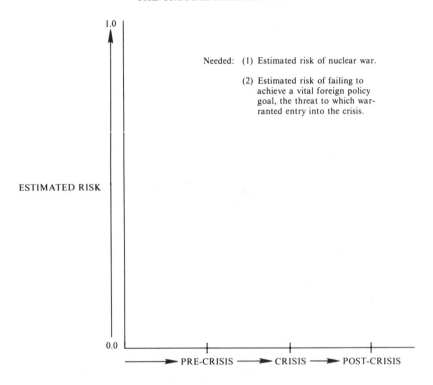

**Figure 7.1.** The basic dilemma of nuclear crisis management.

eliminate this base. I don't think we [can?] sit still . . . if we make it clear that, uh, what we're doing is eliminating this particular base or any other such base that is established [then] we ourselves are not moved to general war, we're simply doing what we said we should do if they took certain action. . . . I think we'll be facing a situation that could well lead to general war; that we have an obligation to do what has to be done but do it in a way that gives, uh, everybody a chance to, uh, put the [word unintelligible] down before it gets too hard.[7]

By the next day, EXCOMM had reached a consensus that Rusk was correct. This is revealed in a memo for discussion of that day by presidential aide Theodore Sorensen: "It is generally agreed that the United States cannot tolerate the known presence of offensive nuclear weapons in a country 90 miles from our shore."[8] Then, in a concluding section he called "other questions or points of disagreement," Sorensen described with striking prescience the more dangerous horn of the dilemma of crisis management, and in doing so he suggested immediately why the missile crisis involved what Richard Neustadt has called "a new dimension of risk."[9] Sorensen shows clearly that from the onset of the missile crisis, the dilemma of crisis management was of a sort and extent that were unprecedented: the danger was nuclear, and the enemy was inadvertence of various sorts. Here, in the telegraphic prose of a staff memo from Sorensen, is the litany of feared nuclear inadvertence:

> Whether Moscow would be either able or willing to prevent Soviet missile commanders from firing on United States when attacked, or Castro and/or his Air Force or any part of it attacking U.S. mainland. This includes the further question of whether, if a military strike is to take place, it must take place before these missiles become operational in the next 2 weeks or so.
>
> Whether Soviets would make, or threaten in response to any note, an equivalent attack on U.S. missiles in Turkey or Italy—or attack Berlin or somewhere else—or confine themselves to stirring up UN and world opinion.
>
> What our response would be to such a Soviet attack or a Soviet defiance of blockade—and what their response would be to our response.
>
> Whether Castro would risk total destruction by sending planes to U.S. mainland—or be able to control all his planes.[10]

It is fair to say, in light of this and other documents detailing EXCOMM's deliberations, that "McNamara's fear," as I have referred to it, was not his alone. These were matters of intense concern to and discussion among the entire group, the President included. The point to be emphasized here is that the basic dilemma of crisis management in this nuclear crisis was, throughout, the fear of the participants, and that the ultimate fear was the fear of an inadvertent nuclear war. The missiles must be removed, all were agreed, and within two weeks. But what would be the cost of getting them out? Indeed, how could one even estimate the risks of taking the various paths? How could one guess, for example, whether Castro could (or would) restrain his air force or whether Khrushchev could control his Strategic Rocket Forces, especially when it was plausible to assume that neither Castro nor Khrushchev could answer such questions with certainty? As I noted in the previous chapter, risk was only a part of the fear equation and, according to McNamara, not the most important part, which was the stakes: what could be lost, and the premonition of having to be responsible for such a loss. So began the uncertain journey to remove the missiles and to grope into a new dimension of risk, and therefore of nuclear fear.

## B. The Perception of Possibility: The Crystal Ball Effect

The outbreak of World War I is often proposed as the prototype of an inadvertent war and, by analogy, as the case whose structural features will probably most closely resemble those of an inadvertent nuclear war, should one ever occur. In her book *The Guns of August,* which became a worldwide best-seller only months before the missile crisis, Barbara Tuchman advanced this thesis most persuasively. In her view, World War I was a war no one really wanted, a war which all the major participants may be said to have lost, and a war in which the seeds were sown for a far greater and more calamitous conflagration a generation later. By late July 1914, preparation for war on all sides— what today we dignify with the name "deterrence"—could no longer be stopped by force of human will, or at least not the will of anyone in charge of the major protagonists. By the last day of July, according to Tuchman:

> War pressed against every frontier. Suddenly dismayed, governments struggled and twisted to fend it off. It was no use. Agents at frontiers were reporting every cavalry patrol as a deployment to beat the mobilization gun. General staffs, goaded by their relentless timetables, were pounding the table for the signal to move lest their opponents gain an hour's head start. Appalled upon the brink, the chiefs of state who would ultimately be responsible for their country's fate attempted to back away, but the pull of military schedules dragged them forward.[11]

The July crisis led to the guns of August, according to Tuchman, because in their attempt to protect what they took to be their interests, leaders on all sides failed to consider the possible costs of such protection, costs that would accrue inadvertently, but no less tragically.

This is the sort of scenario many observers now regard as the most likely path to a major nuclear war.[12] Yet there is at least one immense difference between the evolution of psychological life in the leaders who led their nations into World War I and any leaders who may find themselves poised on the brink of what they believe to be an inadvertent nuclear war. Whereas leaders in 1914 could not foresee the extent of the catastrophic results of a war, the leaders of the nuclear superpowers can hardly fail to imagine the catastrophic results of a nuclear World War III. This is "the crystal ball effect" that guarantees that no matter what situation leaders of the superpowers may find themselves in, they will, if they have not gone mad, see in the crystal ball the same irremediable nuclear catastrophe.[13] This crystal-clear foresight of the total doom accompanying any major nuclear war has led, in periods of peaceful competition, to a degree of prudence probably unprecedented among great powers as intensely adversarial as the United States and the Soviet Union during most of the nuclear age.

Would a leader in a nuclear crisis foresee the shattering of the crystal ball within the same categories that characterized the writing of so many of those who tried in the 1920s to come to terms with the Great War? The most significant characteristic of this literature, and according to some it represented a real departure in the public consciousness of the citizens of the Western world, was irony. As Paul Fussell has written, the first generation of writers after World War I, looking backward with hindsight at the horror of the trenches, used irony to articulate the meaning of their experience, in order to exemplify its "means . . . so melodramatically disproportionate to its presumed ends."[14] But leaders in a nuclear crisis will face a situation far more ironic than anything one might have imagined in the trenches. This was recently stated, poignantly, by the wife of one of the key members of President Kennedy's EXCOMM: "When I discovered the situation we were in," she recalls, "I couldn't help wondering whether those few missiles in Cuba were really worth risking the destruction of our civilization, which had taken as long and so much dedication to construct."[15] Former Undersecretary of State (and EXCOMM member) George Ball recalls:

> I felt a keen sense of the macabre by Saturday evening, October 27. It was just absurd. Here was this beautiful sunset on a perfect Autumn evening, and we were going to blow up the world? It was absurd. That is what moved me to say to Bob McNamara that evening that the whole scene reminded me of one of those Georgia O'Keeffe paintings, with a rose coming up through an oxskull.[16]

And of course, nothing could be more ironic than the remark that ended the EXCOMM meeting of October 27: "Suppose we make Bobby mayor of Havana."[17]

Two other distinguishing features of the nuclear crystal ball effect suggest that the sense of irony in any nuclear crisis might be, in its way, even more anxiety-provoking than anything faced by reflective veterans of World War I. First, the leaders are looking into the future, not reading the record or drawing on memory. This crystal ball does not yield predictions; it provides only the general outline of a possible catastrophe. Events are contingent. Ends are invisible. Means are uncertainly efficacious. Second, and related, leaders peering into a nuclear crystal ball will feel the full force of their own responsibility for avoiding the colossal irony of nuclear war. This powerful sense of seeing oneself moving among the ruins in the foreseeable future comes out in many ways in the material deriving from EXCOMM meetings to which we now have access. For example, we now know that on October 27, some discussion occurred regarding civil defense measures in the event of a nuclear attack on the United States. Robert McNamara suggested that, in the event of a massive air strike on Cuba, leaflets should be dropped first to warn civilians in Cuba to take cover. Five million of them were made up but were never used.[18] McNamara, as we have already seen, was powerfully motivated by the fear that he might become "responsible for the worst disaster in the history of this country."[19] And Dean Rusk believes that a public official in his position had a responsibility to put himself in the President's shoes, which he greatly regrets not having done before the Bay of Pigs debacle, and which he is glad he did during the Cuban missile crisis because it "injected an element of caution into my approach to the matter."[20] All these factors—the immensity of the horror in the nuclear crystal ball, the highly uncertain means and ends, and the sense of personal responsibility for the potential horror to come—seem in the missile crisis to have led to the leaders' fear of nuclear inadvertence that was psychologically analogous to the potential physical effects of the weapons under their control.

According to Robert Kennedy, the ironic component of the crystal ball effect worked both backward and forward in the missile crisis, due to the President's immersion at the time in Tuchman's best-seller, *The Guns of August*. Recalling the inadvertent rush to disaster of 1914, the President reportedly told his brother: "I am not going to follow a course which will allow anyone to write a comparable book about this time, *The Missiles of October*."[21] No one will ever know how seriously President Kennedy took the presumed analogy between the first and third world wars. But Tuchman's book seems to have had an impact on him and, presumably, on the conduct and outcome of the crisis.

If so, we ought to observe a remarkable piece of learning on the part of a president in a very short time. For President Kennedy's generation grew to maturity in the 1930s; for them, the lessons of history were chiefly the lessons provided by the failure of appeasement at Munich in 1938 and the failure of deterrence in the Pacific, December 7, 1941. Indeed, President Kennedy justified the naval quarantine of Cuba to the American people in just those terms. Speaking on national television on October 22, he said: "The 1930s taught us a clear lesson: aggressive conduct, if allowed to grow unchecked and unchallenged, ultimately leads to war."[22] Thus, he endorsed the quarantine, which was designed to squeeze the Soviet missiles out of Cuba. But, perhaps stimulated by Tuchman's book and certainly reinforced by the many scenarios of nuclear inadvertence spelled out in the Sorensen memorandum of October 17, he also understood, by the final weekend of the crisis, the lessons of 1914 as well. "If anybody is around to write after this," he reportedly told his brother Robert, "they are going to understand that we made every effort to find peace and every effort to give our adversary room to move. I am not going to push the Russians an inch beyond what is necessary."[23]

The psychological evolution brought on by the crystal ball effect is represented in Figure 7.2. In sum, it indicates the leaders' unavoidable awareness of the qualitative difference between an old-fashioned, war-threatening crisis and a situation they regard as a potentially *nuclear* war-threatening crisis. They will see clearly that in a major nuclear war, they will bear some responsibility for their nation having been annihilated beyond repair. They will see, as Richard Neustadt has said, that the "irreversible [will] become irreparable."[24] The Kaiser knew eventually that von Moltke's mobilization timetables were irreversible. American and Soviet presidents will understand that an irreversible action might provoke the end of civilization.

## C. Intensification of the Crystal Ball Effect: The Radical Divergence of Political and Military Calculi

The nuclear crystal ball effect works on all of us, whether presidents or ordinary citizens. We all see clearly that a major nuclear war is not worth fighting. But let us focus briefly on some specifically presidential responses to the horror of an imagined nuclear conflict. The president will, as we have seen, have to face the nuclear version of the basic dilemma of crisis management: to avoid a nuclear war (which will

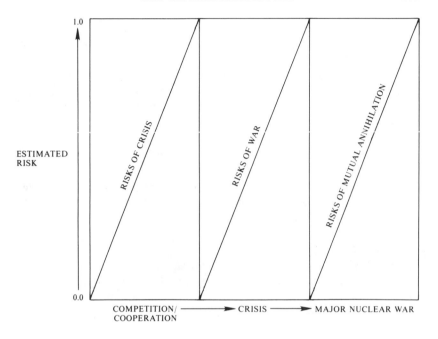

**Figure 7.2.** Stages in the evolution of the crystal ball effect.

Source: Hannes Adomeit, *Soviet Risk-Taking and Crisis Behavior* (London: Allen and Unwin, 1982), p. 43.

probably mean avoiding any substantial armed conflict with the Soviet Union), and also to protect or secure some interests held to be vital by the American government and the American people. As a nuclear crisis wears on, therefore, the crystal ball effect will intensify for the president. How should we understand the structure of some such intensification? A president's confrontation with an intensifying crystal ball effect is unlikely to be simply a matter of putting his hands to his mouth and gasping, "Oh, my God; look what might happen if we do 'X'!" (A president may in fact do this. According to Robert Kennedy, the President did turn pale and shudder visibly at the horrible possibilities he confronted.)[25] By what process might a president arrive at this point? How might he arrive at the conclusion that any plausible scenario for nuclear war would be catastrophic? In short, how does a president think his way into the shattering of the crystal ball?

The missile crisis provides interesting clues. By approximately Oc-

tober 27, 1962, the President and his closest advisers apparently
believed that war might be a finite number of moves away. But this
meant that nuclear war was, in their judgment, perhaps only one or
two (or three) steps beyond that. We know, from real-time data on the
transcripts of the October 27 EXCOMM meetings, from Sorensen's
discussion memo of October 17, and from many recollections, that
tremendous uncertainty existed regarding the degree and nature of
Soviet escalation that would probably result from an American air
strike against the Soviet missile bases in Cuba. Would one or more
Soviet missiles be launched? Would Castro authorize an attack on the
American mainland? Did he have the capability and inclination? and
so on, through all sorts of feared inadvertence. But even if none of
these fears materialized immediately, there remained the great danger
of the momentum of the crisis itself.

Richard Neustadt and Graham Allison discussed this issue with the
President and many EXCOMM members shortly after the crisis. They
have constructed an interesting composite of the President's thinking
in those fateful moments in a way that emphasizes the preoccupying
concern: that, in fact, the superpowers *could* recapitulate the errors of
July 1914 and gradually squeeze one another into a war whose disastrous proportions were totally unacceptable. What if the intensifying
crystal ball effect were an insufficient deterrent to nuclear war in such
a situation as leaders faced by October 27, 1962? This is how Neustadt
and Allison imagined that the President confronted this ghastly possibility:

> If the Russians held their course for a mere seventy-two hours, we would
> have to escalate a step, probably by bombing Cuban sites. In logic, they
> should then bomb Turkish sites. Then we . . . , then they . . . the third
> step is what evidently haunted Kennedy. If Khrushchev's capability to
> calculate and to control was something like his own, then neither's might
> suffice to guide them both through that third step without holocaust.[26]

By this time, therefore, the President would have had to progress
through something like the following series of beliefs:

> Nuclear first-use is virtually impossible.
> Nuclear first-use is improbable but not impossible.
> Nuclear first-use is probable, if X, Y . . .
> X or Y . . . is increasingly probable.
> Nuclear first-use is increasingly probable. If nuclear first-use occurs,
> escalation to catastrophe is highly probable.

The key to understanding the horror with which a president gazes into his crystal ball in a nuclear crisis is the final belief: that nuclear first-use leads almost inevitably to a catastrophic nuclear war, a war ironical in extremis, a war that no supposed foreign policy objective could possibly be worth. How, by what means, would a president reach such a frightening conclusion? Figure 7.3 is meant to suggest some such process by which the President concludes that, as former Kennedy White House aide Arthur Schlesinger wrote, once a nuclear war begins in the midst of a superpower crisis, "the game is over."[27]

Figure 7.3 represents the logical outcome of the point emphasized

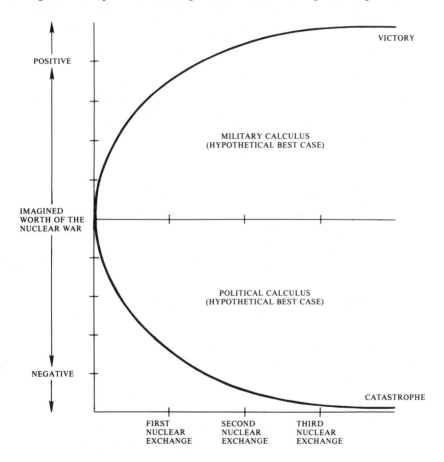

**Figure 7.3.** Military and political calculi of an imagined major nuclear war.

by Jervis, that the very essence of the nuclear revolution lies in the fact that neither superpower could defend itself against a nuclear attack from the other.[28] Thus, as a nuclear crisis deepens, traditional (that is, relative) notions of victory will be seen by a president and those who try to take a presidential perspective to apply not at all to the situation. As "victory" in relative military terms is approached, catastrophic damage will occur to the American homeland a president is elected to preserve and protect. Thus, as nuclear first-use seems to become ever more likely, so does nuclear catastrophe, because few "exchanges" of nuclear detonations are required to produce a catastrophe "beyond history," to quote McGeorge Bundy.[29] In fact, it will become clear after a relatively "limited" nuclear war that military victory equals political catastrophe. Bundy calls this effect "the inverse calculus of gain and pain," according to which "whether the two sides exchange a few weapons or tens or hundreds, or more, the real loss to each will outweigh by orders of magnitude any 'gain' it may have aimed at in the exchange."[30] No one has expressed Bundy's principle with more poignancy than Khushchev. In an interview with American journalist Norman Cousins shortly after the missile crisis, he asked: "What good would it have done me in the last hour of my life to know that though our great nation and the United States were in complete ruins, the national honor of the Soviet Union was intact?"[31] This effect is summarized in Figure 7.4

It is illuminating to dwell for a moment on the psychological implications of Bundy's emphasis on the leaders' grasp in the missile crisis of "the *real* loss to each." For if we try to "thicken" our phenomenological description of psychological evolution in a nuclear crisis, we may notice some profoundly moral undertones.[32] American and Soviet leaders notice an element of personal responsibility that others may not see. Or others may see the responsibility and even be able to articulate it, but they will not feel it as profoundly because they will not feel responsible for it.

As the imagined force of the disaster to result from a nuclear war confronted President Kennedy in October 1962, he began, according to his brother Robert, to talk like a moral philosopher, trying to bring the possible destruction of millions of innocent people within the bounds of his moral categories. But he could not imagine any gain that might counterbalance such pain. Robert Kennedy's account of his brother's intense moral anguish on October 27 makes this clear:

> The thought that disturbed him most, and that made the prospect of war much more fearful than it would otherwise have been, was the specter of

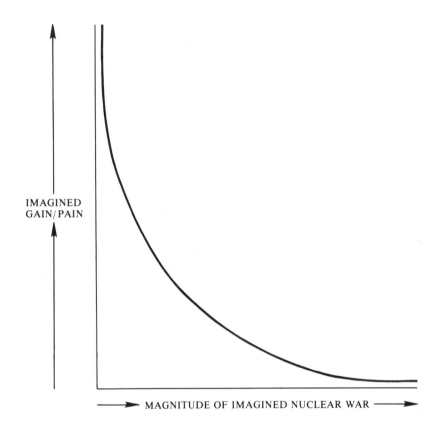

**Figure 7.4.** The inverse calculus of gain and pain imagined to be derived from a nuclear war.

the death of the children of this country and all the world—the young people who had no role, who had no say, who knew nothing even of the confrontation, but whose lives would be snuffed out like everyone else's. They would never have a chance to make a decision, to vote in an election, to run for office, to lead a revolution, to determine their own destinies.

Our generation had. But the great tragedy was that, if we erred, we erred not only for ourselves, our futures, hopes and countries, but for the lives, futures, hopes and countries of those who had never been given an opportunity to play a role, to vote aye or nay, to make themselves felt.

It was this that troubled him most, that gave him such pain.[33]

Someone might object that this was, after all, the President's brother writing, and that such a statement ought to be disregarded as merely an attempt by RFK to place JFK in the best possible light. Is it really plausible, one might ask, that President Kennedy, the pugnacious cold warrior, would be *most* troubled by the thoughts and feelings his brother ascribes to him? I think it is highly probable, for several reasons. One of the most important was the remarkable turnabout in the President's rhetoric and stance toward the Soviet Union following the missile crisis, a subject I take up toward the end of the following chapter. The crisis shook him profoundly, as indeed it shook Khrushchev. The plausibility of the passage is also supported by some of the best recent thinking on the subject of nuclear ethics. Joseph Nye, for example, believes that the key to fulfilling our moral obligations in the nuclear age is to construct policies that maximize the probability that we can pass on to succeeding generations a range and quality of opportunities and possibilities at least equal to our own in their capacity for personal happiness and public fulfillment.[34] As we have just seen from Robert Kennedy's memoir, his brother's distress was extreme because any nuclear holocaust would prevent succeeding generations from enjoying the opportunities that were available to his own. And according to Dean Rusk, it would be with complete justification after a nuclear war that "the first band of shivering survivors who get their hands on the President and Secretary of State . . . will hang them to the nearest tree."[35] Here is a remarkable case, I suggest, of the application of a philosophical principle before the principle was even clearly stated. It may be that those who understand what would be the magnitude of their failed responsibility can hardly avoid thinking these sorts of thoughts. Kennedy wanted most of all to deal with succeeding generations fairly, a goal made increasingly improbable, in his view, as the likelihood of inadvertent nuclear war continued to rise. This may be a way people in that situation deal with the "radical thought" of eternity referred to by Kierkegaard—when a "person will think it and he dares not to think it" (see Chapter 1).

But this is not to say that the phenomenology of these insights, by a president and by ethical philosophers, were identical. What is different about the President's grasp of this moral maxim is that he felt it, and would feel responsible for violating it, should the crystal ball shatter. Clifford Geertz gives us an idea of the sort of thing that must have happened to President Kennedy as he tried without success to fit an inadvertent nuclear war into his moral categories. The horror must have "arrive[d] . . . across a sequence of clashing imaginations and discomfited sensibilities. . . . This is how anything imaginational grows in our minds, is transformed, socially transformed, from something we merely know to exist . . . somehow or other, to something which is properly ours."[36]

Here is the key: the potential reality and responsibility for nuclear catastrophe became, for President Kennedy, *properly his*. He became directly and fully acquainted with it, in a way only one other leader—Nikita Khrushchev—ever has. When an inadvertent nuclear war became transformed for the President from an abstract possibility to a contingent probability, it also became something he owned, and it was therefore horrifying. Presidential counsel Theodore Sorensen once referred to the Cuban missile crisis as "the Gettysburg of the Cold War."[37] The analogy is an apt one in at least one respect: in his address at Gettysburg, Lincoln looked *backward* in horror and revulsion at the slaughter that had taken place there. His address is an attempt to extract some justification, some meaning, from the bloodshed. But Kennedy looked forward in horror and could not derive any justification from the inadvertent nuclear war that seemed ever more probable. Thus this "Gettysburg of the Cold War" was a Gettysburg of the imagination only.

## D. The Evolution of Situational Perversity

John Kennedy is the only American president to have gazed into the nuclear crystal ball at a moment when there seemed to be a real danger of it shattering. Only he actually experienced the "new dimension of risk" noted by Neustadt; only he and his closest advisers have faced the very real prospect of catastrophic damage to the United States as a consequence of some actions they might undertake. He was not, however, the first chief executive to express his revulsion at the prospect of using nuclear weapons. Both of Kennedy's presidential predecessors in the nuclear age, Truman and Eisenhower, were far from enthusiastic about the use of nuclear weapons. For example, Truman was greatly disturbed, when he learned that most of those killed on August 6, 1945, at Hiroshima were civilians. On August 10, the day after the bombing of Nagasaki, he ordered that atomic bombing be stopped. Henry Wallace recorded in his diary that, to Truman, "the thought of wiping out another 100,000 people was too horrible." He just couldn't bring himself, so he said, to order more killing of "all those kids."[38] For his part, Eisenhower, when asked by his advisers to consider using nuclear weapons to prevent the fall of the French garrison at Dien Bien Phu in 1954, said: "You boys must be crazy. We can't use those awful things against Asians for the second time in less than ten years. My God!''[39] It seems clear that the enormous and indiscriminant destructiveness of nuclear weapons impressed upon both Truman and Eisenhower that nuclear weapons were devices appropriate only for deterrence. President Kennedy shared this view. As Dean Rusk noted, after a briefing on the effects of war plans, the President turned to him and said: "And they call us human beings.''[40] With the possible (but not probable) exception of Richard Nixon, every president since John Kennedy has also shared this revulsion against using nuclear weapons.[41]

Despite President Kennedy's continuity with past and future presidents in this respect, it would still be a mistake *not* to focus on the uniqueness of his situation in the missile crisis when he was the first (and perhaps will be the only) president to stare down what Sorensen called "the gun barrel of nuclear war.''[42] Truman and Eisenhower had only to consider further nuclear use against a nonnuclear and beaten enemy like Japan, other nonnuclear powers (the Soviets during the blockade of Berlin in 1948, or against China during the Korean War, or at Dien Bien Phu, or against China in the offshore islands conflict in 1958). Nuclear use depended upon cold-blooded human calculation, thus there existed no danger of an inadvertent mutual catastrophe. But all this seemed to change during the Berlin crisis of 1961. And in the Cuban missile crisis, fear of inadvertent nuclear war was sufficiently intense to shock all those primarily responsible for its outcome, making it the greatest nuclear learning experience to date.

The analogy of gazing into a crystal ball in this situation is apt. For inherent in crystal-ball gazing is the desire to learn an uncertain future. If you believe you are completely in control of your situation, you don't need a crystal ball. But when control erodes, and especially when one has reason to expect the worst, we resort to gazing at "crystal balls." So, whereas Truman could order the atomic bombing to stop, and Eisenhower could order the atomic bombing of Vietnam never to begin, and both could expect thereby to avoid a catastrophic nuclear war, Kennedy came to believe that his orders, and possibly Khrushchev's too, would be insufficient to avoid a nuclear war. When this possibility arose during the missile crisis, the revulsion over nuclear first-use was heightened by the sinister specter of the shattered crystal ball, the fear that one might actually become, in the phrase Oppenheimer borrowed from the *Baghavad Gita,* the "shatterer of worlds."

Writing not long after the missile crisis, Thomas Schelling recognized that the situation faced by Kennedy and Khrushchev during the missile crisis was indeed unprecedented. In a nuclear crisis, Schelling noted, the competition between the superpowers was governed not so much by military gains and losses, but by what Schelling called "competition in risk-taking."[43] As he saw it, both the United States and the Soviet Union had during the missile crisis conducted their attempts at coercion mainly by psychological means. Instead of manipulating armies and navies, Schelling said, risk was used as the coercive instrument. The winner in such encounters, he concluded, is the leader and government that is more ready to risk the mutual catastrophe neither side desires. By this yardstick, Schelling calculated that Kennedy had beaten Khrushchev; he had pushed the Soviets to the brink, and they had backed off. Schelling was prescient, in my view, to seize upon the unprecedented, highly psychological character of the competition in the missile crisis. But because of his commitment to the rational actor psychological outlook, he was blind to the look and feel of nuclear danger in the management of the crisis whose outcome he was trying to explain. What is missing from Schelling's account, in short, is the phenomenology of the competition in risk-taking during the crisis.

Schelling also noticed something else about the missile crisis that provides the clue to where to look for the missing phenomenology. He saw that making what he called "threats which leave something to chance" has a peculiar and unexpected effect in the nuclear context: the threats are just as threatening to the threatener as they are to the side that is threatened. In such a situation, Schelling wrote, the threat becomes "more impersonal, more 'external' to the participants; the threat becomes part of the environment rather than a test of will between two adversaries."[44] This important insight has received insufficient attention, even from Schelling himself. For leaders who become viscerally aware of their total vulnerability to, and ultimate responsibility for, a nuclear catastrophe but who nevertheless feel compelled to apply force to an adversary in order to protect some nonnegotiable vital interest, will eventually come to recognize that they are participating in the construction of a situation over which they are exerting progressively less control, which may eventually turn on them, like Frankenstein's monster, and destroy them. The phenomenology of such a situation, its look and feel, includes a perception of increasing shortage of time, a shrinking list of acceptable options, and the feeling of losing control. And it is very frightening.

On the final weekend of the missile crisis, both Khrushchev and

Kennedy demonstrated that they were feeling the pressure of evolving situational perversity. On October 26, Khrushchev wrote his famous "Friday letter" to the President, arguing that both sides had by then become tied in a "knot of war," with both sides pulling and the knot tightening until, said Khrushchev, one side or the other might eventually feel forced in desperation to cut it, when, he said, mutual extermination would begin.[45] This evolving situation, the escalating sense of loss of control and the disappearance of noncatastrophic options, is a direct psychological result of the phenomenon noted by Schelling: the adversary's migration to "the environment." In the final stage of the missile crisis, the fear of nuclear inadvertence became all-consuming: fear of losing control oneself, fear of the adversary losing control, fear of the adversary's fear (of one's own fear, and so on). The situation, Khrushchev clearly saw, was becoming thoroughly perverse. The President, moreover, concurred publicly with Khrushchev's private assessment when he wrote to Khrushchev on October 28, welcoming his peace proposal as a message that had come just in time, because "developments were approaching a point where events could have become unmanageable."[46]

Figure 7.5 illustrates the evolution of situational perversity. As a nuclear crisis evolves, the risk of inadvertent nuclear war will seem to rise as pressure is applied (or resisted) to achieve whatever goal seemed vital enough to warrant entry into a crisis in the first place. Figure 7.5 illustrates why this is so: because prediction and control of the situation appear to be evaporating. The situation will appear to resemble, in a real and dangerous sense, that which resulted from a famous social psychological experiment of some years ago. Stanford psychologist David Rosenhan taught several of his students to mimic the responses of psychotics to standardized tests, so as to gain entry under false pretenses to mental institutions. The purpose was to determine to what extent the "insane" behavior typical of mental patients is actually a function of the way they are labeled and treated by the professional staff of these institutions. But once admitted to the hospitals, the students were instructed to resume "normal" behavior. The results were unexpectedly severe. Having been labeled as crazy by the staff, virtually all the behavior of the students that was presumably normal was nevertheless responded to as if it were yet further evidence of the "patients'" pathology. Many participants in the exercise reported a feeling of entrapment that they had never known before. No matter what they did or said, they were treated as if they were insane. The phenomenology of "being sane in an insane place," as Rosenhan

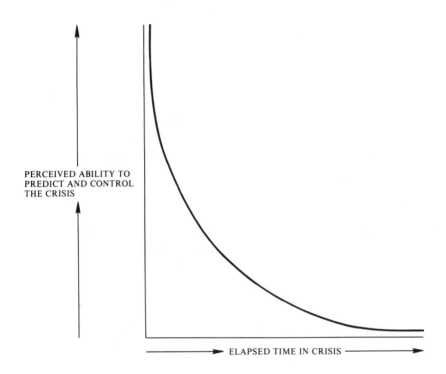

PERCEIVED ABILITY TO
PREDICT AND CONTROL
THE CRISIS

ELAPSED TIME IN CRISIS

**Figure 7.5.** The evolution of situational perversity in a nuclear crisis.

called this phenomenon, was frightening. In effect, the pseudo-patients came to believe (correctly, it turned out) that in the crazy, perverse world they found themselves in, they had lost control of their own lives and that it was virtually impossible to predict the results of even a simple request for food or toilet privileges.[47]

The students' sense of being sane but entrapped in an insane place, of having an unpredictable, not quite identifiable, enemy, and of being totally vulnerable to the environment's apparent capriciousness seems to have much in common with the perverse situation of the superpower leaders during the climactic phase of the Cuban missile crisis. They did not doubt their own sanity or the sanity of their adversary. But the nuclear environment that, in normal times, is calmly referred to as the means of deterrence appeared to be losing its responsiveness to the wishes and control of the deterrers. It was a Kafka-esque nightmare and, like the unfortunate graduate students of David Rosenhan, they themselves had made it that way.

Thus one may doubt, for example, whether it was mere hyperbole, as some have claimed, tnat caused Robert Kennedy to recall the shootdown of an American U-2 reconnaissance plane over Cuba the morning of October 27, 1962, as an event that "was to change the whole course of events and alter history."[48] One did not know how to interpret such an event. Did the Soviet leaders order it? Did some faction, either among the Soviets or perhaps even the Cubans, order the shootdown to sabotage any chance for a peaceful settlement on American terms?[49] Was it just a mistake, like the mistaken American U-2 overflight of Siberia on the same day? If Americans responded in kind, according to their own sense of "an eye for an eye," by bombing the SAM-site responsible for the shootdown, how would *that* be interpreted? And so on.

The manner of recollecting the U-2 shootdown neatly divides the hawks in the Kennedy EXCOMM from the President and his top advisers, all of whom have come to be known as the missile crisis doves. One's reaction to the shootdown, at least as it is recalled later, seems to be almost entirely a function of whether one believed at the time that the situation was not under control and that inadvertent nuclear war was a worrisome possibility. Two of the most significant hawks, Paul Nitze and Douglas Dillon, see the event simply as what Dillon has referred to as "an isolated incident."[50] In any military action, according to Dillon, one must expect a few such occurrences. To Dillon, the significance of the shootdown died with its pilot; it did not mean anything beyond the fact. Of course, Dillon was aware that such incidents would speed the process of deciding to attack Cuba. But he was convinced that this eventuality was both inevitable and no cause for worry unless it involved an invasion, which he feared would stir cries of "Yankee imperialism" across Latin America. Nitze concurred with the view expressed by Dillon, and he seems to have been both perplexed and irritated because, with regard to the shootdown, "from a political standpoint it was clear that we would lose by magnifying a thing beyond its true significance."[51] In other words, for the hawks the crescendo of crisis created by the U-2 shootdown was artificial, manufactured, and perhaps the most regrettable example during the entire crisis of the "flap in the White House."

As one can discover from the portion of the October 27 transcript cited in Chapter 3, the U-2 shootdown was noted and discussed (in apparently angry tones by, for example, John McCone and Alexis Johnson), and then the discussion was moved by McNamara and the President to the issue of the Turkish missiles. While the shootdown seemed important to some of the discussants, one cannot derive from the transcript anything like Robert Kennedy's sense that the U-2 shootdown was the watershed event of the crisis. What is the meaning of this claim? Let us consider a portion of the context.

It is late afternoon. The Turkish missile trade, required by Khrushchev, looks impossible. The Cubans are shooting incessantly at low-level reconnaissance planes. Taylor and McNamara have said that the low-level flights must cease, which is foolish, or they must go in with "a cover on," that is, with fighter protection. These are the facts. But—and this would appear to be key—if you are already aware that any untoward development will raise the likelihood of catastrophe, the U-2 episode will be very disturbing. If you believe the Soviets ordered it, you simply must ask yourself: Are they crazy? Are *we* crazy? Are we at war, a war we cannot control? As the transcript shows, the incident is discussed only briefly. But to the so-called doves, to those who were staring into a shattering crystal ball, the key passages come from McNamara, and they are questions: "How do we interpret this?" and "This is a change of pattern, now why it's a change of pattern we don't know."[52] Were events *now* out of control?

Whether or not the shootdown altered history, it has, in Robert Kennedy's recollection of it, altered our understanding of history. When the October 27 transcript became available, some scholars tended to accuse RFK of playing fast and loose with the facts, for an alteration of history via the U-2 shootdown is not what one finds in it. But a bit of informal phenomenological analysis suggests that the debunkers may be missing the point: that the U-2 episode is a kind of "flashbulb memory," as some psychologists refer to such things, that epitomizes and crystallizes an inchoate remembered sense of great fear and apprehension.[53] It was, or seemed to be, or has been remembered as, a turning point, the point at which, as RFK remembers it, the hour seemed darkest. One guesses that, in having no answer to the questions posed by McNamara, some, including Robert Kennedy, did imagine that the crystal ball had begun to shatter. That sort of material will not show up on any transcript but, if it happened and if its effect was to force the mission later that night to Dobrynin, then RFK would be absolutely correct. The shootdown did alter history because it altered men in EXCOMM and, as we now know, in the Kremlin to end the crisis. If the missile crisis was the Gettysburg of the Cold War, the shootdown is the high-water mark of tension and uncertainty; this was as far as you could go, as much as you could take.

In the end the Kennedy administration learned something profound.

At its outset, the point of the crisis they had willingly entered was simply to remove the Soviet threat from Cuba. This was stated forcefully by the President in his concluding remarks to the first meeting of his EXCOMM on October 16:

> I don't think we got much time on these missiles. They may be . . . so it may be that we just have to, we can't wait two weeks while we're getting ready to, to roll. Maybe just have to take *them out,* and continue our other preparations if we decide to do that. That may be where we end up. I think we ought to, beginning right now, be preparing to . . . because that's what we're going to do *anyway.* We're certainly going to do number one; we're going to take out these, uh, missiles. Uh, questions will be whether, which, what I would describe as number two, which would be a general air strike. That we're not ready to say, but we should be in preparation for it. The third is the, is the, uh, the general invasion. At least we're going to do number one.[54]

In other words, the day the President received word that Soviet missiles were in Cuba, he seems to have had no doubt that they *had* to be bombed, and bombed as soon as possible.

But at the height of the crisis, on October 27, the President resisted tremendous pressure from his military advisers, and from some civilians, too, to bomb *just one* Soviet missile site. Several members of EXCOMM preferred the risk of bombing Cuba to the political risks to NATO of what would appear to be selling out an ally if the United States consented to a public trade of Cuban for Turkish missiles. We now know from the transcript of the October 27 tapes that the President disagreed with this advice. No one in the room, not even McNamara, seemed more keenly sensitive to the danger of a strike on Cuba. Kennedy finally said, with characteristic irony, that he didn't believe the Turks, who vehemently rejected any trade proposal, really understood what was, or might be, about to happen. Before adjourning the meeting in the early evening for a short dinner break, he said:

> But it seems to me we *ought* to have this discussion with NATO about these Turkish missiles, but more generally about sort of an up-to-date briefing about where we're going. . . . We can't very well invade Cuba, with all its toil, and long as it's going to be, when we could have gotten them [the Soviet missiles] out by making a deal on the same missiles in Turkey. If that's part of the record I don't see how we'll have a very good war.[55]

We now have reason to believe that this war, one that on October 16 seemed to be a foregone conclusion, was a war that President Kennedy, by October 27, simply would not permit. For in February 1987, Dean Rusk revealed that after the last EXCOMM meeting late in the evening of October 27, the President had instructed him to open up a channel to the UN through which, if the President gave Rusk the signal the following day, the public trade might commence.[56] He was no longer willing to do what he had called "number one" on October 16, because the world had changed. He would risk, so his critics within EXCOMM suggested, the disintegration of NATO before he would bomb Cuba. For as McNamara had said in the same meeting of October 27, it was just too "damned dangerous!"[57] The situation had, in his view, grown too fragile to permit it.

The President told Arthur Schlesinger on the morning after the crisis had ended that he was afraid people would draw all the wrong conclusions from the missile crisis, especially that if you just hung tough with the Russians, they would cave in.[58] To him this would misrepresent what had happened. In fact, both sides felt mightily squeezed, and both sides had to compromise: Khrushchev withdrew the missiles; Kennedy promised to leave Castro alone and to remove American missiles from Turkey (the latter being a private pledge, made through his brother Robert to Soviet Ambassador Dobrynin on October 27). This, as he saw it, was the ultimate act of sanity in an insane situation.

In fact, the situation the leaders of the superpowers believed they were fast approaching by October 27, 1962, is a perfect example of what the ethical philosopher Thomas Nagel has called a "moral blind alley." Nagel asks: "What if the world itself, or someone else's actions, could face a previously innocent person with a choice between morally abominable courses of action, and leave him no way to escape with his honor? . . . Given the limitations on human action, it is naive to suppose that there is a solution to every moral problem with which the world can face us."[59] The instigation for Nagel's question was the situation American soldiers found themselves in at My Lai, when they were ordered to kill the women and children of the village. Is this not an example, Nagel asks, of a "moral blind alley" devoid of acceptable options? What does a soldier, who has been taught to follow the orders of his superiors, do when he is asked to do something so revolting, so repugnant to his moral sensibilities, that he cannot under any circumstances regard it as acceptable? What does one do when the situation presents these options: kill the innocent, or be killed for insubordination? This, Nagel suggests, is the fundamental moral problem of war and massacre.

This is not too different from the situation of the superpower leaders in the Cuban missile crisis. As they looked down the road, they seemed to see a situation leading inexorably, by one path or another, to massacre—to indiscriminant nuclear war. They imagined with ease, and I believe with considerable accuracy, an environment that might soon provide no further acceptable options. That was the meaning of McNamara's "damned dangerous." It is the meaning of Robert Kennedy's dramatic characterization of the U-2 shootdown. And it is the meaning of the President's instruction to Rusk to prepare to trade missiles publicly. The nuclear crystal ball had begun to shatter, and it was time to try to escape with honor.

# 8

# The Shattered Crystal Ball: Fearing and Forgetting Nuclear Catastrophe after Robert Kennedy's "Statement of Fact"

> If in this situation he did not behave falsely towards possibility, if he did not attempt to walk around the dread which would save him, then he received everything back again.
>
> Kierkegaard,
> *The Concept of Dread*, 1844

The Cuban missile crisis was resolved quickly, peacefully, and unexpectedly over the final weekend in October 1962. This is not what the Kennedy administration apparently believed would happen as they entered the crisis after discovering the Soviet missiles in Cuba. On October 22, in his televised speech to the nation, the President had warned that "this is a difficult and dangerous effort on which we have set out. No one can foresee what course it will take or what costs or casualties will be incurred. Many months of sacrifice and self-discipline lie ahead . . . months in which many threats and denunciations will keep us aware of our dangers."[1] None of this happened. The acute period of crisis ended less than a week after the President's speech; the sacrifice consisted of one American death, Major Rudolf Anderson, shot down on a reconnaissance mission over Cuba; and the crisis ended without even the expected Cold War recriminations from either side. In fact, the resolution of the missile crisis marked the end of the most dangerous phase of the Cold War. No wonder this potentially dangerous event, with a resolution so totally unexpected, has been the subject of more explanations, from more participants, scholars, and journalists, than any other crisis of the Cold War era.

One senses that even now, a quarter century after the event, many of the key participants in the missile crisis are still perplexed by the way it transpired and the way it was resolved. Writing shortly after the crisis, presidential counsel Theodore Sorensen invoked an analogy that reveals a great deal. "Just as missiles are incomparably faster than all their predecessors," he said, "so this worldwide crisis had ended incredibly faster than all its predecessors."[2] Why? EXCOMM member and former Undersecretary of State George Ball recently confided in his memoirs that as time has elapsed, he has experienced more, rather than less, difficulty writing about the crisis. He reports being stymied by a bewildering array of theories and angles meant to explain the event.[3] This sense among its participants that the resolution of the missile crisis was inexplicable was illustrated recently by a remark of then National Security Adviser McGeorge Bundy. The remark was made in a videotaped discussion of the missile crisis during which excerpts were played from President Kennedy's speech of October 22, 1962. Bundy said, after listening to the President ask the American people to prepare for months of sacrifice: "I had forgotten that we all thought the thing was going to last for a very long time."[4] Few, if any, of the American managers of the crisis expected the episode, as Sorensen later said, to become the diplomatic mirror image of the ballistic missiles that provided the focal point of the crisis.

I will make and develop three central points in this chapter. First, I will formalize an argument that was introduced in the preceding chapters, namely, that the fear of inadvertent nuclear war caused this crisis, which most observers anticipated would be long and perhaps bloody, to become short and scary, but peaceful. Second, in light of these considerations of the nature and role of feared nuclear inadvertence, I will reexamine the act that seems to have brought the missile crisis to its unexpectedly rapid and conciliatory conclusion: Robert Kennedy's conversation with Anatoly Dobrynin on the evening of October 27, 1962, in which he conveyed what the Soviets understood to be the final offer from the Americans. Finally, I will speculate on the psychological life of leaders on that final evening of the crisis. I think something occurred during those tense hours that is psychologically more profound than is generally realized, even by the participants themselves.

In the title of his fine memoir, EXCOMM member George Ball has articulated the problem that most needs addressing as we try to understand, finally, what made the missile crisis so unusual, so unexpected in so many of its dimensions, so very much like a missile of a crisis rather than, so to speak, the bomber that had been anticipated. Ball's title, *The Past Has Another Pattern,* derives from T. S. Eliot's "The Dry Salvages":

> It seems, as one becomes older,
> That the past has another pattern, and ceases to be a mere sequence—
> Or even development: the latter a partial fallacy,
> Encouraged by superficial notions of evolution,
> Which becomes, in the popular mind, a means of disowning the past . . .
>
> We had the experience but missed the meaning . . .[5]

I believe that, with one or two exceptions, the multitudinous explanations of the resolution of the missile crisis have indeed "missed the meaning" by "disowning the past," a past dominated in the end by the fear of inadvertent nuclear war.

This past as we have been encouraged to think of it—a couple of weeks of high-stakes poker and a culminating hand during which the Soviet bluff was called—has been reconstructed by analysts and participants alike, according to one or another pattern that is more consistent with this or that received academic wisdom, or simply less frightening to recall than the way events actually seemed to be as they transpired. This observation—that, looking backward, "the past has another pattern" from the confused and often fearful chaos that constitutes the daily crawl of life—is not meant to be an accusation of duplicity or incompetence. The reconstruction of the past so as to drain it of its fearful content is every bit as adaptive an act as fearful responsiveness to events occurring in the present. It is an attempt to bring our experience within the bounds of our understanding. In this sense, as Eliot (and Ball) suggest, we are all of us, all the time, having the experience but missing the meaning. But the standard accounts of the resolution of the Cuban missile crisis seem to be so at odds with ordinary common sense, and this discrepancy is so heavy with implications for our understanding of what it is really like to manage a nuclear crisis, that it is more than worth the effort to take a few halting steps toward recapturing the meaning of those darkest hours of "Black Saturday" and of the following Sunday morning when the whole world awoke to learn that the most dangerous confrontation of the nuclear age was over. I hope that by restoring even a small part of the meaning—what the fear was about and what it was like to be fearful in that context—we will better understand why Robert Kennedy conveyed his frightening message on the evening of October 27, why the members of EXCOMM were so pessimistic about its chances for success, why it did succeed and, finally, why so many EXCOMM members appear to have received the news of Khrushchev's acceptance with disbelief, which yielded immediately to giddy relief and delight.

*  *  *

Let us now try to reenter the final weekend of the crisis. By October 27, the missile crisis had moved forward for nearly a week following President Kennedy's televised speech on October 22, in which he announced an immediate naval quarantine of Cuba that would remain in place until the Soviet government agreed to remove all offensive nuclear missiles from Cuba. In fact, the quarantine was not successful. Soviet ships bound for Cuba had halted on October 24, just before reaching the quarantine line, and ships were allowed to pass through that were carrying cargo not proscribed by the President's orders. Despite the quarantine, the Soviets continued their round-the-clock uncrating and assembling of the missiles, under the close surveillance of American reconnaissance planes. By October 27, the missiles were deemed by American intelligence to be either ready for possible launching or only a few days from the point of readiness.

But the quarantine was, in effect, only the tip of the iceberg of the Kennedy administration's military efforts to compel the Soviets to remove their missiles. For the quarantine was regarded as only the initial step. If the Soviets did not relent, then an air strike, probably followed by an invasion, was planned. In a retrospective report to Secretary McNamara, dated February 13, 1963, Adam Yarmolinsky summarized the preparedness of the U.S. Army invasion force this way: "The Army forces which were alerted, brought up to strength in personnel and equipment, moved, [and] prepared to execute the Cuban operation, were a part of the largest U.S. invasion force prepared since World War II. The remainder of Army units were prepared to carry out any other assigned missions, such as the reinforcement of Europe."[6] Slightly hidden in this statement was a great fear of many EXCOMM members: that if the United States actually bombed and invaded Cuba, the Soviets would move against West Berlin. Thus, the movement of troops for "the reinforcement of Europe."

We now know, on evidence contained in the transcript of the October 27 EXCOMM meetings, that Berlin was a cause for great worry. In the event of a Soviet move against the city, Allied conventional forces would be overwhelmed almost immediately, creating the need for a decision no one wanted to face: whether to respond with nuclear weapons. The vulnerability of Berlin had been the overwhelming foreign policy preoccupation of the Kennedy administration since the Vienna summit in June 1961. Then Khrushchev had issued an ultimatum to Kennedy that amounted to a threat unilaterally to abrogate the Four-Power governance of the city that had existed since World War II and implied that all Western access to the city would be terminated. No one was more concerned about Berlin than Kennedy. On October 27 he said to EXCOMM members opposed to a public trade of missiles that "because we wouldn't take the missiles out of Turkey, then maybe we'll have to invade or make a massive air strike on Cuba which may lose *Berlin*. That's what concerns me."[7] The anticipated action against Cuba would, he believed, have worldwide consequences.

Nowhere were the consequences of the American military alert more obvious and ominous than in the preparations (for possible nuclear war) within the Strategic Air Command. After the President's speech on October 22, SAC was placed, for the first and only time, at Defense Condition (DEFCON) 2. Scott Sagan has summarized what this meant in operational terms:

1. Battle staffs were placed on 24-hour alert duty.

2. All leaves were canceled and personnel recalled.

3. 183 B-47 bombers were dispersed to 33 preselected civilian and military airfields.

4. The B-52 airborne alert training program was expanded so that an eighth of the force was airborne in a continuous series of 24-hour flights with an immediate replacement for every bomber that landed. Fifty-seven bombers and 61 tankers were airborne. Forty-nine of the B-52s, with 182 nuclear weapons on board, were on airborne alert.

5. Additional B-52 and B-47 bombers and tankers were placed on enhanced ground runway alert. The ground alert force totaled 672 bombers and 381 tankers, with a total of 1627 nuclear weapons on board.

6. Ninety Atlas and 46 Titan ICBMs were placed at a heightened state of readiness.[8]

All this occurred following the President's speech of October 22. Sagan has summarized the numbers inherent in that order: "Within 24 hours of that alert order," he has calculated, "SAC was expected to have 172 missiles and 1200 bombers with 2858 weapons on alert. The aggregate destructive power available in this SAC-generated force alone in October 1962 was over 6000 megatons—higher than the entire American strategic arsenal today."[9] Only the tip of this American military iceberg was noticeable to the general public. (Television coverage that week centered on the UN, where a memorable confrontation occurred between American Ambassador Adlai Stevenson and Soviet Ambassador Valerian Zorin).

The Soviets, for their part, reciprocated only minimally. Yarmolinsky reported to Secretary McNamara after the crisis that the Soviets, like the Americans, had canceled military leaves and that "an advanced state of alert was established" within the military forces of the Warsaw Pact and the Red Army itself. He also reported, however, that American intelligence sources reported nothing resembling the full-scale *nuclear* alert in the Soviet military under which the American armed services had been placed by October 27.[10] American Sovietologist Arnold Horelick has said that he always believed the Soviets were too frightened to go to a nuclear alert, fearing that this would evoke a preemptive strike from the vastly superior American nuclear forces. Horelick's hypothesis was recently confirmed by former Khrushchev speechwriter Fyodor Burlatsky.[11] In light of these few facts and of others mentioned in Chapter 2, when one speaks of a unique and overpowering sense of nuclear danger in the Cuban missile crisis, it is clear that one is not exaggerating. The situation was grim indeed. There was an operational basis for fearing that the world was poised on the brink of inadvertent holocaust. Hundreds of American bombers aloft, carrying hundreds of missiles with the capacity to unleash thousands of megatons if so ordered, and dozens of Soviet nuclear missiles and bombers, apparently ready for their missions only 90 miles from the American mainland, provided ample reason for the fear of nuclear inadvertence.

Within this worldwide context of nuclear danger, even more ominous events occurred on October 27. A new Soviet ship was reported to be approaching the quarantine line. Photo-reconnaissance revealed that work on the Soviet missile sites had been, if anything, speeded up. Some nuclear warhead storage bunkers were now being built. Then the two events occurred that were, to many members of EXCOMM, portentous precursors of what lay ahead. First was the shootdown of the unarmed U-2 reconnaissance plane over Cuba and the death of its pilot. I indicated in Chapter 7 why we ought to take seriously Robert Kennedy's claim that the downing of the U-2 was "to change the whole course of events and alter history."[12]

Next was the news that an American piloting a U-2 had made a navigational error, overflown Siberia, and drawn a host of Soviet fighters (but no fire) before returning safely to his base in Alaska. This incident, or rather the American and Soviet reactions to it, illustrates better than any other the effect of the look and feel of nuclear danger on the American and Soviet leaders during the missile crisis. Accidental overflights occur with great frequency and, as a rule, little or nothing is made of them beyond the local level where the overflight has occurred. The President and McNamara were both reported to be very disturbed by this episode.[13] According to Sorensen, members of EXCOMM were deeply concerned because they believed such an overflight might convince the Soviets that the United States was beginning to survey Soviet airbases in preparation for a preemptive nuclear attack, perhaps thereby initiating a Soviet damage-limiting preemptive attack.[14]

Khrushchev *did* wonder about the overflight in his October 28 letter to Kennedy: "How should we regard this?" he asked. "What is this, a provocation? One of your planes violates our frontier during this anxious time we are all experiencing, when everything has been put into combat readiness."[15] Such were the heightened sensitivities in both leaderships. Both sides were quite ready to fight a conventional war of some sort, and the United States was overtly ready to launch a nuclear war. By "ready" I do not mean to imply that anyone close to either Kennedy or Khrushchev desired a conflict to occur. But as war-readiness was heightened by incidents that seemed to be harbingers of more dangerous episodes, it became obvious that, in a sense, the readiness itself was becoming a large, and perhaps the central, problem. How many more shootdowns or overflights could occur before retaliation resulted, unleashing the military forces already close to the shorthand term then in use for Defense Condition (DEFCON) 1: "Cocked pistol."[16] On DEFCON "Zero," so to speak, the pistol would be fired and war between the superpowers would commence. Khrushchev wrote to Kennedy on October 26: "What that would mean I need not explain to you." But he said it anyway: it would be "dooming the world to thermonuclear catastrophe."[17]

Theodore Sorensen has captured with great poignance the look and feel of nuclear danger in EXCOMM on October 27, as the group confronted the possibility that events were about to snowball and defeat their best efforts to remove the missiles without a war. At a meeting that evening, according to Sorensen, tempers flared and the President had to adjourn his advisers until calmer heads prevailed. Here is what the situation looked like to Sorensen on the evening of October 27:

> Everything was in combat readiness on both sides. The conventional and the nuclear forces of the United States were alerted worldwide. Both air-strike planes and the largest invasion force mounted since World War II were massed in Florida. *Our little group seated around the Cabinet table in continuous session that Saturday felt nuclear war to be closer on that day than at any time in the nuclear age.* If the Soviet ship continued coming, if the SAMs continued firing, if the missile crews continued working and if Khrushchev continued insisting on concessions with a gun at our head, then—we all believed—the Soviets must want a war and war would be unavoidable.[18]

The President later told Sorensen that he had believed on October 27 that the odds that the Soviets would go all the way to war were "somewhere between one out of three and even."[19] These "presidential" odds have been much discussed and often discounted as "irrational" or as mere "hyperbole."[20] But the evidence suggests that the President and his inner circle of advisers were indeed afraid on "Black Saturday" that war was imminent. This appears to have been the frightening phenomenology of the situation. And in light of what lay behind Sorensen's remark that "everything was in combat readiness on both sides," a strong argument can be made to suggest that the President's odds and Sorensen's fears were based on an accurate reading of the situation they themselves had helped to create.

In the early evening of October 27, the President sent his brother Robert to convey to Ambassador Dobrynin, thence to Khrushchev, what may have been the final American offer: that the missiles would be removed from Cuba in exchange for a public American pledge not to invade Cuba and a private assurance that, sometime shortly after the crisis was resolved, a group of (obsolete) Jupiter missiles in Turkey under Turkish custody would quietly be removed. These terms had, in general, been proposed by Khrushchev in his two letters to the President of October 26 and 27. The principal difference between what Khrushchev said he required (in the letter of October 27) and what Kennedy proposed was that there would be no "deal," at least none publicly agreed to, in which Soviet missiles in Cuba were "traded" for American missiles in Turkey. The American government was willing to give a private assurance that the Turkish missiles would be withdrawn, but would deny that any such pledge had ever been given if the

Soviets should make the American offer public. This was the content of Robert Kennedy's message to Dobrynin, as RFK reported it.

The Americans were very pessimistic about Khrushchev's response to their offer. Many felt that, far from reaching an accord based on their offer, they were instead about to enter an unprecedented phase of nuclear danger. Sorensen reports that he did not believe they would succeed and that McNamara was so pessimistic that he decided to stay up much of that night to draw up American options short of invasion. CIA Director John McCone was equally pessimistic.[21] And Robert Kennedy recalled: "the President was not optimistic, nor was I. He ordered twenty-four troop-carrier squadrons of the Air Force Reserve to active duty. They would be necessary for an invasion."[22]

The situation seemed very close to the outbreak of war. We now have a clearer idea why the President and his advisers were so pessimistic. For example, it is obvious from the October 27 transcript that Kennedy could scarcely believe that Khrushchev would accept an American acceptance of an offer the Soviets made *privately, yesterday,* when another offer had been made *publicly, today.* For this reason, together with the apparent military escalation in Cuba, the situation seemed to the President to require a public trade, as suggested in the public and more recent proposal from Khrushchev. But many of his aides told the President that the trade was a bad idea: it would severely damage NATO solidarity, and even then the President would be unable to guarantee to the Turks and the world that the Soviets would remove their missiles from Cuba. There seemed to be no way out of this conundrum and, with the shootdown of the U-2, no time to find one. Llewellyn Thompson, the Soviet expert, finally convinced the President to give the ploy a try, overnight.[23] They would accept Khrushchev's first, private offer. But the President also would send Robert Kennedy to deliver, via Ambassador Dobrynin, a personal message to Khrushchev emphasizing the urgency of the situation.

Robert Kennedy recounts in his memoir just how desperate the President and his advisers believed the situation had become. He recalls telling Dobrynin this:

> We had to have a commitment by tomorrow that those bases would be removed. I was not giving them an ultimatum but a statement of fact. He should understand that if they did not remove those bases, we would remove them. President Kennedy had great respect for the Ambassador's country and the courage of its people. Perhaps his country might find it necessary to take retaliatory action; but before that was over, there would

be not only dead Americans but dead Russians as well. . . . Time was
running out. We had only a few more hours—we needed an answer
immediately from the Soviet Union. I said we must have it the next day.[24]

After months of suspicion about Soviet intentions in Cuba, after the
October 15 discovery of offensive missile sites, after a week of intense,
secret discussions between President Kennedy and his advisers, after
the carefully calibrated political and military maneuvering of the preceding week, and after the proposal to the Soviets of a resolution
almost (but not quite) identical to one proposed previously, the Cuban
missile crisis came down to this: the Soviets were given 24 hours to
agree to what was presented as the absolutely final American offer or
risk being plunged into the first shooting war between the nuclear
superpowers.

Why, in the view of the President and his advisers, had it come to
this? *Why the hurry?* As we saw in the previous chapters, the attitudes
and expectations of the men in the White House have mystified many
critics because the so-called "flap in the White House"—their allegedly irrational fear of nuclear war—prevented the United States from
doing what, in their view, ought to have been done right away: bomb
the missile sites, invade the island, and throw out Castro's Communist
government. For these critics, including several missile crisis hawks,
the American "ultimatum," as they like to think of it, was probably
too little and certainly too late.[25] Yet another group has criticized
Robert Kennedy's "ultimatum" of October 27 as being needlessly
unequivocal and hasty. Even McGeorge Bundy remains perplexed, in
hindsight, by the rapid escalation of concern evident, for example, on
the transcript of the October 27 EXCOMM meetings.[26] "Why hurry?"
strikes him as a very important and potentially revealing question.

It is unfortunate that the answers usually given to this question are
often reductively psychological and suggest that the President and his
circle of advisers needlessly lost their composure, or that the forcing
of the crisis to what they regard as a premature conclusion is evidence
of some deep psychopathology in the President and, perhaps, in his
advisers. Much of this amateur psychologizing is scathing on the point
of the Turkish missiles. Why, the critics ask, didn't the President
simply yield to the "fair" Soviet request to trade a missile for a
missile? Adlai Stevenson was sympathetic to this view during the crisis.
But the President was not, and the critics of Robert Kennedy's ultimatum have been harsh. Garry Wills, for example, sees it as evidence
of the President's desire "to rub Khrushchev's nose in the dirt."

According to Wills, "Kennedy would even risk nuclear war rather than admit that a trade of useless missiles near each other's countries was eminently fair.[27] But perhaps the most scathing attack on the President, one that is typical of irrational actor psychology applied to the Robert Kennedy message of October 27, comes from Bruce Miroff. According to Miroff:

> Talk of gradual, step-by-step escalation was abandoned; Kennedy was within two days of plunging into the most dangerous conflict the world would ever witness. This extraordinary haste has never been satisfactorily explained . . . There is no more telling commentary on Kennedy's "crisis mentality" than this preparation for apocalypse on the eve of the crisis resolution. . . . At the height of the crisis, he abdicated control over the outbreak of hostilities to Khrushchev's sense of restraint. This was hardly the stuff of political greatness; in the final analysis, Kennedy's conduct in the missile crisis was neither responsible not justifiable.[28]

According to this account Kennedy, in firm control of the crisis situation, chose to raise the ante needlessly at the last minute because, due to the American military preponderance around Cuba and at the strategic nuclear level, he thought he could get away with it. That he did "get away with it," in this view, does not justify the needless risk of forcing, via his brother's message to Dobrynin, a premature conclusion to the crisis.

But this view is no more in contact with the reality of the Cuban missile crisis than its mirror image—the view that the Americans could safely have bombed and invaded Cuba, at any time and without any significant danger, but for the irrational "flap in the White House." Neither of these views takes seriously Robert Kennedy's account that he went to Dobrynin bearing not "an ultimatum but a statement of fact," implying that he and his colleagues had their backs to the wall. Grossly improbable assumptions are required to sustain this sort of misreading of the evolving psychological life in the crisis, the President's motives, and his brother's account. Miroff claims the President "abdicated control" over how and when war would break out. But this would require us to believe that by the evening of October 27, with 125,000 troops poised in Florida to invade Cuba, with Castro declaring that he would order his forces (who controlled the anti-aircraft batteries around the missile sites) to shoot down everything in sight, with one U-2 already destroyed and its unarmed pilot killed by a Soviet missile, with the recent Siberian overflight, with the antisubmarine activity around the quarantine line becoming overly aggressive, with the knowledge that more than 8,000 nuclear weapons were ready to be used and, perhaps most significant, with the suspicion that Khrushchev faced analogous difficulties, the President was in control of the situation. Only a fantasy could justify the claim that the President and his advisers, by giving Khrushchev 24 hours to "take it or leave it," had willfully "abdicated control" over the situation.

In fact, this kind of criticism is very common, for all its psychological absurdity. This is so primarily because its advocates fail to distinguish between (what amounts to) a "God's eye" view of human action (viewed backward with knowledge of the outcome) and the viewpoint of the experiencing person, in this case the American president. This is mistaking the perspective of the analyst for the perspective of the analyzed. In my view, we should ask some questions before rushing to judgment: Why did the actors in a given instance believe they had to act as they did? What was the situation *they* believed they faced? And what is the likelihood that anyone faced with that situation would have believed the same and thus acted similarly? If we do not ask these questions, if we make little or no attempt to enter the psychological reality of the lived experience, our conclusions will necessarily be derived mainly as deductions from some preconceived theory.

One can see this psychologically naive approach at work repeatedly in interpretations of Robert Kennedy's pivotal (so-called) "ultimatum." From the right-leaning critics comes the following deduction:

Most politicians are afraid of using military force. President Kennedy (and his civilian advisers) were politicians.
Therefore:
President Kennedy was afraid to use force in the missile crisis, even though (as General Curtis LeMay said) the Soviet response would have been "nothing."[29] *The President was "chicken."*

And from the left:
Many politicians are obsessed with power. President Kennedy was a politician who was particularly obsessed with power.
Therefore:
President Kennedy used a completely unnecessary degree of force and pressure to end the missile crisis. *The President was "macho."*

What these explanations have in common is their commitment to a priori theories or ideologies and their blithe disregard for the look and feel of the situation the actor thought he was in. In other words, rather than attemping *intentional* explanations of action *first,* these explainers jump to a mode of deductive explanation typical of physical science. But in physics, attempts are first made to get the facts straight. In interpreting the Robert Kennedy message of October 27, therefore, we ought to get our psychological facts—the psychological context in which the message was delivered—straight before we proceed to further analysis and evaluation. This, of course, is exactly what is lacking: an attempt to experience the look and feel of nuclear danger to a small group of men in the White House (and Kremlin too) on October 27, 1962. This is the first reason Robert Kennedy's statement of fact has been so widely and diversely misinterpreted: an insidious concatenation of rational/irrational actor psychologies and powerful ideologies of left and right have prevented vicarious reentry into the situation faced by EXCOMM.

A second powerful reason for the relative absence of the fear of inadvertent nuclear war in discussions of the resolution of the Cuban missile crisis is this: almost every fiber in our nature rebels against the idea that our lives need not have evolved as they did, that chance and happenstance are pivotal and, most of all, that we ourselves fell into this circumstance or that out of fear of the unknown. When we try to account for the circumstances of our lives, we give our past a meaning, coherence, and rationality it never had in the living. This is George Ball's point, borrowed from T. S. Eliot, that "the past has another pattern," one it does not have when it is lived—when it is the elusive present—but only when it is truly the past and we have the luxury of viewing it as a series of snapshots, each scene leading naturally, as in a well-told story, into the next.

In his recent volume of poems called *The Past,* Galway Kinnell suggests the most significant class of omissions from our tales of our own pasts: "To de-animalize human mentality, to purge it of obsolete evolutionary characteristics, in particular of death, which foreknowledge terrorizes the contents of skulls with, is the fundamental project of technology . . ."[30]

Freud and generations of depth psychologists would concur: of all the tricks played by memory, the most pervasive and necessary occurs in the defense against fear—especially fear of death—in our mental landscape. Freud in fact was one of the first modern psychologists to make Kinnell's point: we require a kind of technology, a set of rules for remembering (or constructing) our fearless victories and forgetting the terror of the unknown.[31] This means it would be surprising if the managers of the missile crisis had recalled the event *primarily* as one in which, at the time of the eventual resolution, fear of the unknown had dominated their thoughts and feelings. The predictable recollection would be one emphasizing mastery of difficult circumstances, the triumph of reason in a situation in which one could have, but did not, give in to fear. And this is generally what one finds. Thus, human nature is part of the reason why fear of inadvertent nuclear war, apparently so powerful and pervasive during the missile crisis, has been analytically almost invisible, a ghost in the rather pat and mechanical explanations of the crisis's resolution. It will always be possible to interpret the events, after the fact, as evidence of rationality or of irrationality on the part of the actors. I merely suggest that on the basis of what we now know about the objective facts of the matter that led to the Robert Kennedy mission to Dobrynin, along with an open-minded appreciation of the probable feel of that situation, it would be surprising if the EXCOMM members, or anyone else, felt that they were in control of the situation, or even that they understood it. They likely believed at the time that the escape had been lucky and very narrow indeed.

But I believe there is a third reason why the fear of nuclear inadvertence is only a ghostly presence in the nuclear debate, and especially in the analyses made of the crisis by some of its central actors. This reason has little to do with organizational inertia or human defensiveness, and everything to do with the full, revolutionary psychological implications of the Cuban missile crisis as it must have been lived forward. It is this: the deep ambivalence with which feared nuclear inadvertence is regarded by most key participants in the missile crisis derives from their having had to confront a situation so unexpected, so profound in its implications, and so unsettling that they have been left in a kind of psychological limbo, unable to disown their fears completely, but also unable to integrate them in any constructive way into their understanding of why the missile crisis was resolved peacefully. For the first and only time, leaders really seem to have believed that they were on the brink of nuclear catastrophe and that, if one came, it would do so despite the intentions of all concerned with the management of the crisis. In a sense, the leaders are nuclear-age exemplars of Kierkegaard's uncertainty principle: life must always be lived forward but understood backward. They fully expected, I believe, that the crisis *would* explode into something—a European crisis? A local war in Cuba? A protracted war of nerves with awful political repercussions? Nuclear war itself? But there was no war, and I believe that few of the participants, and hardly any of their analysts, understand why the expected inadvertent catastrophe never occurred. Because of the depth and the kind of fear they felt, and because of the ultimately peaceful resolution, the participants, I think, remain deeply confused. They know that a statement of fact was indeed delivered from Robert Kennedy to Dobrynin, but they cannot make sense of the outcome without also believing that it was an ultimatum. They cannot—who could?—accept that fear of inadvertence was rampant and also that the crisis remained peaceful. For this would seem to indicate that they were merely lucky. They have no way of causally connecting the fear of inadvertent nuclear war with avoiding all war in the missile crisis.

Of course, I speculate. But at least two reasons suggest why many missile crisis veterans who feared the shattered crystal ball cannot connect it with the outcome. First is the powerful retrospective sense of failed responsibility—fear of the validity of the "plain dumb luck" thesis. The second is purely empirical, derived from dichotomies like those that follow in which those most responsible for the outcome of the crisis can recall their fear, but cannot (or do not) connect it with the resolution of the crisis.

### Robert McNamara

*Fear:*

The sun was setting, in October and I, at least, was so uncertain as to whether the Soviets would accept [our offer] that I wondered if I'd ever see another Saturday sunset like that . . . that may sound over-dramatic, but that was the way I was feeling at the time. It was that serious a problem. That was Saturday night [October 27, 1962].[32]

*Resolution:*

We confronted the Soviet Union with nuclear war over the issue of the offensive weapons [in Cuba] and forced them to remove the offensive weapons rather than engaging in nuclear war.[33]

### Arthur Schlesinger

*Fear:*

Recalling one's own tumult of emotion, . . . I would say, one lobe of the brain had to recognize the ghastly possibility, another found it quite inconceivable. . . . Kennedy's grim odds were based on fear, not of Khrushchev's intention, but of human error, of something going terribly wrong down the line. . . . Even with the justified assumption of reciprocal rationality, a terrible risk remained.[34]

## Resolution:

"There are fewer higher gratifications," Dr. Johnson once said, "than that of reflection on surmounted evils." Kennedy was well satisfied by the performance of his government. The Executive Committee had proved a brilliant instrument of consideration and coordination. He was particularly proud of his brother, always balanced, never rattled, his eye fixed on the ultimate as well as on the immediate. . . . As a whole, the government could hardly have performed better.[35]

### Nikita Khrushchev

## Fear:

I do not know whether you can understand me and believe me. But I wish you would believe yourself and agree that one should not give way to one's passions; that one should be master of them. And what direction are events taking now? If you begin stopping vessels it would be piracy, as you yourself know . . . then we would be forced to take the necessary measures of a defensive nature which would protect our interests . . . why do this? What would it all lead to? . . . If people do not display wisdom, they will eventually reach the point where they will clash, like blind moles, and then mutual annihilation will commence. . . . Mr. President, I appeal to you.[36]

## Resolution:

The Americans knew that if Russian blood were shed in Cuba, American blood would surely be shed in Germany. The American government was anxious to avoid such a development. It had been, to say the least, an interesting and challenging situation. The two most powerful nations of the world had squared off against each other, each with its finger on the button. You'd have thought that war was inevitable. [The crisis was] an episode of world history in which, bringing the world to the brink of atomic war, we won a socialist Cuba. . . . We achieved, I would say, a spectacular success without having to fire a single shot.[37]

I have already noted Theodore Sorensen's remark that the members of EXCOMM on October 27 "felt nuclear war to be closer on that day than at any time in the nuclear age.''[38] In fact, Sorensen's writing on the missile crisis is the most ambivalent of any about the fear of inadvertent nuclear war. No one has been more effective at reconstructing the vast uncertainties EXCOMM faced and the way these uncertainties led to fears of an unprecedented sort. At the same time, there has been no stronger advocate than Sorensen for the thesis that the missile crisis was resolved as it was because one man—the President—was in total control throughout, that he applied the proper amount of pressure at the proper time, and thus that he achieved unquestionably the greatest victory of the nuclear age. Nowhere in the literature of the missile crisis do we find such clear and compelling arguments for the salience *and* irrelevance of feared nuclear inadvertence. In his biography of President Kennedy, Sorensen conveys on consecutive pages his memory of the way he felt (disbelief) when he learned that the crisis was resolved, and his analysis of the resolution brought about by the control and almost superhuman rationality of the President.

### Theodore Sorensen

*Reaction to the resolution*

Upon awakening Sunday morning, October 28, I turned on the news on my bedside radio, as I had each morning during the week. In the course of the 9 A.M. broadcast a special bulletin came in from Moscow. It was a new letter from Khrushchev, his fifth since Tuesday, sent publicly in the interest of speed. Kennedy's terms were being accepted. The missiles were being withdrawn. Inspection would be permitted. The confrontation was over.

Hardly able to believe it, I reached Bundy at the White House. It was true . . . it was a beautiful Sunday morning in Washington in every way.

With deep feelings of relief and exhilaration, we gathered in the cabinet room at eleven, our thirteenth consecutive day of close collaboration. Just as missiles are incomparably faster than all their predecessors, so this worldwide crisis had ended incredibly faster than all its predecessors.[39]

*Explanation of the resolution*

John Kennedy entered and we all stood up. He had, as Harold Macmillan would later say, earned his place in history by this one act alone. He had been engaged in a personal as well as national contest for world leadership and he had won. . . . the hard lessons of the first Cuban crisis [the Bay of

Pigs] were applied in his steady handling of the second with a carefully measured combination of defense, diplomacy and dialogue . . . and caution and precision with which he had determined for thirteen days exactly how much pressure to apply.[40]

Much has been made of the allegedly self-serving nature of explanations such as Sorensen's, which attributes this "finest hour" of the Kennedy Presidency to the superior resolve, intelligence and cleverness of President Kennedy.[41] But to cast them aside as *merely* self-aggrandizing is also, I believe, to miss a great deal about the psychological reality of the last weekend of the acute phase of the Cuban missile crisis. In particular, these attempts to discredit explanations emphasizing courage, brilliance, and above all rational planning and calculation show just how little some of these critics appreciate what those men went through in thirteen days. If we try to reenter the key moments during the crisis—and I count at least five such moments—we discover that by the final weekend, they were thoroughly confused by their inability to predict and control the course the crisis seemed to be taking, and were startled when they received the utterly unexpected news that the irascible and belligerent Khrushchev had agreed to terms.

Moreover, so anxious was Khrushchev to convey to the Americans his acceptance of the American terms that he had broadcast his letter over the radio to assure quick and accurate transmission of his message[42]. This must have been the final straw of confusion for EXCOMM. No one, as far as I know, had been confident that Khushchev would agree to terms. To explain it they, like anyone surrounded by anomalous events, attributed the resolution to the sorts of qualities that had always been required when good triumphed over evil. There is no reason to suspect they did not believe this. After all, what other explanations were available? Fear of inadvertent nuclear war fell by the wayside, perhaps to be regretted but not an important part of the cause of the resolution. The experience of living the crisis forward must have given way immediately to backward-glancing explanations.

The experiences themselves are gone forever. Neither participants in the missile crisis nor anyone else can ever unearth them for, in fact, the mind is not like the earth, and remembering is not like removing dirt to uncover treasure chests preserved intact across the years. Memory is far too constructive. We remember by means of constructive narratives that make sense and that conform to whatever we take to be the relevant and demonstrable facts of the matter.[43]

Any attempt at the recovery of the psychological life during the pivotal weekend of the missile crisis must therefore remain at a fairly general level, and we must turn for help to *analogies* to the missile crisis. In fact, this is done all the time. The paradigmatic analogy is that of a game. The missile crisis, according to this view, is like poker, chess, or "prisoner's dilemma," and nuclear policy analysts are in general agreement on this point. But this analogy won't suffice if we seek deeper entry into the look and feel of nuclear danger during the missile crisis. The participants certainly did not believe they were in a game. In fact, in a heated exchange between Robert McNamara and a former high-level official in the Nixon administration who is now a senior foreign policy analyst, the analyst asked McNamara if he agreed that, after all, the missile crisis was "just a game of chicken" that had been resolved because Khrushchev "chickened out." McNamara stared at his interlocutor, eyes wide, unspeaking for a long moment until he exploded: "It was not a game and there were no 'chickens.' That's not the way it was." Moreover, McGeorge Bundy has recently written that he is sure that the missile crisis represents for *all* the participants the most intense and profound experience of their public lives.[44]

Instead, it is only by completely ignoring the evolving psychological reality of the missile crisis that one can treat it as a game. This point was emphasized vividly by Richard Neustadt at a critical oral history conference in March 1987. At the conclusion of the conference, participants were asked to say what they believed were the most important lessons of the missile crisis. Several academics spoke of what they regarded as the significance of urging high-level decision makers, before assuming offices with nuclear responsibilities, to think ahead about the danger of nuclear crises. A consensus seemed to form around the idea that gaming exercises, if subtle and nuanced, might help a president and his senior advisers to prepare for a superpower crisis. This brought the following response from Neustadt:

[President Kennedy's] subjective estimates of risk may be opaque, but let me give you a concrete example of the kind of thing he had to think about. In the Civil War, out of a total population of 31 million, 600,000 people died. Bob McNamara's account of the prospective civilian deaths that could have been anticipated if Soviet nuclear weapons fell on the United States was roughly proportionate to that. It took this country a hundred years to recover from the Civil War. President Kennedy saw nothing worth even a low risk of that. At the end of a TV interview he did in 1962, Kennedy said, "The President bears the burden of the responsibility; advisers can move on to fresh advice." I have been tremendously impressed at how you participants have been able to do that and at how the academics present can't resist thinking of this affair as one of Tom Schelling's games. I'm sure Kennedy didn't.[45]

Whatever insights may be derived from game analogies are gained only by annihilating the psychological life of the crisis.

But if it wasn't like a game, what was it like? Specifically, are there any analogies to the missile crisis that can help us explain why the fear of the shattered crystal ball, so central to the experience, is absent from the explanations of the episode? Can analogies help us articulate an explanation of the resolution of the missile crisis and, at the same time, account for why the actual participants have been unable to do so? I believe that the answer to all these questions is "yes" and that the proper intentional analogies to the missile crisis are so obvious that one has only to pose the intentional question to discover the answer. We ask: What, in general, must the missile crisis have been *like?* The answer, while obvious, is also fruitful: living through the look and feel of nuclear danger in the missile crisis would have been something like living through *other sorts of crises.* We would expect the structure of evolving psychological life in the missile crisis to display many of the same characteristics we find in other sorts of crises—classes of events about which a good deal is known, psychologically. Thus, to end this chapter we will look briefly at three sorts of crises, each of which sheds a slightly different light on the psychological life of the managers of the missile crisis. These are scientific crises, medical crises, and personal crises. My far-from-comprehensive treatment will merely suggest that if we focus on the missile *crisis,* we may reach some insights and conclusions that will be psychologically real to its participants, discrepant from many of their own explanations of it, and thus, perhaps, catalysts to learning some lessons that derive from the experience of having lived through the episode.

In his work on scientific crises and scientific revolutions, Thomas S. Kuhn has taught an entire generation of scholars a new way of understanding radical shifts in thinking about the world. Although Kuhn, a physicist, draws most of his own data from physics, his vocabulary—anomaly, paradigm, revolution, and so on—has proven to be applicable to any enterprise in which people must come to grips with some part of the world that (or who) behaves in unpredictable and unexpected ways. Kuhn's work provides a framework and nomenclature for understanding the structure of psychological life when expectations clash violently with observed facts. According to Kuhn, when this happens, i.e., when a prediction about which one cares deeply turns out not to be confirmed, we enter a state of crisis. Now, one could agree that this may be true of science, but foreign policy-making is not a science, which is a much more detached, ethereal activity. But one should not, Kuhn emphasizes, overdraw the difference between science and ordinary life. Scientists are also human beings who tend to fall in love with their theories and be crushed when their data are at variance with them. Kuhn cites a remark of Nobel laureate Wolfgang Pauli who, in the mid-1920s, became thoroughly frustrated by his inability to grasp the latest developments in physics. He wrote to a friend: "At the moment physics is again terribly confused. In any case it is too difficult for me, and I wish I had been a movie comedian or something of the sort and had never heard of physics."[46] This physicist found himself in a state of crisis brought on by the failure of the world to conform to his predictions.

An important basis for the analogy between scientific crises and the missile crisis is that many scientific crises do not begin with actual experiments, but with thought experiments. Let us place ourselves vicariously in the shoes of the members of President Kennedy's EXCOMM during the thirteen days of the acute phase of the missile crisis, and carry out what must have been their most significant thought experiments during the crisis.[47] We will find that from the beginning of the crisis to its conclusion, we are faced with anomalies—with failed predictions. Here in outline are five of the most perplexing and significant:

1. *October 16: Soviet offensive nuclear missile in Cuba*
No one in EXCOMM other than CIA Director John McCone predicted this. As Robert Kennedy recalled the first EXCOMM meeting on October 16, "the dominant feeling at the meeting was one of stunned surprise."[48] They had, they believed, been absolutely clear that such weapons would never be permitted; the Soviets would never dare do such a thing. The crisis was launched when the advisers examined the anomalous but incontrovertible data on the morning of October 16.

2. *October 23: No Soviet countermove to the U.S. quarantine*
After the President's speech the previous evening, almost everyone had gone to bed expecting a significant Soviet escalation of the crisis. Perhaps the Soviets would block the autobahn between West Germany and West Berlin; perhaps they would bomb the Turkish missile bases;

perhaps they would begin to move troops through the Dardenelles. But they did nothing. On the morning of October 23, Dean Rusk found George Ball asleep on the couch in his office at the State Department. In waking him Rusk said: "We have won a considerable victory. You and I are still alive."[49] All in EXCOMM were perplexed by the absence of a Soviet countermove.

3. *October 24: Intensification of the Crystal Ball Effect*

At 10:00 AM on October 24, the quarantine went into effect. Soviet ships were sailing toward it with a submarine escort. Fears escalated rapidly in EXCOMM that some sort of untoward incident at sea would inadvertently spark the war all wanted to avoid. Robert Kennedy recalls that in those moments he wondered: "Was the world on the brink of a holocaust? Was it our error? A mistake?"[50] Again, anomaly prevailed. Nothing happened. The Soviet ships reversed course and headed back to the Soviet Union.

4. *October 27: The Crystal Ball begins to shatter*

No one in EXCOMM, I believe, expected the events of this day: the U-2 shootdown and overflight, the second, less hopeful letter from Khrushchev, the presence of a large convoy of Soviet ships steaming toward the quarantine line, and the clear indications from Castro that his forces would try to shoot down every American plane in sight. No one expected that by evening they would have given the Soviets twenty-four hours to agree to American terms "or else." No one expected to feel that they would be, as Sorensen recalled, closer to nuclear war than at any other moment in the nuclear age.

5. *October 28: The peaceful resolution of the crisis*

No one predicted it. Some were already drawing up contingency plans for whatever the next move was to be following Khrushchev's expected refusal of their terms. Then the message came through Sunday morning over the radio. Few, if any, could believe it.

In the course of the crisis, five critical thought experiments failed, five predictions were disconfirmed, and five sources of profound confusion emerged. The President and his advisers had expected no missile crisis, had expected the Soviets to respond belligerently once the crisis had begun, had expected inadvertent war on the high seas, had not expected events suddenly to appear to career out of control, and had not, finally, expected their "final" offer to the Soviet ambassador to be accepted. Every one of their most critical predictions had been disconfirmed. Thus one might with some justice describe the psychological evolution of these men during the missile crisis as the evolution of ever more profound and disturbing confusion. Cause and effect, our handles on reality, suddenly seemed to have become detached from events. Episodes came and went, but who knew why?

Just such situations as these have interested Thomas Kuhn. He believes that thought experiments of profound significance, such as those conducted by the members of the EXCOMM, have four very distinct stages: the prediction, the anomalous results, the crisis, and the all-important response to the crisis—the new or old explanation. In situations in which the expectations of the thought-experimenters are embedded in powerfully held beliefs and their expectations are not met, the seeds are sown for a psychological *revolution*—a new way of understanding the world that comports with the new data and which, importantly, thereby transforms anomalies into expectable occurrences. According to Kuhn:

> A crisis induced by the failure of expectation and followed by revolution is at the heart of the thought-experimental situation . . . Thought experiment is one of the essential analytic tools which are deployed during crises and which then help to promote basic conceptual reform. . . . Full confusion came only in the thought-experimental situation and then it came as a prelude to its cure . . . the thought experiment informed our subjects what was wrong. That first clear view of the misfit between experience and implicit expectation provided the clues necessary to set the situation right.[51]

This description has interesting similarities with the revolution in thinking during the missile crisis. Participants were awash in anomalies; everyone was aware that a deep crisis was upon them. In particular, no one expected the two features of the crisis that seem to have astonished the participants the most: the intensification of the crystal ball effect, with its concomitant heightened fear of inadvertent nuclear war, and, the sudden and unexpected resolution. These occurred on consecutive days, following in Kuhn's terms, "full confusion" due to "the misfit between experience and implicit expectation." But the participants could not connect these two central constituents of their confusion. Thus, I would argue that while the final weekend of the missile crisis was certainly revolutionary in the sense that nothing quite like it had ever happened before, the explanations of the event were not revolutionary. Rather, they were epistemologically conservative. The fear of the shattered crystal ball, the fear of inadvertent nuclear war, and the unexpectedly peaceful resolution of the missile crisis have been "explained" (and explained away) by the participants as simple anomalies that do not fit into their causal explanations of the event.

In this way, I conjecture, many of the participants in the missile crisis, even those who recall vividly their rising fear of inadvertent nuclear war, have felt obliged to annihilate their own psychological life during the missile crisis. They can make no explanatory sense of it. In a similar way, perhaps, many of the participants who had the experience have also missed the meaning that it had for them, as they lived through it. That is why I believe that most of them still regard the mortal fear of nuclear inadvertence as something to be suppressed and overcome, rather than the heart and soul of nuclear crisis resolution in October 1962. The missile crisis, they would (and do) argue, was resolved despite fear and trembling in the face of nuclear danger, rather than because of it.

But while it is true that the analogy between scientific crises and the Cuban missile crisis may shed some light on the cognitive side of evolving psychological life during the crisis, it does not allow us to appreciate the extent and implications of its intensity. The missile crisis, we must always keep in mind, provided not only the "full confusion" noted by Thomas Kuhn in his remarks on scientists; it also provoked tremendous fear. The crisis was unexpected, meteoric, short, and dangerous. Robert McNamara recalls wondering if he would live out the week following October 27. George Ball remembers his wife, Ruth, stocking their basement with canned goods, to be used in the event of a Soviet nuclear strike on Washington.[52] Robert Kennedy recalled wondering if they weren't on the brink of a worldwide nuclear holocaust. Such intensity and gravity is characteristic neither of science nor of everyday life; life is not lived by most people as if one were in the midst of a crisis. A crisis, as we characteristically use the term, connotes a state of mind and a situation that differ qualitatively from the normal course of affairs.

One crisis with which we are all somewhat familiar, that by its usual definition connotes danger, discomfort, and fear, is a medical crisis. In the history of medicine, a "crisis" has come to refer to a critical moment in the progress of an illness, often connected with a feverish, incoherent state. The peak of the medical crisis is the point beyond which a patient will become demonstrably better and ultimately recover, or will deteriorate and die. It is the point at which the fever will either "break" or overwhelm the patient, leading to death. This situation and state of mind are very frightening. Let us consider whether the psychological life characteristic of medical crises can shed some light on the way fear of inadvertent nuclear war might have operated in the psychological lives of the managers of the missile crisis. Let us ask what we can learn by analogy and apply to the emotive side of feared nuclear inadvertence that can help us construct an intentional explanation of the resolution of the missile crisis.

The German philosopher Jurgen Habermas has discussed medical crises in a way that is particularly sensitive to what seems to be the central feature of the evolution of feared nuclear inadvertence: the sense of losing control of a situation in a way and to an extent that have potentially catastrophic consequences. According to Habermas:

> The crisis cannot be separated from the one who is undergoing it—the patient experiences his powerlessness vis à vis the objectivity of his illness only because he is a subject condemned to passivity and temporarily deprived of the possibility of being a subject in full possession of his powers. We therefore associate with crises the idea of an objective force that deprives a subject of some part of his normal sovereignty. To conceive of a process as a crisis is tacitly to give it a normative meaning— the resolution of the crisis effects a liberation of the subject caught up in it.[53]

Keeping in mind that the relation of this passage is one of analogy to a nuclear crisis rather than a description of it, let us examine its pertinence to our subject. A nuclear crisis is psychologically a crisis of the imagination, a crisis brought on by informed thought experiments whose results lead one to conclude that an inadvertent nuclear war is becoming increasingly probable. Leaders begin to imagine that, at some point in the near future, they will, in Habermas's words, be condemned to passivity and deprived of full possession of their powers. This is one way to describe the psychological concomitant of Thomas Schelling's neglected insight, that in the Cuban missile crisis, the enemy was perceived by both sides to migrate from the other superpower out into the political-military "environment." Because the causation of nuclear risk has moved mysteriously onto a stage where the actors' intentions no longer seem to control the direction of the unfolding drama, leaders begin to imagine themselves deprived of their normal sovereignty as leaders and as managers. This is why any resolution of the crisis will be accompanied by intense feelings of "liberation of the subject caught up in it." Leaders will find themselves suddenly extricated from their nascent confusion and powerlessness.

They will be keenly aware that their situation seems to be returning to its more familiar, more predictable, less dangerous state, accompanied by feelings of a Houdini-like escape, of relief and joy, like that of a prisoner condemned to the gallows but who is unexpectedly pardoned.

Here is a rudimentary analogical framework we may use to comprehend the emotive side of the resolution of the missile crisis the weekend of October 26 to 28, 1962. Specifically, it strengthens the psychological context of Robert Kennedy's message to Dobrynin. He said: "I was not giving them an ultimatum but a statement of fact." This statement, which will seem cowardly, mendacious, foolish, or self-serving if viewed as a component of some superpower "game," takes on a somber credibility when we appreciate the elements of what must have been an important part of the inner life of the crisis. Rather than being an ultimatum, an attempt to manipulate the risks so as to force Khrushchev to cave in, it is instead a recognition of the fact that all concerned were rapidly being reduced to helpless passivity, carried along by events toward an awful war.

It seems clear that Khrushchev had no doubt that he was receiving a "statement of fact," in this same sense: a declaration that, in the American view, the crisis was spinning out of control. In his memoirs, he recalled those final days of the crisis, leading up to the resolution: "I remember a period of six or seven days when the danger was particularly acute . . . I spent one of the most dangerous nights at the Council of Ministers office in the Kremlin. I slept on a couch in my office—and I kept my clothes on . . . I was ready for alarming news at any moment, and I wanted to be ready to react immediately."[54]

While Khrushchev was sleeping on a couch in the Kremlin, George Ball was doing likewise at the State Department, and Robert McNamara, the highest ranking "desk officer" in the history of the Defense Department, was spending every night, all night, at the Pentagon.[55] When news of Robert Kennedy's visit to Dobrynin reached Khrushchev, moreover, he found the message perfectly believable. It is interesting, in fact, that Khrushchev found not only the content of the message but also the demeanor of its bearer credible. According to Khrushchev, Dobrynin reported the following:

Robert Kennedy looked exhausted. One could see from his eyes that he had not slept for days. He himself said that he had not been home for six days and nights. "The President is in a grave situation," Robert Kennedy said, "and he does not know how to get out of it. We are under very severe stress. In fact we are under pressure from our military to use force against Cuba. . . . President Kennedy implores Chairman Khrushchev to accept his offer."⁵⁶

Was Robert Kennedy acting? Was this merely the last in a series of carefully crafted, fully controlled moves to force the Soviets either to fold or to call the President's bluff? Or was Robert Kennedy's message a genuine attempt to convey to the Soviets the American fear that the crisis was moving rapidly and inexorably toward war, with nuclear war a live possibility? No one can now say for certain, of course. But all the psychological data bearing on the crisis as it was lived forward are on the side of the "statement of fact." Khrushchev seems clearly to have believed that Kennedy believed that he, Kennedy, was running out of options. So should we.

Another, third sort of analogy ought to cause us to take Robert Kennedy as seriously as Khrushchev took him when he said he came bearing a "statement of fact." This is the *identity crisis*. Here is how Habermas describes the central point of such deeply personal upheavals: "Fate is fulfilled in the revelation of conflicting norms against which the identities of the participants shatter, unless they are able to summon up the strength to win back their freedom by shattering the mythical power of fate through the formation of new identities."⁵⁷ This central analogical point is critically important: people are necessarily and profoundly changed by participating in terrifying crises. The missile crisis marked the end of the most dangerous phase of the Cold War, after which relations between the superpowers improved dramatically. The participants seemed to have learned that deep crises between them simply had to be avoided. The great fear of forgetting the cardinal rule of the nuclear age seems to have provoked the integration of the rule far more deeply than before into superpower relations. The profundity of the learning from that nuclear crisis has matched the profundity of the fear that gave rise to it.

Psychologists from William James to Erik Erikson have agreed with Habermas that a changed conception of personal identity is at the psychological core of all really profound learning in which great fear is ultimately involved.⁵⁸ How might this transformation of identity have worked its way out in the evolving psychological life of the key American participants in the missile crisis? Probably the most important concomitant of their attempt to "win back their freedom" would have been the necessity of becoming collaborators with the government of the Soviet Union. In order to resolve the Cuban missile crisis, the leaders on both sides eventually worked together. This was no minor border dispute, trade agreement, or even an arms-control treaty. This was a terrifying experience for all, one that challenged some of their most basic assumptions about their abilities and the nature of "the enemy" in the nuclear age. Kierkegaard once said that those who are "educated by dread [and] educated by possibility . . . will then interpret reality differently."[59] The nature and extent of the learning wrought by fear in the missile crisis may be seen in even a brief chronology of superpower interactions during the Kennedy presidency. The first two years of John Kennedy's presidency were marked by a series of episodes that were characterized by Cold War bitterness. In early 1961, a military clash between Soviet-supplied and -advised forces and their American-led counterparts was narrowly averted in Southeast Asia. In October 1961, American and Soviet tanks faced each other at point-blank range on either side of the newly constructed Berlin Wall. Ultimately, neither side saw fit to open fire and the crisis abated, although it was far from resolved. Finally, during the missile crisis the superpowers came closer than before or since to a large-scale military engagement. If war had broken out, most leaders on both sides believed nuclear war was likely to follow.

Deeply shaken by the missile crisis, Kennedy and Khrushchev did a turnabout. In a commencement address at American University, June 10, 1963, President Kennedy announced that discussions were underway in Moscow to work out the details of an agreement that would eliminate atmospheric testing of nuclear weapons by the United States, the Soviet Union, and Great Britain. He further announced that the United States would henceforth forego atmospheric testing unilaterally, as long as the other nuclear powers refrained from doing so. The Soviets reciprocated. Moreover, for the first time in memory they opened their airwaves to Western broadcasts by permitting the entire text of the President's speech to be broadcast, in Russian and unjammed, throughout the Soviet Union. In the weeks that followed, they ceased altogether to jam foreign broadcasts in the Russian language, no matter what the subject or content.[60] Finally, during a speech in East Berlin on July 2, 1963, Khrushchev endorsed the atmospheric test ban. On July 26, Kennedy introduced the atmospheric test-ban treaty in a televised address to the nation, arguing that "the achievement . . . is not a victory for one side, it is a victory for mankind."[61] The limited Test Ban Treaty was signed on August 5 and ratified by the American Senate on September 24 by a vote of 80 to 19.

It is worthwhile to pause briefly to consider just how unexpected and remarkable the turnabout in superpower relations seemed at the time. In his inaugural speech of January 1961, President Kennedy had asked the American people to "bear any burden," to "pay any price" in the "long twilight struggle" against Communism.[62] The conceptual distance between that Cold War rhetoric and attitude and that expressed in his most famous post-missile crisis speech is absolutely remarkable. Here, in his 1963 American University address, is how President Kennedy expressed what he had learned since 1961 and, I believe, in the missile crisis:

> If we cannot now end our differences, at least we can help make the world safe for diversity. For, in the final analysis our most basic common link is the fact that we all inhabit this planet. We all breathe the same air. We all cherish our children's future. And we are all mortal . . . confident and unafraid, we labor on—not toward a strategy of annihilation, but toward a strategy of peace.[63]

This turnabout in word and deed, reflecting a deep transformation in the perception of nuclear risk, would have been inconceivable without the Cuban missile crisis. Erik Erikson, the great theorist of the personal identity crisis, has argued that "a new life task presents a *crisis* whose outcome can be a successful graduation, or alternatively, an impairment of the life cycle which will aggravate future crises."[64] It seems clear in retrospect that the altered identities forged in the key actors during the missile crisis did indeed constitute a "successful graduation" in Erikson's terms. Since 1962, there has been no event of comparable nuclear danger. It appears, therefore, as if the life histories of the men in the White House and Kremlin in late October 1962 have become central constituents of the broader historical moment of the nuclear age of the late twentieth century.

There is no plausible way to account for this development, this learning, without accepting three propositions that are antithetical to the whole tradition of nuclear strategy and policy and to the interpretation of the missile crisis. The first is that the missile crisis, in its resolution phase, was not like any other international crisis, although it may have psychological analogues in other sorts of crises. Second, Robert Kennedy did believe he was delivering a "statement of fact" to the Soviets on the evening of October 27, 1962, a statement behind which lay a week of the most profound confusion and, finally, fear of inadvertent nuclear war. Finally, the uniqueness and inscrutability of the psychological transformations the occurred during the missile crisis make it more, rather than less, interesting as an object of still further study and learning about nuclear danger. In that pivotal crisis, the participants were able to connect their fear in the event with their actions in adaptive ways. But they, and we, have had great difficulty connecting their fear with the outcome of the crisis. *Why* fear of the shattered crystal ball *should* have led to the learning required for the resolution isn't obvious, because the theories we customarily use to account for it, be they formal or informal, tell us that fear is either irrelevant or bad. In the next chapter I offer an outline of a rationale for believing that, in the Cuban missile crisis, fear was adaptive.

# PART FIVE: PROSPECTS

# 9

# Looking Backward: The Adaptive Role of Fear in the Cuban Missile Crisis

So soon as psychology has finished with dread, it has nothing to do but deliver it over to dogmatics.

Kierkegaard,
*The Concept of Dread*, 1844

At the end of the nineteenth century, a popular movement known as "mind-cure" arose among U.S. educated classes. Using what we today might call "pop psychology," mind-curers emphasized the usefulness of looking on the bright side, of using verbal and mental tricks to banish uncomfortable thoughts and feelings and, in general, of glorifying the virtues of mental discipline. Christian Science became the most influential and long-lived exponent of this sunny and optimistic view of human nature and human ability. The emotions were a constant source of embarrassment to these seat-of-the-pants rationalists, and of all the emotions, fear troubled them the most. Giving in to fear, in their view, meant relinquishing one's hold on the higher, rational faculties— faculties that, despite what the outrageous Charles Darwin had been saying, distinguished human beings from ordinary beasts. Fear could never, as they saw it, be good or adaptive. Man could reason, and reason, for man, was adaptive. In his classic *The Varieties of Religious Experience*, William James, showing his typical virtuosity in uncovering obscure but interesting sources, cites one Horace Fletcher's recommendations to mind-curers for getting rid of that embarrassing,

149

maladaptive anachronism, fear. According to Horace Fletcher, one must perform a verbal switch:

> Fear has had its uses in the evolutionary process, and seems to constitute the whole of forethought in most animals; but that it should remain any part of the mental equipment of civilized life is an absurdity. . . . To assist in the analysis of fear, and in the denunciation of its expressions, I have coined the word *fearthought* to stand for the unprofitable element of forethought . . . in order to place it where it really belongs, in the category of harmful, unnecessary, and therefore not respectable things.[1]

The important thing for Mr. Fletcher and his fellow mind-curers, apparently, was to purge themselves of fearful emotion, to have (as Fletcher refers to it in the title of his pamphlet) "forethought minus fearthought," and thus to exert rational control over whatever situation one might be facing or anticipating.

I believe the conduct and outcome of the Cuban missile crisis refute the view of the mind-curers and their intellectual descendants, the rational/irrational actor psychologists. Fear was pervasive, from the American President and Soviet Chairman to the ordinary citizens, and fear was efficacious. Without the rise of what I have called the intensifying crystal ball effect, it is hard to imagine that the missile crisis could have been resolved peacefully. And although this is my own view of why this most dangerous crisis in history transpired as it did, the vast majority of the participants and analysts with opinions on this issue come down hard near where the mind-curers came down in the nineteenth century: emphasizing "forethought minus fearthought," so to speak.[2] I tried to show in the previous chapter how and why the key participants have such difficulty connecting the great fear they recall with the event (the resolution of the missile crisis) they seek to explain. Despite their (implied) protestation, I have tried to demonstrate that feared nuclear inadvertence drove the missile crisis to its dramatic, only partially comprehensible, and quite amicable conclusion. The emphasis was on the phenomenology of nuclear inadvertence. In this chapter, I will look more closely at the adaptive role of fear in this nuclear crisis. Obviously, there is something valid and useful in the attempts of people like the mind-curers to rationalize human action, for fear is not always adaptive. But often it is, and I believe the resolution of the missile crisis is a significant case in point.

But to believe these things is, within the present climate of nuclear studies, to risk appearing to promote the virtues of irrational actors in nuclear crises, which is nonsensical. To put the matter plainly, fear (and the emotions generally) are regarded by nearly all exponents of "nuclear crisis management" as, to quote the estimable Horace Fletcher, "not respectable things." This is not the place for a full-blown critical history and analysis of nuclear crisis management as a discipline, but some points are clear. First, the discipline was born shortly after the missile crisis when, according to Coral Bell, Robert McNamara said in testimony to Congress: "There is no longer any such thing as strategy; only crisis management."[3] By "crisis management," moreover, was meant (at least as McNamara was interpreted) the systematic attempt to rationalize the conduct of international crises. Finally, the reconstructed Cuban missile crisis became the *sine qua non* of crisis management. It is typically described by specialists in crisis management as the calmest, coolest, most measured and laudable example of exerting rational control over a complex and dangerous international situation. Emotion is rarely mentioned, except perhaps by pointing out that the EXCOMM members were, after all, human and may occasionally have lost their tempers. Even the hottest debate in this field is carried on between people such as Alexander George, who believe that prospects for rationalizing (and thus resolving) nuclear crises are, if not exactly good, then at least possible, and those like Richard Ned Lebow, who believe that such prospects are poor at best.[4] The point I wish to emphasize is that all parties to this controversy seek to expunge "fearthought from forethought," both in their interpretations of the missile crisis and in whatever applications they envision in some future crisis. To all of them, following what they have imagined to be McNamara's own analysis of the missile crisis and his alleged endorsement of crisis management, fear is bad, because it is maladaptive and can lead only to bad management. This of course means that in a nuclear crisis, increased fear will lead to an increased likelihood of nuclear holocaust. Because fear is so widely believed to be maladaptive by participants in the missile crisis and analysts alike, anyone arguing for the *adaptive* importance of fear will not have an easy time of it.

The problem here, as elsewhere in the study of nuclear crises, is this: participants and analysts alike have for various reasons failed to appreciate the vast difference between a rational reconstruction, derived by looking backward at a selected, distorted, artificially coherent set of mental snapshots of the past, on the one hand, and, on the other, the uncertain phenomenology of living the event forward without the slightest idea of how it will turn out. This tilting toward rational reconstruction amounts to the widespread inability among all manner of students of the missile crisis, and of the discipline devoted to the study of crises, to believe that fear was thick in the psychological texture of the missile crisis and, even more important, that this fear was and remains unprecedented. It was a profound fear, and that fear was not fear of calculated attack, as one characteristically finds at the psychological root of conventional deterrence failures, but was largely fear of inadvertence—of *fate,* if you will. I believe that if we try to step backward *into* the missile crisis and look forward with the confused and fearful participants, we see inadvertent nuclear danger and fear of the shattered crystal ball. Without this look and this feel, the resolution of the missile crisis cannot be explained satisfactorily. The advocates of the rational/irrational actor psychologies who dominate the discussion cannot explain it because they don't understand the adaptive role of fear in the resolution. If we better comprehend what the missile crisis was like for the key participants, the adaptive role of fear will become more obvious, as will the justice of holding that the goal of leaders in a nuclear crisis ought not to be to expunge "fearthought from forethought," but to encourage it, and that such encouragement would be an altogether adaptive attitude to take.

It is important to understand an important conceptual and methodological foundation for the vast and rapidly expanding work on psychology and avoiding nuclear war: the Cuban missile crisis was *not* psychologically unique. Beginning with this assumption, investigators are free to roam far and wide in search of data, which they gather mostly from analyses of other international crises, but also increasingly from the literatures of scientific psychology. In an important sense, therefore, they do not regard other crises as analogous to the missile crisis, so much as they consider all of them to be cases that will one day be shown psychologically to be examples of the same general principles of the conduct of international crises, whatever they turn out to be. The method is therefore intrinsically comparative. For example, in the introduction to a highly regarded comparative study of this sort, *Psychology and Deterrence,* Robert Jervis has summarized his and his colleagues' findings regarding what they call "motivated biases":

Motivated biases arise from the emotions generated by conflicts that personal needs and severe situational dilemmas pose. These biases serve important psychological functions, primarily minimizing . . . discomfort. . . . The individual will pay a high price in the future as reality inescapably shapes and defeats the policy, but in the interim he or she avoids intolerable psychological stress and conflict.[5]

This conclusion derives from viewing the analyses of many failures of nonnuclear deterrence through a prism provided by the rational/ irrational actor psychologies. The proponents find this repeated pattern: errors compound errors as decision makers, fearing the worst, cave in to stress, retreat into fantasy, exercise poor judgment, and lead their nations into disastrous wars. Important for our purposes, these authors (like nearly everyone writing on the subject of international crises) seek to generalize their findings on failed conventional deterrence, for which data are plentiful, to the missile crisis and to some hypothetical future nuclear crisis. The psychological evolution that forms the underlying pattern for the repeated failure of nonnuclear deterrence is what they fear most about a nuclear crisis. The psychological rule of thumb seems in general to be: if nonnuclear deterrence can fail often and easily due to fear and its psychological side-effects, then nuclear deterrence in a crisis will be even more psychologically fragile, because the fear will be so much greater. As Jervis says: "Motivated biases arise from the emotions." Emotion, he and his colleagues usually find, is bad, and fear is particularly bad. Fear, in an important sense, is really the psychological enemy in a nuclear crisis, according to this view.

It is worth taking a closer look at the hypothetical psychological causal sequence if this canonical, maladaptive path to the failure of deterrence is to lead, in the worst case, to nuclear holocaust. The sequence is summarized in Figure 9.1.

If the psychological parallel between failure of conventional deterrence and failure of nuclear deterrence is to hold water, then something like the following must occur. We begin with entry into a crisis and its immediate psychological corollary, heightened fear of attack. Thus begins the activation of the so-called "spiral model" of crisis escalation articulated some years ago by Jervis.[6] Fear of attack leads to an upward spiral of preparedness for war which, in turn, creates ever higher levels of fear in the adversary, leading to a new round of still more menacing-looking preparations. The psychological state that results from this process is stress, a concept central to the scenarios for nuclear war imagined by advocates of the rational/irrational actor psychologies. The contribution of stress to this process of psychological devolution is to render policy makers progressively less rational than they might be under noncrisis conditions. Eventually, stress

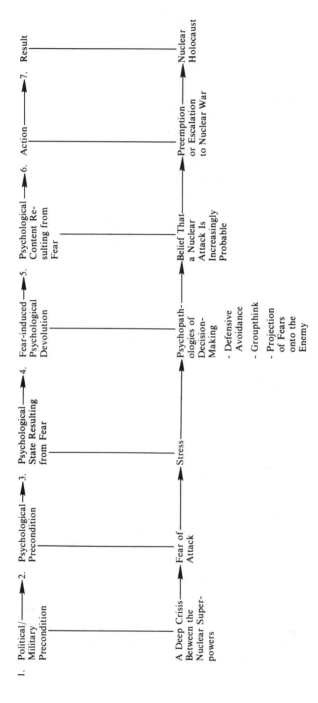

**Figure 9.1.** The *maladaptive* psychological path to holocaust in a nuclear crisis.

becomes intolerable, and leaders seek to escape from it as quickly and completely as possible. Thus it is claimed, in effect, that the problem situation of leaders is fundamentally altered by the presence of stress: they shift from seeking to achieve this or that foreign policy goal to seeking an escape from intolerable stress. This shifts leaders' attention inward, clouds perception of the outside world, and leads ultimately to wholesale miscalculation and misperception.

As the attention of leaders shifts inward, according to this view, we will begin to notice the whole range of defensive psychopathologies first described in a formal way by Sigmund Freud and Anna Freud.[7] In psychoanalytic terms, the ego defends itself against threatening stimuli by warding off, filtering, and otherwise ignoring information that might lead to further stress. The overall political-military result of this process of psychological self-defense has been stated by Richard Ned Lebow: "The psychological stress that arises from . . . decisional dilemma[s] is usually received by the adoption of defensive avoidance as a coping strategy. Leaders commit themselves to a course of action and deny information that indicates that their policy might not succeed."[8] It should be emphasized that leaders under stress, wallowing defensively as they try to avoid threatening information, are not coping primarily with the objective contingencies of the crisis situation. Rather, they are coping mainly with inner discomfort. And this, finally, is what renders this whole fear-driven process so maladaptive: leaders under stress seek to adapt to inner psychological states rather than to objective reality. In short, their policies are unconsciously but powerfully motivated by the need to *escape* hard decisions rather than to *make* effective ones.

Psychological devolution of this sort is generally believed to be the most likely cause in a nuclear crisis of rising risk of nuclear holocaust. An attack, a nuclear attack in that instance, is believed to be increasingly probable. Actions taken by a group of leaders to bolster nuclear deterrence will be seen by fearful and stress-ridden leaders on the other side as preparations for attack. At some point, never before reached in the nuclear age but much feared by students of the alleged relation between psychological stress and nuclear danger, the pressure of the crisis will lead inexorably to a panicky attempt to escape the intolerable stress by attacking first. Leaders will by then have become exhausted, confused, and frightened by their recursive participation in a mind-game described many years ago by Schelling: "He thinks we think he thinks we think . . . he thinks we think he'll attack; so he thinks we shall; so he will; so we must."[9] By some similar psychological process, leaders will have initiated the nuclear war that, at the outset of the crisis, all sought to avoid. And at the psychological fountainhead of this process will have been fear leading to stress and its associated psychopathologies, which will together have been responsible for transforming leaders' beliefs from total opposition to initiating nuclear war, to going ahead and authorizing nuclear first-use, either in a preemptive strike or in some initially more limited escalatory action.

This central prognostication and concern of proponents of the rational/irrational actor psychologies presently circumscribe discussions of nuclear policy. We should note two of its characteristics. First, while nuclear war would be arrived at inadvertently, in the sense that the decision to end the crisis by launching nuclear weapons was not anticipated at the time of entry into the crisis, the fear that drives the psychopathologies has nothing to do with inadvertence but is simply fear of being attacked. In other words, according to this view, leaders in a nuclear crisis will, in all probability, learn nothing significant and certainly nothing revolutionary, as they try to manage it. It will seem to them, as it seems to these analysts, to be conceptually identical to a nonnuclear crisis. The conclusions reached by rational/irrational actor psychologists about the psychological devolution leading to nuclear war derive largely from the extrapolations to nuclear war of their psychological analyses of failures of conventional deterrence. The comparative method, they believe, must be employed if we are ever to understand how nuclear deterrence might be brought psychologically to the failing point.[10]

Second, we should note the direct connection in a nuclear crisis between the position that we have little to fear other than fear itself and the central tenets of the dominant rational/irrational actor psychologists. The goal of all these individuals is to rationalize a nuclear crisis, to develop ways to manage it that give rise to fewer fears and more rational analysis. All its proponents begin without concern about what the look and feel of nuclear danger would be like during a deep nuclear crisis. Or perhaps it would be slightly more charitable to say that none of these analysts seems to believe there is, or would be, much difference between a rational reconstruction (or preconstruction) of nuclear crisis and the construction of it as one moves uncertainly and creatively through it. They all begin with the same assumption with which Schelling began many years ago: rational actors will not initiate a nuclear war that is demonstrably suicidal. But whereas Schelling and most members of the strategy and arms-control community seem to believe that rationality will remain relatively and sufficiently robust even in superpower crises, a large chorus of voices has recently arisen to warn us that this may not be so: in a nuclear crisis, they say, rationality may become profoundly and tragically degraded. Some worry about a "conspiracy of circumstantial craziness" (as I referred to it in Chapter 4); some do not. This difference is probably due to rational actor psychologists like Schelling having placed heavy emphasis on nuclear force structure as a deterrent to nuclear war in a crisis, while the irrational actor psychologists worry that fear-driven, stress-producing psychological devolution may swamp the influence of any force structure, no matter how robust it may seem in noncrisis situations. Despite these differences, one searches the landscape of nuclear discourse almost in vain for someone who does not believe that fear will be at the psychological core of the momentum that will transform the next nuclear crisis into a nuclear war.

For all these worriers over the psychological mechanisms that may lead us into nuclear war, the Cuban missile crisis ought to stand as the foremost anomaly. It ought to, but it does not. Instead, this psychologically unique crisis, which tells us a great deal about the relation between fear and learning in a nuclear crisis, is regarded as just another crisis. The nature, extent, and role of fear in its outcome is ignored, usually totally, in the dozens (or perhaps hundreds) of explanations regarding the event. The fear is minimized, the crisis is normalized, and psychological theories of international crises are confirmed left and right. But it is simply a fact that the missile crisis is the empirical flaw in any attempt to apply to nuclear crises the rational/irrational actor psychologies whose data are derived from, and can be demonstrated to apply to, instances of failed conventional deterrence. Their advocates must, I believe, predict the wrong outcome in the missile crisis. Fear in that instance did not lead to holocaust or even to war. The maladaptive psychological path to oblivion was not taken by the managers of the missile crisis.[11]

How *do* the rational/irrational actor psychologists come to grips with the uncomfortable (for their theories) juxtaposition of the ultimate nuclear danger and a peaceful resolution? Schelling, Lebow, and other outspoken analysts tend to reach the same basic, highly paradoxical, and deeply disturbing conclusion: the missile crisis transpired and concluded as it did because its key participants were "irrational." Schelling appears at times to hold a version of Dean Acheson's view that the Kennedy administration's handling of the crisis was greatly abetted by having "plain dumb luck" on its side.[12] Acheson believed the rational thing would have been to attack the Soviet missile bases in Cuba quickly and without warning. To fear the consequences of some such attack was, according to this view, plainly irrational because the United States then had overwhelming superiority in both strategic nuclear forces and in conventional forces in the Caribbean.[13] Schelling has gone further and suggested that if the President really believed (as Theodore Sorensen reported) that during the final weekend of the crisis the risk of war with the Soviet Union was "between one out of three and even," then the rational thing would have been to preempt Soviet nuclear forces, which were vastly inferior in size to American forces. The President did not, and thus, in Schelling's view, he could not really have believed in those odds or, more likely, he simply behaved irrationally by not ordering a preemptive strike against the Soviet nuclear forces.[14] Similarly, Lebow has written that Khrushchev was irrational to place the missiles in Cuba, for he should have known such an act would never be tolerated, and also that Kennedy was irrational (and irresponsible) in electing to force their removal.[15] In effect, both hawks and doves unite around the theory that the resolution of the missile crisis *is* anomalous, explicable only by invoking the "irrationality" of its central cast of characters. But of course this auxiliary hypothesis—"X was irrational"—is required because the rational/irrational actor psychological theories predict the wrong outcome. In theory, we should have had no missiles in Cuba but, once there, they should have provoked an American preemptive strike. So both the cause—the deployment—and the outcome—the peaceful compromise—are attributed to the irrationality of Khrushchev and/or Kennedy.

The explanatory cul-de-sac that the missile crisis presents for the rational/irrational actor psychologies is insufficiently appreciated. On the one hand, it is widely believed that the psychological event most to be feared in a nuclear crisis is a degradation of rationality. Rational actors, it is believed, simply will not go to nuclear war because they will understand fully the catastrophic consequences of such an act. Irrational actors, however, quaking with fear and caving in to stress, might somehow forget that nuclear war is suicidal, or might simply become so overwhelmed by the fear of a nuclear first strike against them, that they might somehow decide it is in their best interest to go to nuclear war. Yet, the missile crisis did not lead to nuclear war, either (according to Lebow) despite the irrationality of the leaders or (according to Schelling) *because* they were irrational. The theory not only predicts the wrong result, but this result is explained in exactly the same way that the opposite (actual) result would be explained. That is, if a nuclear war had occurred, its occurrence would have been interpreted as a function of degraded rationality, having occurred as a function of fear-driven stress. So, hypothetical irrationality is held to account for a nuclear war *not* having occurred in the missile crisis, and for the nuclear war that probably *will* occur in some future crisis. In science, and indeed in everyday life, one regards with extreme skepticism a theory that can explain opposite outcomes in an identical fashion. In fact, it is impossible to specify the conditions under which the theory might conceivably be regarded as mistaken. In the face of such a theory, one must suspect that something is fundamentally wrong with its approach to its subject matter. This is certainly true in this instance. The *actual* psychological evolution during the missile crisis is a square peg that cannot be made to fit plausibly into the round hole provided for it by the rational/irrational actor psychologies.

Let us take a systematic look at (what I am calling) the "actual" psychological evolution during the missile crisis. By "actual" I mean nothing as extravagant as the accurate and complete record of psychological life during the episode. No such thing will ever exist. By "actual" I merely mean keeping the phenomenological prerogative foremost. As we try to reconstruct the past, we do so insofar as possible with a view to looking vicariously forward, in this case into the look and feel of nuclear danger. Also, we should begin with the data-based conviction that fear in the missile crisis was adaptive; it was connected in some way with the peaceful resolution. No evidence supports the psychological domino theory that a nuclear crisis necessarily leads to fear of attack, thence to stress and psychopathology, then to the raised risk of holocaust and, in the worst case, to holocaust. As I have suggested, the outcome, conduct, and apparent psychological life of leaders during the missile crisis simply refutes this. Instead, we begin with what we have discovered so far: the missile crisis led to overpowering fear of nuclear inadvertence, and this response was adaptive. At the end of this chapter I will offer some thoughts as to why this may have been so.

An outline of the adaptive psychological path to peaceful nuclear crisis resolution is given in Figure 9.2.

The first thing we note is the fear of inadvertent nuclear war that seems to have preoccupied leaders on both sides as the missile crisis evolved. President Kennedy and Chairman Khrushchev both seem to have feared that events would outpace their own ability to control them. But the missile crisis surely was stressful. In a recent interview,

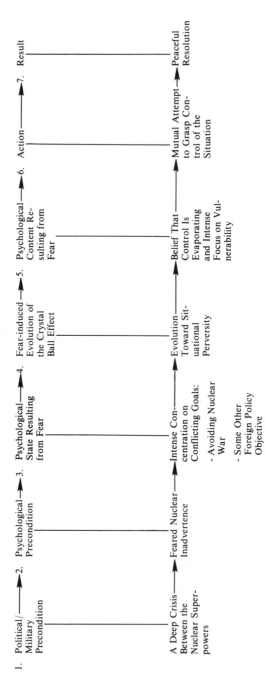

**Figure 9.2.** The *adaptive* psychological path to peaceful resolution in a nuclear crisis.

Dean Rusk spoke for all the key members of EXCOMM when he recalled: "We sustained a crisis at a very high level of intensity for some thirteen days. How long can human beings sustain a crisis at that level before sleeplessness, weariness, fear of the unknown, suspicion and accident begin to play a role?"[16] The answer is: probably not much longer than the thirteen days to which Rusk refers.

Yet despite the obvious tension, weariness, and stress (recall Khrushchev's report of the distraught, disheveled Robert Kennedy whom Dobrynin reported had visited him on October 27), the available evidence suggests that, as the crisis evolved, the participants engaged in less stereotyped thinking, increased empathy with the plight of the adversary, and greatly diminished tendencies toward "groupthink" or other typical indications that leaders are caving in to stress. Rusk, McNamara, Robert Kennedy, Sorensen, and Bundy were particularly effective at helping EXCOMM to avoid the sort of premature movement toward ill-thought-out consensus that seemed to have characterized the process by which the Bay of Pigs fiasco was planned. Even in the first day's sessions, for example, McNamara cautioned against premature endorsement of military force against Cuba: "Mr. President, this is why I think tonight we ought to put on paper the alternative plans and the probable, possible consequences thereof in a way that State and Defense could agree on . . . Because the consequences of these actions have *not* been thought through clearly."[17]

A particularly striking example from the transcript of these secretly made tapes is the cautionary warning with which Bundy drew the first meeting of October 16 to a close. President Kennedy had just summarized where he believed the consensus lay. He seemed to believe, at that point, that option "number one" (the air strike to take out the missile sites) would have to be exercised, regardless of what else was decided upon.

JFK:    At least we're going to do number one, so it seems to me that we don't have to wait very long. We, we ought to be making *those* preparations.

BUNDY: You want to be clear, Mr. President, whether we have *definitely* decided *against* a political track. I, myself, think we ought . . . to work out a contingency on that.[18]

In fact, contingencies were worked out on many different tracks, and these were summarized in Theodore Sorensen's discussion memo of October 17. Caution was the byword right from the discovery of the

missiles. The fear generated by *nuclear* danger was obviously behind
it. This is also evident from the start. One can almost feel the tension
crackling as Robert Kennedy thought out loud at the first day's meeting
about the problems with even a minimal use of force, like a blockade:

McNAMARA:    You have to put a blockade in following any . . . limited
             action.
RFK:         Then we're going to have to sink Russian ships.
McNAMARA(?): Right.
RFK:         Then we're gonna have to sink . . . Russian submarines.[19]

But of course that would mean outright war with the Soviet Union.
It may have been in the course of some similar reflection or of his
mission to Dobrynin on October 27 that Robert Kennedy began to
wonder: "What, if any, circumstance or justification gives this government or any government the moral right to bring its people and possibly
all people under the shadow of nuclear destruction?"[20]

Here we come to the heart of the psychological matter, viewed from
a phenomenological perspective, from the standpoint of individuals
who were groping forward into an unknown and dangerous future: the
evolution during the missile crisis of the crystal ball effect. Here we
may see the deep wisdom of Schelling's neglected insight based on his
reading of the events in October 1962—that in the missile crisis, the
enemy shifted from the nuclear adversary to the nuclear "environment." Feared nuclear inadvertence was in that instance the fear of a
process and an outcome that was abhorred by both sides, thus creating
a *de facto* but powerful common enemy against which both sides must
unite to keep the nuclear crystal ball from shattering. One psychological result of this process seems to be the turning *outward* onto the
whole environment of potentially dangerous events, rather than a
turning inward in defensive avoidance, as the psychological domino
theory of rational/irrational actors predicts. Instead of becoming less
sensitive to the perceptions and needs of the adversary, leaders in
October 1962 were obsessed with how their actions would be perceived
by the adversary. This is emphasized by the unanimous assertion of
the key American leaders that the unsung hero of the missile crisis was
Llewellyn Thompson, on whom EXCOMM depended for insight into
Khrushchev and his colleagues.[21] The reason for this preoccupation
with the adversary's perception of the situation is obvious now, but it
is ignored by the purveyors of the rational/irrational actor psychologies: both sides believed control was slipping away, both sides began

to experience viscerally their absolute vulnerability to holocaust, and thus both sides came finally to appreciate their identical nuclear predicaments. This, I believe, is why in the final days of the missile crisis both sides reached out to grasp hold of their situation before it destroyed them both. This seems to me, more than anything else, to explain the peaceful resolution: a growing tacit understanding of the mutuality of shared nuclear danger, implicit in the Soviet government's order to its ships to stop before reaching the quarantine line on October 24, and explicit in Khrushchev's October 26 letter to Kennedy and by the American "statement of fact" delivered by Robert Kennedy to Dobrynin the following evening. This explanation has the virtue of being consistent with the psychological facts of the matter, as they have emerged from the critical oral history of the Cuban missile crisis. The main participants came to fear greatly inadvertent nuclear war, they became determined not to allow it to happen, and they succeeded. Fundamental to this explanation is the adaptive role of fear. Without fear—fear of nuclear inadvertence—it would have been almost impossible to have had a settlement of the Cuban missile crisis with only one death. The more likely event would have been a conflict in degree somewhere between a sizable conventional war on at least one, and possibly more, fronts and a major nuclear catastrophe. The presence of great fear helped leaders avoid these results.

It may be useful to notice some important distinguishing features of an explanation in which feared nuclear inadvertence is central. First, it resembles, I imagine, a commonsense explanation of the crisis, and as such it differs in content, emphasis, and form from the paradigmatic rational/irrational actor psychological interpretations. A phenomenological approach seeks to stay close to what, in this post-Freudian age, we now tend to think of as the "surface" of psychological life—the look and feel of nuclear danger as we believe it must have appeared to the actors who were trying to manage the missile crisis. It is important that we do not begin with some "model" of what counts as rational behavior and then try to explain some action as the conceptual distance between the expected (assuming "perfect rationality") and the observed. In other words, there is no a priori reason in the phenomenological account why fear must be regarded as irrational, hence defined as maladaptive. We instead leave it as an open question, at first.

But as we look at the missile crisis unblinded by the arbitrary assumptions of the rational/irrational actor psychologies, it becomes clear that fear in this instance was adaptive; indeed, it was decisively adaptive. We may recall Horace Fletcher, with whose denunciation of "fearthought" this chapter began. According to Fletcher, although "fear had its uses in the evolutionary process, [it is absurd] to assume it need (or can) play any positive role for us now."[22] Fletcher, like the rational/irrational actor psychologists, was for "forethought minus fearthought." But in the Cuban missile crisis, contrary to the theories of Fletcher and his modern-day sympathizers (but happily for the world in general), the evidence suggests that forethought was driven by "fearthought."

The most important difference between the rational/irrational actor accounts of the Cuban missile crisis and the one proposed here, a difference reflected in the similarity of the phenomenological account with common sense, is this: each involves a different kind of explanation of human action. I discussed this briefly in Chapters 4 and 6, but it may be worthwhile to reiterate this distinction, because it supplies the reason one mode of explanation cannot account for the fact that fear in a nuclear crisis was adaptive, and one can. The explanations of the rational/irrational actor psychologists follow the same form as do explanations in the sciences. They begin with some general theories (often quite implicit and derived from a highly selective borrowing from this or that branch of psychology, economics, game theory, and so on). These theories are then "applied" to various cases of failed nonnuclear deterrence.

It is important to appreciate that they are *applied,* not *tested.* In this sort of literature we find examples of thus-and-such psychological tendencies in crises, not a test of the theory. If this were science, the theory would be tested. But it is not, so it is "applied"—in this case mainly to nonnuclear deterrence failures. The authors then deduce that "irrationality" is at the base of much of the risk in those situations in which deterrence fails. It is important that this whole framework is applied like a lacquer to history, gluing it in place, without much (or any) regard to the look and feel of those situations that the actors themselves must have experienced when they made their decisions. Then, at last, this conceptual lacquering approach is spread over what is considered to be the plausible range of nuclear crises we may someday face. The past has been viewed from the standpoint of present theory; the future is viewed from the standpoint of a nonnuclear past that may well be irrelevant to a nuclear future; and in neither the account of the past nor of the future do we find any interest in the psychological texture of the fleeting series of "presents" in which all decisions must ultimately be made. The problem with this scientistic approach, in short, is that whereas in physics one tries to explain the behavior of nonconscious entities, in history one must try to understand the actions of people like ourselves, who have views (and fears) that must be causally connected to their eventual actions.

Conversely, the phenomenological approach is distinguished, as I have noted, by intentional explanations. Its central assumption is that our reasons for acting as we do are among the most important causes of our actions. This does not require laying aside the belief that human action is in some sense "lawful"—that it falls into patterns of causal connections, which, with luck and effort, may be partially revealed in the enterprise of behavioral science. It certainly does not require making any assumption of free will, leading to a kind of epistemological anarchy. It does require, however, that we begin any psychological analysis of human action by trying to describe as accurately as possible the psychological reality of the situation as it appeared to the subjects of our inquiry. In an important sense, if we fail to do this, if we fail to begin by situating our subjects as best we can in *their* situation, then whatever explanations we derive will not strictly apply to them. Because we will not have begun with an attempt to reconstruct their reality, any subsequent cleverness is for naught. As Charles Taylor has aptly put this point: "We need to see what has to be explained to get an idea of what it would mean to explain behavior."[23] In the case of the missile crisis, we need to begin with the psychological reality of the fear of inadvertent nuclear war rather than, as has been so often the case, the theoretical reality of the psychological analysts. That way, we can at least hope to offer someday a reasonably complete and accurate explanation of the actual missile crisis, rather than the reconstituted event of the same name that so exercises advocates of the rational/irrational actor psychologies.

The proof of an intentional explanation must finally be in the pudding of prediction. As philosopher and cognitive scientist Daniel Dennett argued, when people are viewed as what he calls *intentional systems*—as integrated systems of intentions, fears, hopes, beliefs, desires, and so on—they may be understood to engage in behavior and thinking that ought to be increasingly predictable, as we learn more about what, in given circumstances, they are in fact intending to do.[24] This, I believe, is exactly what we find when we compare the rational/irrational actor and phenomenological accounts of psychological evolution during the missile crisis. If we are at all successful in seeing and feeling that event as it must have appeared to its participants, we must conclude that fear of inadvertent nuclear war was the controlling factor in their considerations. If we accept this, the rapid, unexpected, and peaceful outcome makes sense; it follows from the phenomenology. If we take the standard view, as I have tried to show, we cannot explain it; it doesn't make sense. We are forced back into pseudo-explanations claiming that the missile crisis was just an anomaly, perhaps the proverbial exception that proves the rule, and that rationality, especially the absence of fear, is the prerequisite to successful nuclear crisis management. But this will only save the theory; it cannot explain what happened in the missile crisis. In that event, the crisis appears to have been resolved because of a great, general, and mutual fear that the participants were about to live out a Nietzschean nightmare in which they, having become enslaved to the momentum of the crisis they had created, would bring on the ultimate catastrophe.

Some may believe that this conclusion—that fear did play an adaptive role in history's deepest nuclear crisis—offers the reader only half an explanatory loaf. For even if one accepts, against the received wisdom, that fear was adaptive, I have not said why this was so. I admit this. One could go on to pose Freudian questions such as: What was the interplay in participants in the missile crisis between "realistic anxiety" and "neurotic anxiety?" Why was the feeling of fear or anxiety in the missile crisis also accompanied by an adaptive "signal" to the participants to engage in what Freud called "protective action?" What was the type and extent of trauma experienced by the participants in the missile crisis?[25] It is possible that in posing such questions, one might derive answers leading to a deeper understanding of why fear was or will be adaptive in a nuclear crisis.

But to pose them, or at any rate to pursue them, is to commit the same psychologists' fallacy that has prevented an entire generation of psychologically informed thinkers from drawing certain obvious, valid conclusions about the missile crisis, and about nuclear crisis management. To put the matter plainly: the participants lived through the Cuban missile crisis, not a "trauma." The former is the event of interest we want to understand. The latter is a loaded term plucked from the psychologists' reality, and a highly theoretical reality at that. I believe that if we stick close to our best guess of the evolving psychological reality of the participants, the causes of common sense and policy-relevance will both be better served. As to how fear became adaptive, or what in general happened to the minds of the participants to make it so, I take William James still to have the last word:

> It probably operates through the subliminal door, then. But just how anything operates in this region is still unexplained, and we shall do well

now to say good-by to the *process* of transformation altogether—leaving it, if you like, a good deal of a psychological . . . mystery—and to turn our attention to the fruits of the condition, no matter in what way they may have been produced.[26]

In other words, let us try to understand and explain "the fruits"—the raw experience of fear in the missile crisis, and its peaceful resolution—not some hypothetical mental processes unknown to crisis participants but alleged by analysts to be "responsible" for the fruits. Perhaps if we students of nuclear issues can focus on what that crisis experience was about and what it was like, then the next generation of analysts will more fully appreciate that the actions of men and women, not mental processes, are what need explaining. If we can learn to look backward at the event by vicariously looking forward with its participants, we ought to derive a much enriched understanding of what they all regard as Lesson Number One: never again. Let the Cuban missile crisis be the first, last, and only event of its kind.

# 10

# Living Forward: The Adaptive Role of Fear in the Crystal Ball Effect

The more difficult the matter becomes, the greater the temptation to hasten along the easy road of speculation, away from fearful dangers.

Kierkegaard,
*Concluding Unscientific Postscript,* 1846

Fear played an adaptive role in the resolution of the Cuban missile crisis, as I have argued in Chapters 1 through 9. At the climax of the crisis, leaders in the White House and Kremlin sensed that they were losing control of the situation they had created; that indeed war might be about to break out between them; and that it was thus possible that they were on the verge of mutual nuclear catastrophe. The profundity of that horrifying experience, I have suggested, accounts both for the striking, unexpected, swift, and peaceful resolution of the crisis, and for the considerable difficulty the leaders have had in integrating their unusual experience into their understanding of the crisis. This book is conceived as a first step toward the integration of the experience and interpretation of a crisis in which fear of the shattered crystal ball came ultimately to supersede all other factors in importance. This was a crisis in which fear was fundamental and adaptive.

If fearful adaptation is the *sense* we ought make of the crisis, to what *use* might this knowledge be put by those who must continue to live indefinitely under the same basic conditions that characterized the nuclear world of 1962? Now, as then, the United States and Soviet Union remain highly competitive; they own nearly all the world's nuclear weapons; and they both retain, consistent with the received wisdom of nuclear deterrence, the capacity to destroy each other as functioning societies. What does a phenomenological analysis of the role of fear in the missile crisis tell us about our nuclear future and how to grapple with it?

First, should we be optimistic, even casual, about the likelihood of fear prevailing in future U.S.–Soviet crises? Can we, should we, rely on something like a psychological firebreak of fear to save us in the next nuclear crisis? The answer is that we should *not*. Two sets of reasons—one historical, the other contemporary (and both psychological)—suggest that we would be foolish to expect a canonical, peaceful replay of the Cuban missile crisis. The historical reason is time. Figure 10.1 summarizes the psychological progression toward adaptive fear during the missile crisis. It took Kennedy and his advisers nearly a week to negotiate the psychological minefield from shock to outrage, to belligerence, to circumspection, to fear, and thence to caution and

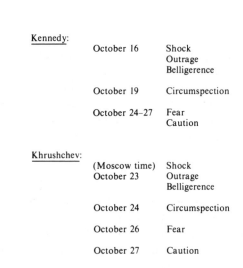

Figure 10.1. Psychological evolution of Kennedy and Khrushchev during the public week of the Cuban missile crisis.

the need to resolve the crisis quickly, with a compromise. Khrushchev had even less time—less than two days before the quarantine of Cuba became effective—and, as we saw in Chapter 2, his psychological evolution may have been barely rapid enough to keep pace with the events in the crisis.

This leads to the second point of (contemporary) wisdom. There is practically no likelihood that leaders in another nuclear crisis would have that much time in which to arrive at the phase of adaptive fear. In post-Watergate and post-Vietnam Washington, an EXCOMM-like group, meeting secretly for six days and nights, would be almost impossible. In Moscow, too, *glasnost,* for all its positive attributes, has already opened up Soviet decision-making to outside scrutiny to an unprecedented degree. But perhaps more important, the weapons systems and procedures have changed dramatically since 1962. We now have short flight times of highly accurate missiles, fewer slow, recallable bombers, and tightly wound and highly interdependent superpower command and control systems. It is possible, therefore, that any future nuclear crisis might be constrained to only minutes, rather than days or weeks, before the systems did what they were made to do, which is launch a nuclear war.[1] It seems quite unlikely that psychological evolution now would keep pace with escalating nuclear danger. These considerations lead directly to the conclusion reached by all participants in the Cuban missile crisis, whether hawks or doves, Soviets or Americans: never again! We must never come that close again! Nuclear crises must be prevented because they cannot be managed reliably.

The question is: What do we *do* about such a conclusion? How do we act on it, in ways that are consistent with what we think we have learned about the resolution of the Cuban missile crisis? In addressing this question, I will refer briefly to the most concentrated and systematic effort to address the question that I am aware of. It derives from the Harvard Nuclear Study Group, subsequently (after 1983) the Project on Avoiding Nuclear War (ANW). In their first book, *Living with Nuclear Weapons,* this group identified and named the crystal ball effect, which is the central factor in their conclusion that we not only must continue living with nuclear weapons but we can expect to do so.[2] The crystal ball effect amounts to foreknowledge of the effects of any major nuclear war. Foresight, knowledge, and understanding are, in this view, adaptive. Knowledge of the highly probable effects of a nuclear war leads to the equally (highly) probable propensity to avoid one, leading to reduced probability of a superpower crisis, hence to reduced likelihood of war between them, and therefore to reduced odds of a nuclear war. The crystal ball effect does indeed help to explain why the bitter Cold War that developed after World War II has yet to produce a single nuclear weapon fired in anger.

Soon, however, the members of the ANW Project came to believe that the crystal ball effect, by itself, might be insufficient. In addition to foreknowledge of the unarguably catastrophic effects of a major nuclear war, the ANW Project came eventually to focus its efforts on identifying incremental steps that might reduce the danger of nuclear war. They concluded in *Hawks, Doves, & Owls* that while deterrence is robust, rendering very low the likelihood of surprise attack, much remains to be done about reducing the risk of inadvertent nuclear war in crises.[3] They called these "owlish" measures, in contrast to traditional "hawkish" emphasis on strength and "dovish" inclination toward conciliation. The overall goal was to articulate ways to reduce the probability of nuclear war along various hypothetical paths. The authors concluded by admitting that, in addition to bolstering deterrence, ways must be found to reduce reliance on deterrence over the long run.[4]

This task was taken up in the research effort published as *Fateful Visions*, a comparative, critical study of ten "visions," or possible nuclear futures, in which reliance on nuclear deterrence was greatly reduced.[5] While the ANW Project reached no firm consensus in support of any single "vision," the participants concluded that the key to reducing reliance on the threat of nuclear catastrophe has to be the improvement of the U.S.–Soviet political relationship. We must, they concluded, find ways to move to a more cooperative, trusting competition with the Soviet Union.[6] This, they asserted, will provide the extra measure of confidence needed to continue living with nuclear weapons, and thus to enjoy the stability they appear to have brought to great power relationships, but without unacceptable risk of their actually being used. Thus the ANW Project has concluded that, in addition to the brute, factual force of the crystal ball effect, we need to be constantly at work bolstering deterrence for the short run, even as we improve U.S.–Soviet political relations, reducing the need for deterrence in the long run. Nothing in the foregoing analysis of the resolution of the Cuban missile crisis calls these sensible conclusions into question. We need to become and remain actively involved in augmenting the crystal ball effect, as we constantly try to reduce the probability that rational people will believe it is in their interest to initiate a nuclear war.

Yet, the phenomenological reconstruction of the last hours of the Cuban missile crisis does suggest that the crystal ball effect, however augmented, may be a necessary though insufficient condition for avoiding nuclear crises and nuclear war. For the record shows, I believe, that the crystal ball effect operated profoundly in both the White House of John Kennedy and the Kremlin of Nikita Khrushchev, but did not prove sufficient either to transform U.S.–Soviet political relations or to prevent a deep nuclear crisis. These changes came only after the deeply disturbing, apparently close brush with nuclear catastrophe. It came only after leaders had acquired, in addition to their notional knowledge of the probable effects of a major nuclear war, a sense of its real possibility and of each one's terrible responsibility in the event of nuclear catastrophe. To the foreknowledge implied by the crystal ball effect was added fear of the shattered crystal ball. Once the knowledge was wedded to the fear, a transformation in U.S.–Soviet political relations did occur in the remarkable spring and summer of 1963.

Nothing since the Cuban missile crisis has approached its level of nuclear danger. But, fear is not enough, for next time we may not have a chance to reach the stage in a crisis where it might perform its adaptive transformations. But neither, I think, is foreknowledge enough, because such knowledge, undriven by visceral fear of its possibility, will have a tendency to fall into the trash heap of received wisdom; its acceptance will arrive by rote and not from conviction, and its effect—*the* crystal ball effect—will thus evaporate over time. If this should happen, and if by inadvertence we should once again find ourselves on the brink of a superpower crisis, it may be attributable in large measure to our having forgotten the fear that gripped our leaders the last time around.

Let us therefore not forget the fear, even as we work to bolster and augment deterrence. That fear of inadvertent nuclear war was terrifying, and its salutary effect was fully commensurate with the awesome responsibility for nuclear catastrophe felt by those in charge. If we believe *now,* as we should, that our primary foreign policy goal ought to be the transformation of U.S.–Soviet political relations, let us try to recall vividly why such a transformation occurred *then,* over a quarter-century ago. It will not be easy to learn the lesson without that experience, but we must try. We cannot afford not to, for we cannot afford the direct experience of another full-blown nuclear crisis between the superpowers.

It has long been traditional to visit Hiroshima and Nagasaki to absorb the full shattering force of the crystal ball effect, to understand with one's mind and heart that such catastrophes must never happen again. It is a rare person who, in that setting, knowing that history, does not shed tears for what happened in August 1945. But to add the other necessary ingredient, the fear of the shattered crystal ball, we should develop ways to revisit the Cuban missile crisis, phenomenologically, as it appeared and felt at the time. It is hard historical and psychological realism that leads me to hope we will eventually find ways to move us closer to, if not tearfulness, at least shattering fearfulness as we step backward into the forward-moving events of October 1962.

I began the phenomenological part of this volume with the analogy, in Chapter 5, of a driver who stops his car in fear of an apparition in the road. The analogy had several purposes: to introduce the concept of fear into the discussion; to show that if we try to recover psychological life, rather than annihilate it, we explain the action of interest very differently; and to suggest that the process of psychological recovery requires interpretation, by which one tries to get even further inside the viewpoint of the experiencing person. But however adequate (or inadequate) the analogy may be methodologically, it hardly captures the kind or depth of fear to be found in the participants of the Cuban missile crisis. It refers to fear for oneself, and it is momentary. In the missile crisis, the fear was associated with responsibility for a catastrophe, and it was shattering. I will therefore conclude with another analogy about a different car and driver, in a different kind of situation, that has several of the key psychological constituents of the situation faced by leaders in the White House and Kremlin in October 1962.

Leamus had managed to get an air passage to Cologne and picked up a car at the airport. It was still quite early in the morning and he'd hoped to miss most of the autobahn traffic to Karlsruhe, but the heavy lorries were already on the move. He drove 70 km. in half an hour, weaving between the traffic, taking risks to beat the clock, when a small car, a Fiat probably, nosed its way out into the fast lane forty yards ahead of him. Leamus stamped on the brake, turning his headlights full on and sounding his horn, and by the grace of God he missed it, missed it by a fraction of a second. As he passed the car he saw out of the corner of his eye four children in the back waving and laughing, and the stupid frightened face of their father at the wheel. He drove on, cursing, and suddenly it happened, suddenly his hands were shaking feverishly, his face was burning hot, his heart palpitating wildly. He managed to pull off the road into a lay-by, scrambled out of the car and stood, breathing heavily, staring at the hurdling stream of giant lorries. He had a vision of the little car caught among them, pounded and smashed until there was nothing left, the bodies of the children torn like the murdered refugees on the road across the dune. He drove very slowly the rest of the way and missed his meeting with Karl. He never drove again without some corner of his memory recalling the tousled children waving to him from the back of that car and their father grasping the wheel like a farmer at the shafts of a hand plough.[7]

Let this be our goal: to find ways to encourage leaders on whose shoulders nuclear responsibilities may one day ultimately rest to remember what (the fictional) Leamus and Kennedy, Khrushchev, and their advisers remember (or remembered). It might have happened. It might have been otherwise. It would have been their responsibility. And let us begin where the actors began, in the event of a very near miss, by focusing on the experience of the nearness and deemphasizing explanations of the miss.

# Notes

## Foreword

1. Arthur Schlesinger, Jr., *A Thousand Days* (New York: Fawcett, 1965), chap. 31.
2. Albert Carnesale, Paul Doty, Stanley Hoffmann, Samuel P. Huntington, Joseph S. Nye, Jr., and Scott D. Sagan, *Living with Nuclear Weapons* (New York: Bantam, 1983).
3. Ibid., 254–255.
4. Graham Allison, Albert Carnesale, and Joseph S. Nye, Jr., eds., *Hawks, Doves & Owls: An Agenda for Avoiding Nuclear War* (New York: W. W. Norton, 1985).
5. These are enumerated in Chapter 5, note 9.
6. Blight and several colleagues at Harvard's Center for Science and International Affairs have now begun The Nuclear Crisis Project, a further look into the missile crisis and also a multiyear investigation of the Berlin crises, 1958–1962. In addition to the present book, a first fruit of the crisis project is Blight and David A. Welch, *On the Brink: Americans and Soviets Reexamine the Cuban Missile Crisis* (New York: Farrar, Straus, & Giroux/Hill and Wang, 1989). In a sense, the Blight and Welch book is the initial "data book" of the crisis project, while *The Shattered Crystal Ball* is its interpretive "theory" book.
7. Theodore C. Sorensen, *Kennedy* (New York: Harper & Row, 1965), p. 705.

## Chapter 1

1. Carnesale, Doty, Hoffman, Huntington, Nye, and Sagan, *Living with Nuclear Weapons*.
2. Jonathan Schell, *The Abolition* (New York: Alfred A. Knopf, 1984), pp. 7–8.

177

3. Carnesale et al., *Living with Nuclear Weapons,* p. 44.

4. Ibid., p. 68.

5. "Anatomy of a Crisis," CBS News special report, October 28, 1962, narrated by Charles Collingwood. Property of CBS News Archives, New York, N.Y.

6. Patrick Pacheco, "The Peace Corps Then and Now," *Ladies Home Journal* (March 1986): 100–102, 197–198.

7. Harold Macmillan, *At the End of the Day: 1961–1963* (New York: Harper & Row, 1973), pp. 214–215.

8. Nikita Khrushchev, "Report on the International Situation," (December 12, 1962). Cited in Graham T. Allison, *Essence of Decision: Explaining the Cuban Missile Crisis* (Boston: Little, Brown, 1971), p. 212.

9. Sorensen, *Kennedy,* p. 724.

10. McGeorge Bundy, interview with the author, August 12, 1987.

11. Blight and Welch, *On the Brink,* pt. 2.

12. Nikita S. Khrushchev, *Khrushchev Remembers,* 2 vols., ed. and trans. Strobe Talbott; intro. by Edward Crankshaw (Boston: Little, Brown, 1970, 1974), vol. 1, pp. 488–505; vol. 2, pp. 509–514.

13. Richard E. Neustadt, *Presidential Power* (New York: John Wiley, 1980), p. 158.

14. Soren Kierkegaard, *The Concept of Anxiety,* ed. and trans. Reidar Thomte and Albert B. Anderson (Princeton: Princeton University Press, 1980), p. 235.

15. Ibid., p. 206.

## Chapter 2

1. William James, *The Principles of Psychology,* 2 vols. (New York: Henry Holt, 1890), vol. 1, p. 1.

2. Those with serious interest in following up this brief introduction to operational nuclear danger should consult the highly detailed and extensively documented work that has emerged so far from the Nuclear Crisis Project, especially Blight and Welch, *On the Brink.* See also James G. Blight, Joseph S. Nye, Jr., and David A. Welch, "The Cuban Missile Crisis Revisited," *Foreign Affairs* 66, no. 1 (Fall 1987): 170–188; David A. Welch and James G. Blight, "The Eleventh Hour of the Cuban Missile Crisis," *International Security* 12, no. 3 (Winter 1987/88): 5–29; McGeorge Bundy and James G. Blight, "October 27, 1962," *International Security* 12, no. 3 (Winter 1987/88): 30–92; David A. Welch, ed., "Proceedings of the Hawk's Cay Conference on the Cuban Missile Crisis" and "Proceedings of the Cambridge Conference on the Cuban Missile Crisis," both produced in April 1988 and available from the Center for Science and International Affairs, Harvard University. In addition one should also consult the fine work done by two former Kennedy administration officials who have been writing on the missile crisis and participating in

the conferences sponsored by the Nuclear Crisis Project: McGeorge Bundy, *Danger and Survival: Choices About the Bomb in the First Fifty Years* (New York: Random House, 1988); and Raymond L. Garthoff, *Reflections on the Cuban Missile Crisis* (Washington, D.C.: The Brookings Institution, 1987), and "Cuban Missile Crisis: The Soviet Story," *Foreign Policy* 72 (Fall 1988): 61–80.

3. Sorensen, *Kennedy;* Schlesinger, *A Thousand Days;* and Robert F. Kennedy, *Thirteen Days* (New York: W. W. Norton, 1971). None of these books contains any footnotes, which normally constitute the scholar's roadmap into the treacherous business of evaluating an author's claims, based on their correspondence with the documentation. For many years, however, this was simply impossible, because there were neither notes nor documents to work with.

4. Marc Trachtenberg, ed., "White House Tapes and Minutes of the Cuban Missile Crisis," *International Security* 10, no. 1 (Summer 1985): 164–203; and Bundy and Blight, "October 27, 1962."

5. See Blight and Welch, *On the Brink,* pp. 6–8 and 137–138.

6. William James, *Principles of Psychology,* vol. 1, pp. 221–223.

7. Blight and Welch, *On the Brink,* pt. 3.

8. H. R. Trevor-Roper, "The Lost Moments of History," *New York Review of Books* 35, no. 16 (October 27, 1988): 61–67, p. 61. Trevor-Roper's title is borrowed from Frances Yates.

## Chapter 3

1. Bundy and Blight, "October 27, 1962." This edited version contains, in addition to editorial commentary, half of the material in the unedited transcript, which may be obtained from the John F. Kennedy Library, Boston.

2. Tim O'Brien, *The Nuclear Age* (New York: Alfred A. Knopf, 1985), pp. 39–40.

3. Spencer R. Weart, *Nuclear Fear: A History of Images* (Cambridge: Harvard University Press, 1988), p. 259. These reactions were noted with considerable interest by officials within the Kennedy administration. State Department Legal Counsel Abram Chayes recently recalled how deeply divided and emotional were congressional discussions of Cuba; and presidential counsel Theodore Sorensen recalls demonstrations in Washington during the crisis both for and against attacking Cuba. See Blight and Welch, *On the Brink,* pp. 40–41 and 73–74.

4. An important testimony to the power of theory lay in the fact that several interpreters of the crisis have been making my point for nearly a quarter-century. Recalling Kennedy's remark to Sorensen that the risk of war on October 27, 1968, may have been "between one out of three and even," for example, Arthur Schlesinger has argued that "Kennedy's grim odds were based on fear, not of Khrushchev's intention, but of human error, of something

going terribly wrong down the line . . . even with the justified assumption of reciprocal rationality a terrible risk remained" (*Robert Kennedy and His Times* (New York: Ballantine, 1979)), pp. 570–571. See also a similar remark by Richard Neustadt in his *Presidential Power,* pp. 158–159. These men, while close to the President and his key advisers, are not, however, theoreticians, and thus not bound to promote an "approach," however biased they may (or may not) have been due to their close association with the Kennedy administration.

5. Albert Wohlstetter and Roberta Wohlstetter, "Controlling the Risks in Cuba," *Adelphi Paper No. 7,* April 1965. Reprinted in R. J. Art and K. N. Waltz, eds., *The Use of Force: International Politics and Foreign Policy,* 2nd ed. (Lanham, Md: University Press of America, 1983), pp. 307–343, p. 328.

6. John F. Kennedy, "Message in Reply to a Broadcast by Chairman Khrushchev on the Cuban Crisis," October 28, 1962. In *Public Papers of the Presidents* (Washington, D.C.: U.S. Government Printing Office, 1963), pp. 814–815, p. 814 (italics added).

7. Wohlstetter and Wohlstetter, "Controlling the Risks in Cuba," p. 329.

8. Richard Ned Lebow, *Between Peace and War* (Baltimore: Johns Hopkins University Press, 1981), p. 303.

9. Richard Ned Lebow, *Nuclear Crisis Management: A Dangerous Illusion* (Ithaca: Cornell University Press, 1987), p. 147.

10. Trachtenberg, ed., "White House Tapes and Minutes of the Cuban Missile Crisis," pp. 201–203.

11. Bundy and Blight, "October 27, 1962," p. 35.

12. Ibid., pp. 66, 67, 71, 72, 74, 75, 91, 92.

13. William James, "The Compounding of Consciousness," in J. J. McDermott, ed., *The Writings of William James: A Comprehensive Edition* (Chicago: University of Chicago Press, 1977), pp. 546–561, p. 560. (1909)

14. William James, "Bergson and His Critique of Intellectualism," in McDermott, ed., *Writings of William James,* pp. 561–581, p. 573. (1909)


*Chapter 4*

1. Ronald Reagan, "Radio Address to the Nation," April 17, 1982.

2. Thomas C. Schelling, *Arms and Influence* (New Haven: Yale University Press, 1966), p. 259.

3. Joseph S. Nye, Jr., "Nuclear Learning and U.S.–Soviet Security Regimes," *International Organization* 41, no. 3 (Summer 1987): 371–402.

4. Thomas C. Schelling, "What Went Wrong with Arms Control?" *Foreign Affairs* 64, no. 2 (Winter 1985/86): 219–233, p. 233.

5. Thomas C. Schelling, "Arrangements for Reciprocal Reassurance," in H. Roderick and U. Magnusson, eds., *Avoiding Inadvertent War: Crisis Management* (Austin, Texas: LBJ School of Public Affairs, 1983), pp. 123–129, p. 124.

6. Works that are now often regarded as classics from a bygone "golden age" of nuclear strategy are Albert Wohlstetter, "The Delicate Balance of Terror," *Foreign Affairs* 37, no. 2 (January 1959); Bernard Brodie, *Strategy in the Missile Age* (Princeton: Princeton University Press, 1959); and Thomas C. Schelling, *The Strategy of Conflict* (Cambridge: Harvard University Press, 1960).

7. This is the title of chapter one in Schelling's *Strategy of Conflict*.

8. Schelling, "What Went Wrong with Arms Control?"

9. Allison, *Essence of Decision;* John D. Steinbruner, *The Cybernetic Theory of Decision* (Princeton: Princeton University Press, 1974).

10. John D. Steinbruner, "Beyond Rational Deterrence: The Struggle for New Conceptions," in Klaus Knorr, ed., *Power, Strategy, and Security* (Princeton: Princeton University Press, 1983), pp. 103–125, p. 119. (1976)

11. An excellent critical review of the burgeoning literature of psychological radicalism on nuclear issues may be found in Stanley Hoffmann, "On the Political Psychology of War and Peace: A Critique and an Agenda," *Political Psychology* 7, no. 1 (March 1986): 1–22. See also my own articles on psychological radicalism listed in note 9 to Chapter 5 (below).

12. Murray Sayle, "KE 007: A Conspiracy of Circumstance," *New York Review of Books* 32, no. 7, April 25, 1985, pp. 44–54.

13. The standard reference for this point of view is Charles Perrow, *Normal Accidents* (New York: Basic Books, 1984). For an application of this viewpoint to nuclear war, see Todd Gitlin, "Time to Move Beyond Deterrence," *The Nation* (December 22, 1984), pp. 676–679. For a critique of the notion that assessing the probability of nuclear war is like spinning a roulette wheel, see my "Beyond Deterrence or Beyond Utopian Ideology?: Thought Experiments for an Anti-Nuclear Movement in Crisis," Working Paper No. 2 (Center for Science and International Affairs, Harvard University); and Joseph S. Nye, Jr., *Nuclear Ethics* (New York: Free Press, 1986), chap. 5.

14. Helen Caldicott, *Missile Envy* (New York: Morrow, 1984). See also Joel Kovel, *Against the State of Nuclear Terror* (Boston: South End Press, 1983).

15. Morton Deutsch, "The Prevention of World War III: A Psychological Perspective," *Political Psychology* 4, no. 1 (1983): 3–31. The pioneer among psychologists in articulating this point of view was Charles E. Osgood. See his *An Alternative to War or Surrender* (Urbana: University of Illinois Press, 1962). See also Ralph K. White, *Fearful Warriors: A Psychological Profile of U.S.–Soviet Relations* (New York: Free Press, 1984); John E. Mack, "Toward a Collective Psychopathology of the Nuclear Arms Competition," *Political Psychology* 6, no. 2 (1985): 291–321; and Steven Kull, *Minds at War* (New York: Basic Books, 1988).

16. Erik H. Erikson, "Reflections on Ethos and War," *Yale Review* (1984), pp. 481–486. Erikson's remarks about the connection he sees between the pseudo-speciation of the Jews in Nazi Germany and in U.S.–Soviet relations occurred at a conference on "The Psychology of U.S.–Soviet Relations," March 1986, in Big Sur, California.

17. See Irving Janis, *Groupthink*, 2nd ed. (Boston: Houghton-Mifflin, 1982); and Lebow, *Between Peace and War*.

18. See Robert Jervis, Richard Ned Lebow, and Janice Gross Stein, *Psychology and Deterrence* (Baltimore: Johns Hopkins University Press, 1985). See also, for a critique of the psychological approach to nuclear policy in that book, my "The New Psychology of War and Peace," *International Security* 11, no. 3 (Winter 1986/87): 175–186.

19. See Allison, Carnesale, and Nye, *Hawks, Doves, & Owls;* and idem, "The Owl's Agenda for Avoiding Nuclear War," *The Washington Quarterly* 9, no. 3 (Summer 1986): 45–58.

20. This (essentially psychological) characterization of "crisis" is taken from Lebow, *Between Peace and War*, pp. 10–12.

21. Richard K. Betts, "Surprise Attack and Preemption," in Allison, Carnesale, and Nye, *Hawks, Doves, & Owls*, p. 59.

22. J. D. Steinbruner, "Beyond Rational Deterrence," p. 104.

23. See Blight, "Beyond Deterrence or Beyond Utopian Ideology?" and J. S. Nye, *Nuclear Ethics*, chap. 5.

24. Jervis et al., *Psychology and Deterrence*, chaps. 3–5.

25. R. N. Lebow, in R. Jervis et al., *Psychology and Deterrence*, p. 192.

26. Schelling, *Arms and Influence*, p. 166.

27. Thomas C. Schelling and Morton H. Halperin, *Strategy and Arms Control* (New York: Twentieth Century Fund, 1961).

28. See, for example, Richard E. Neustadt and Graham T. Allison, "Afterword" to R. F. Kennedy, *Thirteen Days*, pp. 112–114.

## Chapter 5

1. H. R. Trevor-Roper, "The Lost Moments of History," pp. 61–67.

2. Ibid., p. 61.

3. Ibid., p. 67.

4. R. F. Kennedy, *Thirteen Days*.

5. Trevor-Roper, "The Lost Moments of History," p. 61.

6. On several occasions, Robert McNamara has said that, in his view, the "cottage industry" devoted to explaining various aspects of the Cuban missile crisis is next to worthless. This is despite the fact that most, though not all, of this literature praises his performance and lauds his salutary cautionary influence on President Kennedy. Clearly, one reason he rejects so much of this literature is that the square corners of its theoretical requirements fit so poorly with the rounded contours of his memory of what the experience of the crisis was like for him. For example, at a conference in Hawk's Cay, Florida, in March 1987, McNamara responded as follows to a question from political scientist Alexander George of Stanford: "I don't think we've quite succeeded in re-creating the atmosphere at the time. The questions Alex asked simply weren't framed that precisely back then. There were deep differences of

opinion among us, and very strong feelings about Cuba, and the fact is that we weren't going through an unemotional, orderly, and comprehensive decision-making process. There were tremendous political and military pressures to *do* something." (Blight and Welch, *On the Brink*, p. 51). To many former EXCOMM members present, the scholars' questions just weren't *their* questions, they weren't directed at *their* experience (See *On the Brink*, pt. 1, passim).

7. Robert D. Romanyshyn, *Psychological Life: From Science to Metaphor* (Austin: University of Texas Press, 1982), pp. 134–136.

8. Thomas Nagel, *The View from Nowhere* (New York: Oxford University Press, 1986). See also Nagel's *Moral Questions* (New York: Cambridge University Press, 1979), esp. pp. 53–74.

9. I have attempted critically to assess the emerging discipline of the psychology of avoiding nuclear war (or nuclear psychology) in the following pieces: " 'Limited' Nuclear War? The Unmet Psychological Challenge of the American Catholic Bishops," *Science, Technology, and Human Values* 10, no. 4 (Fall 1985): 3–16; "Toward a Policy-Relevant Psychology of Avoiding Nuclear War: Lessons for Psychologists from the Cuban Missile Crisis," *The American Psychologist* 42, no. 1 (January 1987): 1–18; "Can Psychology Reduce the Risk of Nuclear War? Reflections of a 'Little Drummer Boy' of Nuclear Psychology," *Journal of Humanistic Psychology* 28, no. 2 (Spring 1988); "How Might Psychology Contribute to Reducing the Risk of Nuclear War? *Political Psychology* 7, no. 4 (Winter 1986/87); and "The New Psychology of War and Peace," *International Security* 3, no. 3 (Winter 1986/87): 175–186. Several of these pieces have elicited unusually heated, occasionally illuminating responses from critical reviewers. See, for example, the exchanges in *The American Psychologist* in April 1988; in *The Journal of Humanistic Psychology* in the spring of 1988; and in *Readings: A Journal of Reviews and Commentary in Mental Health,* June 1987. In my view, the policy-irrelevance of nearly all this work is due at bottom to the authors' exhalted regard for the strictures of their disciplines, and their resulting disregard for the perspectives of the policymakers on whom they pass their psychological judgments.

10. William James, *Principles of Psychology,* vol. 2, pp. 442–485.

## *Chapter 6*

1. "Model I" and "Model II" factors derive from Graham T. Allison's original exposition of these constructs in *Essence of Decision,* chaps. 1 and 3. Their application to contemporary questions of nuclear policy are in Allison, Carnesale, and Nye, *Hawks, Doves & Owls,* chap. 8; and idem, "Owl's Agenda." Nuclear strategists Thomas Schelling and Charles Glaser have in conversation expressed to me considerable skepticism about the explanatory usefulness of "Model II" factors, while psychiatrist John Mack and political scientist Richard Ned Lebow have, also in conversations with me, been just as skeptical about the usefulness (and reality) of "Model I" factors.

2. T. C. Schelling, "Arrangements for Reciprocal Reassurance," pp. 123–124.

3. John F. Kennedy, cited in R. F. Kennedy, *Thirteen Days,* p. 40.

4. Robert S. McNamara, videotaped discussion of the Cuban missile crisis, conducted by Richard E. Neustadt, June 1983. (Tapes and transcripts in the possession of the Alfred P. Sloan Foundation, New York, N.Y.)

5. Ibid.

6. William James, "The Stream of Thought," in *Principles of Psychology,* vol. 1, pp. 224–290. See also Gerald Myers, *William James: His Life and Thought* (New Haven: Yale University Press, 1986); and Jacques Barzun, *A Stroll with William James* (Chicago: University of Chicago Press, 1983). Myers gives a very thorough philosophical and psychological exposition of James's ideas on "the stream of thought," though Myers's style is a bit hard to penetrate—he is the very opposite of James in this respect. Barzun, while not as thorough as Myers, offers the skeptical or uninitiated reader many reasons for believing that James is as pertinent as ever—and as lively.

7. I have borrowed these terms from Richard Wollheim, *The Thread of Life* (Cambridge: Harvard University Press, 1984), pp. 33–42. The distinction between direct and mediated knowledge is an old one, however, and very fundamental in epistemology. See, for example, William James's distinction between "knowledge of acquaintance" and "knowledge about" (*Principles of Psychology,* vol. 1, pp. 221–223); and Thomas Nagel's recent illuminating evocation of the difference between what he calls the (objective) "view from nowhere" and the personal and unique "view from somewhere" *(The View from Nowhere).* And for a particularly striking discussion of some of these issues, see Nagel's "What Is It Like to Be a Bat?" in *Mortal Questions* (New York: Cambridge University Press, 1979), pp. 165–180.

8. Robert Jervis, *The Illogic of American Nuclear Strategy* (Ithaca: Cornell University Press, 1984), p. 58.

9. Thomas C. Schelling, "Confidence in Crisis," *International Security* 8, no. 4 (Spring 1984): 55–66, p. 57.

10. Richard E. Neustadt, videotaped discussion of the Cuban missile crisis, June 1983.

11. Maxwell Taylor, videotaped discussion of the Cuban missile crisis with Richard E. Neustadt, June 1983. (Videotape in the possession of the Alfred P. Sloan Foundation, New York, N.Y.) Also in Blight and Welch, *On the Brink,* p. 82.

12. Edmund Husserl, *Ideas,* trans. W. R. Boyce Gibson (New York: Collier, 1962).

13. Charles Taylor, "The Explanation of Purposive Behavior," in R. Borger and F. Cioffi, *Explanation in the Behavioral Sciences* (New York: Cambridge University Press, 1970), pp. 49–79, p. 49.

14. Theodore Mischel, "Psychological Explanations and Their Vicissitudes," in W. J. Arnold, ed., *Conceptual Foundations of Psychology* (Lincoln: University of Nebraska Press, 1975), pp. 134–204, p. 146.

15. William James, *Principles of Psychology,* vol. 1, p. 225.
16. Ibid., p. 192.
17. William James, "Pragmatism's Conception of Truth," in J. J. McDermott, ed., *The Writings of William James,* pp. 429–443, p. 420.
18. This conference is described in detail in Blight and Welch, *On the Brink,* pt. 1.
19. See ibid., pp. 148–149.
20. Ibid., p. 169.
21. Ibid., p. 192.
22. Ibid., p. 188.
23. Ibid., pp. 107–108.

## Chapter 7

1. Plato, *Meno* (Jowett translation) in R. M. Hutchins, ed., *The Great Books of the Western World* (Chicago: Encyclopedia Britannica, 1952), vol. 7: pp. 174–190; p. 179.
2. One of the most recent and important examples of the use of the analogy between nonnuclear and nuclear crises is Jervis et al., *Psychology and Deterrence.* But complementary accounts may also be found in Robert Axelrod, *The Evolution of Cooperation* (New York: Basic Books, 1984), whose framework is the "prisoner's dilemma" game, and Irving Janis, *Groupthink,* whose theoretical basis is psychological research on stress and decision-making.
3. Iris Murdoch, *The Bell.* Cited in J. W. N. Watkins, "Imperfect Rationality," in R. Borger and F. Cioffi, *Explanation in the Behavioral Sciences,* pp. 167–230, p. 229.
4. Blight and Welch, *On the Brink,* p. 182.
5. This information came to light in conversations about the missile crisis between Robert McNamara, McGeorge Bundy, and me.
6. Alexander L. George, "Crisis Management: The Interaction of Political and Military Considerations," *Survival* 26, no. 5 (September/October 1984): 223–234, p. 224.
7. Dean Rusk, statement opening discussion at Meeting No. 1 of "EXCOMM," October 16, 1962. In Trachtenberg, ed., "White House Tapes and Minutes of the Cuban Missile Crisis, pp. 164–203, 171–173.
8. Theodore C. Sorensen, "Memo to EXCOMM Members," October 17, 1962. (Box 49, National Security Files, John F. Kennedy Library, Boston, Mass.), p. 1.
9. R. E. Neustadt, "Basic Issues in National Security Operations," p. 95; and *Presidential Power,* p. 158.
10. Sorensen, "Memo to EXCOMM Members," p. 3.
11. Barbara Tuchman, *The Guns of August* (New York: Bantam, 1976), pp. 91–92. (1962).
12. See, for example, Paul Bracken, *The Command and Control of Nuclear*

*Forces* (New Haven: Yale University Press, 1983), pp. 2–3; and Stephen Van Evera, "The Cult of the Offensive and the Origins of the First World War," in S. E. Miller, ed., *Military Strategy and the Origins of the First World War* (Princeton: Princeton University Press, 1985), pp. 58–107.

13. Carnesale, Doty, Hoffmann, Huntington, Nye, and Sagan, *Living with Nuclear Weapons*, p. 44.

14. Paul Fussell, *The Great War and Modern Memory* (New York: Oxford University Press, 1975), p. 7.

15. The source of this passage prefers to remain anonymous.

16. George W. Ball, interview with the author, Princeton, N.J., May 1, 1987.

17. Bundy and Blight, "October 27, 1962," p. 92.

18. Frank A. Sieverts, "Report" (on the Cuban Missile Crisis), written during the summer of 1963 for the State Department. (Box 49, National Security Files, John F. Kennedy Library, Boston, Mass.).

19. McNamara, *On the Brink*, p. 188.

20. Dean Rusk, in ibid., p. 178.

21. R. F. Kennedy, *Thirteen Days*, p. 105.

22. J. F. Kennedy, "Report . . . on the Soviet Arms Buildup in Cuba," p. 807.

23. R. F. Kennedy, *Thirteen Days*, p. 105.

24. Neustadt, *Presidential Power*, p. 158.

25. R. F. Kennedy, *Thirteen Days*, pp. 47–48.

26. Neustadt and Allison, "Afterword" to Kennedy, *Thirteen Days*, pp. 107–150, p. 118.

27. Arthur M. Schlesinger, Jr., *The Cycles of American History* (Boston: Houghton-Mifflin, 1986), p. 62. (Reprinted from an article in *Foreign Affairs*, 1983, "Foreign Policy and the American Character." Walter Cronkite, in a CBS News special report of October 24, 1962, used the same analogy. As he and his colleagues assessed the situation the evening after the quarantine went into effect, Cronkite remarked that if one of the Soviet ships tried to run through the quarantine line, and if fighting broke out, and if escalation ensued, then, according to Cronkite, "there goes the whole ball game." (Property of CBS News Archives, New York, N.Y.)

28. Robert Jervis, *The Illogic of American Nuclear Strategy* (Ithaca: Cornell University Press, 1984), p. 53.

29. McGeorge Bundy, "To Cap the Volcano," *Foreign Affairs* (October 1969), p. 2.

30. McGeorge Bundy, "Political Leadership and Nuclear Deterrence: Some Claims for the Utility of Truth" (a lecture at the Davies Forum, University of San Francisco, October 25, 1983), p. 9.

31. Nikita Khrushchev, cited in R. R. Pope, ed., *Soviet Views on the Cuban Missile Crisis* (Lanham, Md.: University Press of America, 1982), p. 92.

32. See Clifford Geertz, "Thick Description: Toward an Interpretive Theory of Culture" in C. Geertz, *The Interpretation of Cultures* (New York: Basic Books, 1973), pp. 3–30.

33. R. F. Kennedy, *Thirteen Days*, p. 84.

34. Joseph S. Nye, Jr., *Nuclear Ethics* (New York: Free Press, 1986), p. 65; See also Derek Parfit, *Reasons and Persons* (New York: Oxford University Press, 1984), p. 453.

35. Dean Rusk, in *On the Brink*, p. 184.

36. Clifford Geertz, *Local Knowledge: Further Essays in Interpretive Anthropology* (New York: Basic Books, 1983), p. 47.

37. Sorensen, *Kennedy*, p. 724.

38. Harry S. Truman, cited in Schlesinger, *Cycles of American History*, p. 398.

39. Eisenhower made this statement in an interview with Stephen E. Ambrose. See Ambrose, *Eisenhower: The President* (New York: Simon & Schuster, 1984), p. 184.

40. Dean Rusk, in a videotaped discussion of the Cuban Missile Crisis, January 1983 (a Project of the Alfred P. Sloan Foundation, New York, N.Y., which owns the tapes). See also Blight and Welch, *On the Brink*, p. 183.

41. Richard Nixon claims to be an exception. In a recent interview Nixon told Roger Rosenblatt that he gave the use of nuclear weapons serious consideration on four occasions: (1) during the Vietnam War, (2) during the 1973 Middle East war, (3) during the 1969 Soviet-Chinese border dispute, and (4) during the India-Pakistan War of 1971. See Rosenblatt, *Witness: The World Since Hiroshima* (Boston: Little, Brown, 1985), pp. 78–79. It is hard to know what to make of such claims. In subsequent interviews, however, Henry Kissinger gently suggested that when a president (in this case his former boss) says he "considered" going to nuclear war, one must take it with a grain of salt. It seems doubtful whether Nixon ever "considered" the use of nuclear weapons any more seriously than did Eisenhower in 1954.

42. Sorensen, *Kennedy*, p. 724.

43. Thomas C. Schelling, *Arms and Influence*, p. 166.

44. Ibid., pp. 121–122.

45. Nikita Khrushchev, "Letter to President Kennedy," October 26, 1962. Reprinted in Pope, ed., *Soviet Views on the Cuban Missile Crisis*, pp. 37–49, p. 48.

46. John F. Kennedy, "Letter to Chairman Khrushchev," October 28, 1962. In *Public Papers of the Presidents*, pp. 814–815, p. 814.

47. David Rosenhan, "On Being Sane in Insane Places," *Science* 179, pp. 250–258.

48. R. F. Kennedy, *Thirteen Days*, p. 75.

49. Herbert Dinnerstein has suggested that the shootdown of the American U-2 over Cuba on October 27 may have been the result of efforts of Soviet hard-liners to foil any chances for a negotiated settlement of the crisis, one that would have presumably entailed removal of the missiles from Cuba. See Dinnerstein, *The Making of a Missile Crisis, October 1962* (Baltimore: Johns Hopkins University Press, 1976), p. 229. This is total speculation, however.

Moreover, it was clear during the crisis, and it is even clearer in retrospect, that Castro bitterly opposed any settlement of the crisis that would require removing the missiles. See Tad Szulc, *Fidel: A Critical Portrait* (New York: Morrow, 1986), pp. 584–589. One hears rumors from time to time that Castro even ordered some of his forces to try to take over one of the Soviet SAM-sites, presumably so they could shoot down more American U-2s, thus precipitating a war they preferred, relative to losing the Soviet missiles. These rumors persist though there is little hard evidence to go on. (See Blight and Welch, *On the Brink,* Chapter 6.)

50. Douglas Dillon, in Blight and Welch, *On the Brink,* p. 168.

51. Paul Nitze, in ibid., p. 149.

52. Robert McNamara, in Bundy and Blight, "October 27, 1962," pp. 67, 71.

53. See Ulric Neisser, "Snapshots or Benchmarks?" in Neisser, ed., *Memory Observed: Remembering in Natural Contexts* (San Francisco: Freeman, 1981), pp. 43–48.

54. John F. Kennedy, in Trachtenberg, ed., "White House Tapes," p. 181.

55. John F. Kennedy, in Bundy and Blight, "October 27, 1962," p. 83.

56. Dean Rusk, letter to the author, February 25, 1987; see also Blight and Welch, *On the Brink,* pp. 83–84.

57. Robert McNamara, in Bundy and Blight, "October 27, 1962," p. 75.

58. A. Schlesinger, *Cycles of American History,* p. 415.

59. Thomas Nagel, *Mortal Questions,* p. 74. See also Stanley Hoffmann, *Duties Beyond Borders: On the Limits and Possibilities of Ethical International Politics* (Syracuse, N.Y.: Syracuse University Press, 1981), p. 81.

## Chapter 8

1. John F. Kennedy, "Radio and Television Report to the American People on the Soviet Arms Buildup in Cuba," October 22, 1962. In *Public Papers of the Presidents,* p. 809.

2. Sorenson, *Kennedy,* p. 716.

3. George W. Ball, *The Past Has Another Pattern* (New York: Norton, 1982), p. 286.

4. McGeorge Bundy, videotaped "Discussion of the Cuban Missile Crisis," January 1983 (tapes are the property of the Sloan Foundation, New York, N.Y.).

5. T. S. Eliot, "The Dry Salvages," (from *The Four Quartets,* London: Faber & Faber, 1943); cited in Ball, *The Past Has Another Pattern,* p. xiii.

6. Adam Yarmolinsky, "Department of Defense Operations During the Cuban Crisis" (a Report to the Secretary of Defense, February 13, 1963), ed. by Dan Caldwell in *The Naval War College Review* 32, no. 4 (July–August 1979): 83–99, p. 93.

7. Bundy and Blight, "October 27, 1962," p. 55.

8. Scott D. Sagan, "Nuclear Alerts and Crisis Management," *International Security* 9, no. 4 (Spring 1985): 99–139, p. 109.

9. Ibid., p. 109.

10. Yarmolinsky, "Department of Defense Operations," p. 92.

11. See Blight and Welch, *On the Brink,* p. 90 and chap. 5.

12. R. F. Kennedy, *Thirteen Days,* p. 75.

13. See David Detzer, *The Brink* (New York: Crowell, 1979), p. 281; and Sagan, "Nuclear Alerts," p. 118.

14. Sorensen, *Kennedy,* p. 713.

15. Nikita Khrushchev, "Letter to President Kennedy," October 28, 1962, in Pope, ed., *Soviet Views of the Cuban Missile Crisis,* pp. 58–65, pp. 62–63.

16. Sagan, "Nuclear Alerts," p. 101.

17. Nikita Khrushchev, "Letter to President Kennedy," October 26, 1962, pp. 37–49, p. 49.

18. Sorensen, *Kennedy,* pp. 713–714 (italics added).

19. Ibid., p. 705.

20. See, for example, Richard K. Betts, "Surprise Attack and Preemption," pp. 54–79, p. 66. The argument for President Kennedy's "irrationality" in setting the odds so high derives from Thomas C. Shelling, in a series of verbal and written communications to me.

21. Sorensen, *Kennedy,* p. 716.

22. R. F. Kennedy, *Thirteen Days,* p. 87.

23. Bundy and Blight, "October 27, 1962," pp. 57–62.

24. R. F. Kennedy, *Thirteen Days,* pp. 86–87.

25. See Blight and Welch, *On the Brink,* chap. 3.

26. Bundy, *Danger and Survival,* chap. 9.

27. Garry Wills, *The Kennedy Imprisonment: A Meditation on Power* (New York: Pocket Books, 1983), p. 279. (1982). Other notable expressions of this so-called "revisionist" view may be found in Barton J. Bernstein, "The Cuban Missile Crisis: Trading the Jupiters in Turkey?" *Political Science Quarterly* 95, no. 1 (Spring 1980): 97–126; James A. Nathan, "The Missile Crisis: His Finest Hour Now," *World Politics* 27, no. 2 (January 1975): 256–281; and Richard Ned Lebow, *Between Peace and War.*

28. Bruce Miroff, *Pragmatic Illusions: The Presidential Politics of John F. Kennedy* (New York: David MacKay, 1975), pp. 88–89.

29. Allison, *Essence of Decision,* p. 198.

30. Galway Kinnell, *The Past* (Boston: Houghton-Mifflin, 1985), p. 48.

31. In the Freudian lexicon, this phenomenon is known as "The Compulsion to Repeat," or "The Repetition Compulsion." See Sigmund Freud, *Beyond the Pleasure Principle,* in J. Strachey, ed., *The Standard Edition of the Complete Psychological Works of Sigmund Freud* (London: Hogarth, 1966), vol. 8, pp. 3–64, pp. 14–17. (1920).

32. Robert S. McNamara, videotaped "Discussion of the Cuban Missile Crisis," June 1983 (tapes are the property of the Alfred P. Sloan Foundation, New York, N.Y.).

33. Robert S. McNamara, "Hearings on Military Posture Before the House Committee on Armed Services, for Fiscal Year 1964." (Washington, D.C.: U.S. Government Printing Office, 1963), p. 274.

34. Arthur Schlesinger, Jr., *Robert Kennedy and His Times* (New York: Ballantine, 1978), pp. 570–571.

35. Arthur Schlesinger, Jr., *A Thousand Days: John F. Kennedy in the White House* (New York: Fawcett, 1965), pp. 760–761.

36. Khrushchev, "Letter to Kennedy of October 26," pp. 43–44; 48.

37. Nikita Khrushchev, *Khrushchev Remembers,* pp. 500, 504.

38. Sorensen, *Kennedy,* p. 714.

39. Ibid., p. 716.

40. Ibid., p. 717.

41. See this chapter, note 27, for several references to this "revisionist" literature.

42. See Chapter 2 on the facts surrounding the shootdown, and Blight and Welch, *On the Brink,* chap. 6. Khrushchev believed by the time Dobrynin relayed Robert Kennedy's message, that he had lost control of the situation on the ground in Cuba. So, while Kennedy could not control "his" Turks and give Khrushchev the trade he wanted, Khrushchev had lost control of "his" Cubans and therefore could not protect American reconnaissance aircraft from being shot at.

43. Ulric Neisser, *Memory Observed: Remembering in Natural Contexts,* p. 47. On the constructive nature of memory, also consult Neisser's previous *Cognitive Psychology* (New York: Appleton-Century-Crofts, 1967).

44. McGeorge Bundy, *Danger and Survival,* chap. 9.

45. Neustadt, in Blight and Welch, *On the Brink,* p. 108.

46. Thomas S. Kuhn, *The Structure of Scientific Revolutions,* rev. ed. (Chicago: University of Chicago Press, 1970), p. 84.

47. We are still very far from being able to perform a similar analysis of possible stages of shock and confusion on the Soviet side. But we do know now that Khrushchev was stunned and enraged by the quarantine. See Blight and Welch, *On the Brink,* pt. 3.

48. R. F. Kennedy, *Thirteen Days,* p. 2.

49. Dean Rusk, cited in E. Abel, *The Missile Crisis,* p. 127.

50. R. F. Kennedy, *Thirteen Days,* p. 47.

51. Thomas S. Kuhn, *The Essential Tension: Selected Studies in Scientific Tradition and Change* (Chicago: University of Chicago Press, 1977), pp. 263–264.

52. George Ball, *The Past Has Another Pattern,* pp. 304–305.

53. Jurgen Habermas, *Legitimation Crisis,* trans. Thomas McCarthy (Boston: Beacon Press, 1975), p. 1.

54. Nikita Khrushchev, *Khrushchev Remembers,* p. 497.

55. On Ball, see E. Abel; *The Missile Crisis,* p. 127; on McNamara, consult the Sloan Foundation videotaped discussion of the missile crisis, June 1983.

56. Nikita Khrushchev, *Khrushchev Remembers*, pp. 497–498.

57. Jurgen Habermas, *Legitimation Crisis*, p. 2.

58. The locus classicus is William James, *The Varieties of Religious Experience* (New York: Collier, 1961). (1902). More recently, this theme—the centrality of radical change in the development of human personality—has become the domain of Erik Erikson and his many followers. See especially Erikson's *Young Man Luther* (New York: W. W. Norton, 1958).

59. Soren Kierkegaard, *The Concept of Dread* (Princeton: Princeton University Press, 1957), p. 140. (1844)

60. Theodore Sorensen, *Kennedy*, p. 733.

61. John F. Kennedy, "Radio and Television Address to the American People on the Nuclear Test Ban Treaty," in *Public Papers of the Presidents, 1963*, pp. 601–606, p. 602. Portions of the preceding paragraphs are adapted from my article "Toward a Policy-Relevant Psychology of Avoiding Nuclear War," pp. 16–18.

62. John F. Kennedy, "Inaugural Address," in *Public Papers of the Presidents, 1961*, pp. 1–2.

63. John F. Kennedy, "Commencement Address at American University in Washington," in *Public Papers of the Presidents, 1963*, pp. 459–464, p. 462.

64. Erikson, *Young Man Luther*, p. 254 (italics in original).

*Chapter 9*

1. Horace Fletcher, "Happiness as Found in Forethought *Minus* Fearthought," cited in W. James, *The Varieties of Religious Experience*, pp. 92–93 (italics in original).

2. Robert McNamara, however, has spoken out forcefully on the contrary view. For example: "I think the missile crisis proves beyond a shadow of a doubt that there was enough fear of the consequences of a nuclear war in the American Administration to be deterred. We *were* deterred, plain and simple. So, what you want is enough fear to maintain deterrence in a crisis, and no more. How much is that? Look at the missile crisis. I'll bet the Soviets didn't have more than a few dozen warheads they could deliver on our forces and cities: That was enough. Conclusion? A few dozen is enough." (In Blight and Welch, *On the Brink*, p. 199.) The goal, according to McNamara, is to get rid of what he calls "surplus fear," such as he recalls in abundance—overabundance—in the Cuban missile crisis (ibid., p. 198). It is interesting, however, that McNamara still does seem to connect fear of inadvertent nuclear war with the positive outcome, as much as with the possible, negative outcome. As he says: "People may crack. You do not want to reduce your leaders to quivering, panicky, irrational people, do you?" (ibid., p. 198). Yet there is no evidence of this in American leaders in the missile crisis, although the *fear* of it in Khrushchev, according to some, added considerable gravity to their own deliberations (George Ball, interview with the author, May 1, 1987, at Princeton, N.J.; Dean Rusk, in Blight and Welch, *On the Brink*, p. 178).

3. Coral Bell, *The Conventions of Crisis* (Oxford: Oxford University Press, 1971), p. 2. Bell gives no reference for McNamara's celebrated utterance, one that has become something like Holy Writ for the budding discipline of nuclear crisis management. In fact, I have not been able to discover the source. Whether McNamara actually uttered the statement is less interesting, in my view, than the reliance of an entire generation of aspiring crisis managers on Bell's unreferenced attribution to McNamara. All of them, to a person, cite McNamara (as cited by Bell) to indicate, among other things, just how deeply rooted is crisis management in a single individual's (McNamara's) alleged interpretation of a single event, the missile crisis. Now, however, enthusiasts of crisis management will have to contend with McNamara's total repudiation of the concept. At the critical oral history meeting on the missile crisis in March 1987, McNamara enunciated "McNamara's Law": "It is impossible to predict with a high degree of confidence what the effects of the use of military force will be because of the risks of accident, miscalculation, misperception, and inadvertence. . . . 'Managing' crises is the wrong term; you don't 'manage' them because you *can't* 'manage' them" (Blight and Welch, *On the Brink*, p. 99). He concludes from this that the proper question to ask is: "How do we prevent crises, not how do we manage them?" (ibid., p. 200).

4. See Alexander L. George, "Crisis Management," pp. 223–234; and "Political Crises," in J. S. Nye., ed., *The Making of America's Soviet Policy* (New Haven: Yale University Press, 1984), pp. 129–158. See also Richard Ned Lebow, *Between Peace and War* and *Nuclear Crisis Management*.

5. Jervis, Lebow, and Stein, *Psychology and Deterrence,* p. 4.

6. Robert Jervis, *Perception and Misperception in International Politics* (Princeton: Princeton University Press, 1976), esp. pp. 62–78. More recently, Jervis has updated his earlier analysis with some findings from behavioral decision theory, to provide what he takes to be a canonical path to nuclear war via a spiral of misperception. See "War and Misperception," *Journal of Interdisciplinary History* 18, no. 4 (Spring 1988): 675–700.

7. "Ego psychology" is often portrayed as a distinctly post-Freudian development, a movement away from Freud's alleged too-heavy emphasis on the instinctual, unconscious basis of thinking and behavior. But its roots are clearly present in Freud's late work. See his *The Ego and the Id,* in J. Strachey, ed., *Standard Edition of Freud,* vol. 19, pp. 3–66. See also Anna Freud, *The Ego and the Mechanisms of Defense* (New York: International Universities Press, 1946). (1936).

8. Richard Ned Lebow, "Conclusions" to *Psychology and Deterrence,* pp. 203–232, pp. 213–214.

9. Thomas C. Schelling, *The Strategy of Conflict* (Cambridge: Harvard University Press, 1960), p. 207.

10. Particularly influential examples of the comparative method are Schelling, *Arms and Influence;* Barry M. Blechman and Stephen S. Kaplan, *Force Without War: U.S. Armed Forces as a Political Instrument* (Washington, D.C.:

Brookings Institution, 1978); Alexander L. George and Richard Smoke, *Deterrence in American Foreign Policy: Theory and Practice* (New York: Columbia University Press, 1974); Lebow, *Between Peace and War;* and Glenn H. Snyder and Paul Diesing, *Conflict Among Nations: Bargaining, Decision Making, and System Structure in International Crisis* (Princeton: Princeton University Press, 1977).

11. The psychological literature on the missile crisis is peculiar. By far the most famous such study is that of Irving Janis, *Groupthink*. Janis, who is a thoroughgoing devotee of the view that stress leads to bad decision-making, has nothing but praise for the managers of the missile crisis. Apparently, we are given to believe, they just somehow overcame the stress. Janis's sometime collaborator Richard Ned Lebow, however, sees stress and "groupthink" even in the EXCOMM meetings Janis admires for the absence of "groupthink." See Lebow, *Between Peace and War*, pp. 298–303 and "The Cuban Missile Crisis: Reading the Lessons Correctly," *Political Science Quarterly* 98 (1983): 431–458. To make his case, Lebow emphasizes the short shrift given by EXCOMM to Adlai Stevenson's view that the United States ought to pursue a purely political/diplomatic course. The peculiarity of an argument like this is that it must assert the pernicious influence of "groupthink" over a relatively minor issue—whether to adopt Stevenson's plan—while the outcome of the crisis, a sensible peaceful resolution, is left unaccounted for. By all accounts, the stress was far greater during the second week, when the resolution occurred, than it was during the first week when, in Lebow's estimation, Stevenson was ignored. According to the logic of the stress/decision-making psychopathology linkage, the decision-making flaws should therefore have come at the end of the crisis, rather than at the beginning. The same mistake was made by Richard Harwood, "Kennedy Secretly a Dove in Cuba Crisis, Letter Shows," *The Washington Post,* Aug. 29, 1987. See Blight and Welch, *On the Brink,* p. 333.

12. Dean Acheson, "Dean Acheson's Version of Robert Kennedy's Version of the Cuban Missile Affair," *Esquire,* vol. 71 (February 1969); pp. 44, 46, 76–77.

13. Agreement with Acheson on the point from Nitze and Dillon may be found in Blight and Welch, *On the Brink,* chap. 3.

14. Thomas C. Schelling, personal communication to the author, November 1984.

15. Richard Ned Lebow, "The Cuban Missile Crisis."

16. Dean Rusk, in the Sloan Foundation Videotapes, January 1983. See also Thomas J. Schoenbaum, *Waging Peace and War* (New York: Simon & Schuster, 1988), chap. 10; and Blight and Welch, *On the Brink,* chap. 3.

17. Robert S. McNamara, in M. Trachtenberg, ed., "White House Tapes," p. 189 (italics in original). Warren I. Cohen also points out this propensity in Dean Rusk during the missile crisis; see his *Dean Rusk* (Totowa, N.J.: Cooper Square Publishers, 1980), pp. 152–153.

18. John F. Kennedy and McGeorge Bundy, in M. Trachtenberg, ed., "White House Tapes," p. 181.

19. Robert F. Kennedy and Robert S. McNamara, in ibid.

20. R. F. Kennedy, *Thirteen Days*, p. 106.

21. This comes through with special clarity in the Sloan Foundation videotape of June 1983 (with Robert McNamara, George Ball, McGeorge Bundy, and U. Alexis Johnson). Now, thanks to the release of the October 27 EXCOMM transcripts, we have a clearer idea of what Thompson did. It was Thompson, in fact, who convinced the skeptical President to send the favorable response to Khrushchev's first letter, effectively ignoring the second. He convinced Kennedy, at least for the moment, that Khrushchev would settle for being able to say "I saved Cuba" (from an American invasion). See Bundy and Blight, "October 27, 1962," pp. 59–60.

22. See this chapter, note 1 (above).

23. Charles Taylor, "The Explanation of Purposive Behavior," in R. Borger and F. Cioffi, eds., *Explanation in the Behavioral Sciences*, pp. 49–95, p. 78.

24. Daniel Dennett, *Brainstorms: Philosophical Essays on Mind and Psychology* (Cambridge: MIT Press, Bradford Books, 1978), pp. 3; 238.

25. The study of modern psychological theories of anxiety begins with Sigmund Freud, *Inhibitions, Symptoms and Anxiety*, in J. Strachey, ed., *Standard Edition of Freud*, vol. 20, pp. 77–175. (196). Addendum B ("Supplementary Remarks on Anxiety") is particularly relevant to a Freudian understanding of the kind of fear one might find in a nuclear crisis.

26. William James, *Varieties of Religious Experience*, p. 219.

*Chapter 10*

1. See Bruce G. Blair, *Strategic Command and Control: Redefining the Nuclear Threat* (Washington, D.C.: Brookings Institution, 1985); Paul Bracken, *The Command and Control of Nuclear Forces* (New Haven: Yale University Press, 1983); and Ashton B. Carter, John B. Steinbruner, and Charles A. Zraket, eds., *Managing Nuclear Operations* (Washington, D.C.: Brookings Institution, 1987).

2. Carnesale et al., *Living with Nuclear Weapons*, pp. 43–44.

3. Allison, Carnesale, and Nye, *Hawks, Doves, & Owls*, pp. 206–222.

4. Ibid., pp. 244–246.

5. Joseph S. Nye, Jr., Graham T. Allison, and Albert Carnesale, eds., *Fateful Visions: Avoiding Nuclear Catastrophe* (Cambridge: Ballinger, 1988).

6. Ibid., pp. 215–235.

7. John Le Carré, *The Spy Who Came in from the Cold* (New York: Avenel, 1983), pp. 80–81. (1962).

# Index